Espen Dahl, Jan-Olav Henriksen,
Marius T. Mjaaland (Eds.)

Imagination in Religion

Nordic Studies in Theology
Nordische Studien zur Theologie

Edited by / Herausgegeben von

Prof. Dr. Kirsten Busch Nielsen
(University of Copenhagen)

Prof. Dr. Dr. Jan-Olav Henriksen
(MF Norwegian School of Theology, Religion and Society, Oslo)

Dr. Hans Bringeland
(NLA University College, Bergen)

Volume / Band 8

LIT

Imagination in Religion

Perspectives from the Philosophy of Religion

Edited by

Espen Dahl, Jan-Olav Henriksen,
Marius T. Mjaaland

LIT

Printed with the financial support of Aarhus University Research Foundation

This book is printed on acid-free paper.

Bibliographic information published by the Deutsche Nationalbibliothek
The Deutsche Nationalbibliothek lists this publication in the Deutsche Nationalbibliografie; detailed bibliographic data are available in the Internet at http://dnb.dnb.de.

ISBN 978-3-643-91210-7 (pb)
ISBN 978-2-643-96210-2 (PDF)
ISSN 2311-1194

A catalogue record for this book is available from the British Library.

Flössergasse 10
CH-8001 Zürich
Tel. +41 (0) 76-632 84 35
E-Mail: zuerich@lit-verlag.ch https://www.lit-verlag.ch
Distribution:
In the UK: Global Book Marketing, e-mail: mo@centralbooks.com
In North America: Independent Publishers Group, e-mail: orders@ipgbook.com
In Germany: LIT Verlag Fresnostr. 2, D-48159 Münster
Tel. +49 (0) 2 51-620 32 22, Fax +49 (0) 2 51-922 60 99, e-mail: vertrieb@lit-verlag.de

Table of Contents

Contributors:

Jonna Bornemark, Professor, Philosophy, Centre for Studies in Practical Knowledge, Södertörn University, Sweden.

Espen Dahl, Professor, Systematic Theology, The Arctic University of Norway, Tromsø.

Jan-Olav Henriksen, Professor, Philosophy of Religion, MF Norwegian School of Theology, Religion and Society, Oslo.

Alan Herbert, Post-Doc Research Fellow at the Oxford Centre for Hindu Studies, Oxford University, UK.

Jonas Holst, Associate Professor, Institute of Humanism and Society, San Jorge University, Zaragoza, Spain.

Roomet Jakapi, Associate Professor of History of Philosophy, University of Tartu, Estonia.

Mads Peter Karlsen, Assistant Professor, Department of Management, Politics, and Philosophy, Copenhagen Business School, Denmark.

Marius T. Mjaaland, Professor, Philosophy of Religion, Faculty of Theology, University of Oslo, Norway.

Ulrik Nissen, Associate Professor, Ethics and Philosophy of Religion, Dept. of Theology, Faculty of Arts, Aarhus University, Denmark.

Ritva Palmén, Docent, Lecturer in Philosophy of Religion, Faculty of Theology, University of Helsinki, Finland.

Carl-Johan Palmqvist, Researcher, Department of Philosophy, Lund University, Sweden.

Esben Korsgaard Rasmussen, Doctoral Student, Faculty of Theology, University of Copenhagen, Denmark.

Introduction

Espen Dahl, Jan-Olav Henriksen, Marius T. Mjaaland

Imagine there's no heaven
It's easy if you try
No hell below us
Above us only sky
Imagine all the people
living for today

John Lennon's "Imagine" from 1971 is probably one of the most famous expressions of imagination within popular culture. He asks the listeners to imagine a better world, freed from the bonds of nationalism, capitalism, and, to be sure, from religion. Lennon's lyrics unmistakably draws a clear connection between religion and imagination; on the one hand, by imagining a world where religion is absent, and on the other, in presupposing that religion is essentially about producing beautiful and harmful images, such as heaven and hell. Moreover, as Lennon no doubt sees the overcoming of religion as integral to his image of a better world, his own alternative nonetheless relies on structures of eschatological imagery. At the risk of becoming a dreamer, even installing a community of dreamers, he points us toward a new world beyond destruction and divides. As the refrain puts it: "I hope some day you'll join us. And the world will be as one."

Whatever one might think of Lennon's specific prospects, his song gives a clear indication of the topic of this volume: the relation between imagination and religion. Moreover, it suggests that imagination, especially in its religious application, can be as destructive as it can be constructive. It is hard to deny that imagination occupies a central place in religious life and is integral to the material upon which theology draws. Think of how symbols and myths, poetry and metaphors, parables and aphorisms pervade the Bible. Think of how aesthetic productions have flown from religious inspirations and, in turn, furnished the religious universe in shifting historical circumstances. Or the way memories of God's people or even God's immemorial acts are made alive through imaginative representations, and, correspondingly, how hopes and fears of the unknown future have been and still are nourished by enigmatic symbols or apocalyptic visions. And the list of examples goes on. The point is simply that religion as we know it would be impossible without imagination. Perhaps these examples suggest that imagination provides content to what otherwise escapes discourse and perception, or perhaps that it enlivens events and states that would otherwise be sterile. Either way, imagination opens up a productive realm for creative involvement that keeps religion from sinking into trivialities or abstractions.

If it is clear that imagination has a role in religion, it is also clear that imagination poses serious problems too. At least since Feuerbach's time, the most common objection to religion is that our image of God is best understood as human projections of wishes and longings. Granted that God is an outcome of our imagination, God simply cannot exist as real and independent of us. According to this line of thought, imagination does not permanently refer to real objects, but produces irreal objects without reality or existence. Hence, to rely on imagination seems to undercut God's existence. And there are further related problems, for if imagination is not restricted by any external reality but invents its imagery according to whatever fashion we like, it cannot contain any claims to truth either. There are simply no facts or state of affairs to which the imagined content could possibly correspond, and hence no way to determine whether it is true or false. Religious convictions, however, seem not only to presuppose the possibility of truth, but to think of truth as not at our disposal, certainly not as our inventions, but as somehow given to us, say revealed by divine authorities. Something similar also holds for our moral life. For our deeds and misdeeds can, no doubt, draw on the imagined possibilities, but such a moral imagination seems not to capture precisely what makes acts moral, such as moral goals, strong evaluations or moral restraints.

If there are both good reasons for believing that imagination is part of religious life, and at the same time posing challenges to it, there is all the more reason for welcoming the present contributions that in various ways explore its potentialities and problems. Granted that Lennon is right in suggesting an intimate relationship between imagination and religion, with its perils and promises, we must look for new ways of proceeding. Although conceptual problems and inherent dangers must be observed, we want to propose that there are ways to think again and think differently – which in itself involves the power of imagination. The articles in this volume approach religion and imagination in different manners, but they also express discomfort with ways in which the obstacles to its religious use have been posed above. For it seems that the presented obstacles simply presume that there are clear dividing lines between imagination, conceptual thinking, and perception, and hence between fantasy and reality, fiction and truth. By means of such clear-cut divisions, it becomes possible to think of imagination as having no interference with thinking and perception. From such assumptions, the next step follows: imagination has nothing to do with reality, truth, and morality. As many of the contributions demonstrate, however, such division is far from obvious or necessary; indeed, fresh perspectives open up once we explore the dynamics between various faculties or dimensions of life. Imagination might then be involved in thinking, in perceiving, in contemplation, and in practices – in short, involved in our being-in-the-world as well as being-toward-God. Reality and truth might then turn out to be less clear, but also much more complex and worth disclosing. Imagination is not only – perhaps not even most importantly – a faculty *sui generis* that produces irreal fictions, but rather a power that bestows sense, on the interval between immanence and transcendence, fills in gaps in conceptual thinking, bringing unity to difference, animating meaning to past and future – all of which are important to religious faith.

Admittedly, exploring the productive power of imagination in exchange with other powers of human life is not new in itself. Operating with distinctions between thinking, perception, and imagination, Aristotle already suggests that imagination can play a mediating role between thinking and perceiving. A similar idea is found in Kant, where imagination plays a pivotal role in uniting sensuality and categories (so-called schematism) in the constitution of knowledge. However, Kant also suggests how the productive imagination is at work in aesthetic experience – an idea that was expanded in various Romantic movements, such as in the theological version elaborated by Schleiermacher. While we can conceive of the suggested historical strand as one emphasising the mediating and productive role of imagination, it finds its counterpart in another strand that takes imagination to have a different role, as reproductive. From Plato's reproduction of the original ideas to Sartre's notion of the negation involved in imagination, this second strand regards imaginations as compensating for a certain absence in time and space. However, both the productive and the reproductive notion of imagination assign freedom to it because imagination stretches beyond what is entailed in concepts or given in perception. It, therefore, has the fruitful power of opening us up to realms not seen, pasts not lived, and the future beyond the present. Yet, for the same reason, it comes with dangers of leading astray – which appears more threatening the more unbound and unmediated imagination is taken to be. Therefore, the question we need to address is: Where do we go from such double heritage, and how we can preserve the most fruitful ways of thinking imagination in religion with a critical stance towards its possible misuse?

The current collection of essays spans over theoretical issues of philosophy of religion, practical philosophy (moral and political), reading of historical contributions as well as reflections from non-Christian religions. What binds them together is not only the common investigation of imagination's role in religion but also the common philosophical approach to the subject matter.

The first five contributions are firmly rooted in the continental philosophy of religion. Espen Dahl takes his point of departure in the overly simplified conceptions of both imagination and religion, both of which seem to ban perception from playing any significant role in any of them. Dahl counters these positions by arguing for a more nuanced and less antagonistic understanding of the role perception plays in relation to imagination and religion. His thesis is that imagination designates our ability to perceive more or differently – drawing on possibilities in what is perceived that potentially transfigure our otherwise ordinary reality. By way of careful analysis of positions in phenomenology, he proceeds towards a position in which Ricoeur's notion of a "productive imagination" comes constructively into play. He develops Ricoeur's position further with reference to elements in Wittgenstein and advances a position in which imagination does not represent a way out of the ordinary, but a return to its possibilities "in the face of the actual everyday that is presently lived in illusion and loss."

Jan-Olav Henriksen enters his discussion of imagination from the point of view of how all religion builds on the semiotic character of experience. Accordingly, it also entails that religions build on representations, given that a divine reality cannot be identified with any element in the world as such. Hence, he argues that the inference from an experience of what is understood as a representation towards the represented relies on abduction. However, abduction would not play this role unless it also engaged our ability to imagine the connection between the representation and the represented. Against this backdrop, Henriksen applies Robert Neville's analysis of the fundamental role of imagination to argue that both imagination and abduction are downplayed and not taken sufficiently into consideration in Hegel's understanding of religion as something that eventually will be sublated in philosophy. In short, he argues that imagination and abduction both play a role in religion that cannot be left behind but remain as constitutive parts of the religious content in representations.

Mads Peter Karlsen approaches the topic of this book from another angle: He analyses in detail the discussion in contemporary French philosophy on questions concerning the *myth*. In this discussion, the development of reason is not considered merely as a process in which the myth is left behind. Instead, reason, and the development of science, are seen as interruptions of the myth. With Nancy, he argues that "myth designates something that cannot simply disappear," but on the other hand, the development also entails that the myth becomes transparent *as myth*. Building on his analysis of the French thinkers, Karlsen is then able to bring in the discussion about Bultmann and Ricoeur on the difference between demythologisation and demythization, and link this to the present discussion on deconstruction. Karlsen's careful analysis of the different strata in the French discussion displays the continued role that imagination, as myth, still has in contemporary thinking.

Jonas Holst treats the role of imagination in ethical life, drawing on resources from antiquity. Despite its enormous impact, Holst holds that Plato's allegory of the cave is not helpful in order to shed light on how we can perceive the good as it appears in the world. In contrast, Aristotle's ethics is deliberately designed to account for how the good is part of lived experience. As Holst points out, Aristotle's notion of imagination, *phantasia*, plays a decisive role in deliberating the right action, as it mediates perception and the factual situation. Moreover, *phantasia* also has the capacity to combine perceptual elements in new ways that prepare the agent for a wide range of possible situations. Holst argues that Aristotle's conception is applicable to Christian ethics as well, and he employs the parable of the Good Samaritan as a case in point. In one sense, the story goes beyond Aristotle in stressing the Samaritan's immediate bodily reaction and empathy to the sufferer. Yet, what the samaritan displays, and what the priest and the Levite lack, is an apt use of *phantasia* to grasp the situation and act accordingly. Interestingly, the position Holst reaches draws close to Løgstrup's phenomenology.

Ulrik Nissen offers a discussion of to what extent the so-called Scandinavian creation theology can be "enriched by a broader understanding of creation theology than found in its traditional Nordic representatives." He also argues that imagination can play a key role in the further development of this theology, and thereby, he implicitly also argues that the philosophy of religion is an important contributor to a more elaborate articulation of these theological positions. Nissen argues that the phenomenological thought of the French philosopher Michel Henry is important in this respect. Henry's position can offer a broader understanding of human reality with imagination as a key concept. By combining theology and philosophy in this way, Nissen advances a position in which a Christologically saturated concept of reality does not stand in contrast to creation theology. Thus, this position can "speak more profoundly about a deeper and fuller understanding of life as it is given, imagined, and known in Christ," he argues.

The debate concerning imagination in religion is also present in the analytical philosophy of religion, as the following two contributions give witness to. Roomet Jakapi's article takes its cue from the claim that due to its emphasis on the epistemic status of religious *belief,* the traditional analytic philosophy of religion has mostly overlooked the role of imagination. As an example, he points to Alvin Plantinga's impressive work *Warranted Christian Belief* that "takes beliefs and imaginings to be entirely distinct from each other and therefore does not see religious imaginings as constituents of religious beliefs and faith" However, others, such as J.L. Schellenberg, describe the nature of faith precisely in terms of imagination. By way of an analysis of their positions, Jakapi nevertheless argues that Plantinga and Schellenberg's understanding of proper religious faith shares some common features. Against this backdrop, he challenges the view that it is possible to draw a clear line between religious belief and imagination. Thus, he aims to show the relevance of mental imagery for the epistemology of religion. He concludes by claiming that "the standard conception of beliefs as propositional attitudes is too restrictive and needs revision"

Carl-Johan Palmqvist shares with Jakapi an interest in the account of imagination in J.L. Schellenberg's philosophy of religion, but he uses it for different purposes. Taking his point of departure in the position called non-doxasticism, in which religious faith is considered as being, in one sense, belief-less, Palmqvist argues that this mode of faith becomes vulnerable to the despair-problem that is articulated in the literature on hope. He suggests that the problem can be overcome by adopting Schellenberg's imagination-based account of non-doxastic faith. To advance this claim, he draws on Amy Kind's account of imagination and the understanding of despair suggested by Cheshire Calhoun. Imagination solves the problem of despair, he holds, because "faith excludes despair if both attitudes, faith as well as despair, "are conceived of in terms of holding a phenomenological picture of the world in one's imagination."

Whereas the previously mentioned contributions focus on theoretical issues, the following two articles point to how imagination is crucial to practical philosophy.

The four final contributions reach back to historical sources in order to remind the current debate of the rich resources found in older works, both within the western and eastern traditions. Ritva Palmén argues that the current debate of imagination can profit from lending an ear to the past, particularly medieval philosophy and theology. Much confusion in contemporary philosophy, Palmén holds, stems from the lack of clear distinction between imagination's "transcendent use," by which it goes beyond the given world, and its "instructive use," where it enables us to learn more about the world. Such distinction was, however, central to Richard of St. Victor. With regard to the transcendent use, Richard argues that imagination works as the connecting link that enables human beings to be elevated from visible to invisible realities and eventually to encounter God. In its instructive use, Richard explores the diverse ways in which imagination cooperates with the abilities of the soul in order to enrich our perception of things and grant us access to religious metaphorical language. Eventually, Palmén claims that for Richard, such investigations of the imagination can both teach us more about the soul, but more importantly, also tell us something about the Creator in the image of whom we are made.

Jonna Bornemark retrieves the thinking of Giordano Bruno in order to propose a wider notion of imagination than prevalent modern conceptions allow for. It is precisely the dichotomy of imagination, regarded as the free realm of illusions, and rationality, regarded as formal and calculating, that Bornemark thinks has proved fatal. Bruno's "magical thinking" – prepared in many ways by Nicholas of Cusa – advances beyond such deadlocks and unfolds a more resourceful understanding of imagination. In Bornemark's rendering, Bruno places imagination at the centre of the human mind, not as a faculty that represents things or invents irrealitites, but as our ability to bind elements together and thus to perceive and act in new ways. The imagining mind is part of the universe, which itself is a living and unfolding creative process. In

Bruno's theory, Bornemark argues, God is the very movement itself, "the world soul," that remains incomprehensible for finite beings.

Esben Korsgaard Rasmussen analyses the role of imagination in Thomas Hobbes's *Leviathan.* He argues that the need for the political power to *appear* in a specific way is determined by Hobbes's conception of religion's origins and its roots in human finitude. Because human life is marked by an anxious desire to stay alive, this desire structures both thought and action. This structure is, in turn, determined by a system of *imaginary representations.* These representations have an inherent potential for conflict. Against this backdrop, Rasmussen argues that Hobbes's sovereign state and its grand figure can be seen as an effort "to aesthetically reform divergent systems of religious imaginary representations." Rasmussen explores the imaginations' relation to sensation, passion, and what Hobbes calls "mental discourse." Furthermore, he offers a closer examination of how desire concludes in a never-ending search for power. This desire is at the root of a complex system of social stratification structured by a set of shared imaginary representations, of which religion is an important and historically dominant case. Hence, Rasmussen contributes to understanding how religious imagery and imaginations play a vital role in the political realm, as conceived by Hobbes.

Alan Herbert offers an essential supplement to the previous articles insofar as he deals with material from the Indian context. Thus, his contribution is also a testimony to the contemporary development in the philosophy of religion beyond the Western hemisphere, and with questions that are different from but not unrelated to topics traditionally discussed within the context of that discipline. He analyses a text that seems critical of the role that imagination traditionally was expected to play in religious mediation practice, namely the *Bhakti-sandarbha*, a seminal treatise attributed to the sixteenth-century thinker Jiva Gosvami. Jiva criticises the role that meditation practitioners are encouraged to give imagination when they imagine themselves as being in unity with the deity. Jiva does so by advancing his own alternative understanding of what role imagination plays in religious practice. Herbert's careful analysis of the problems that have emerged in the scholarship concerning this topic allows him to display how religious imagination and religious practice are deeply intertwined and have an impact on doctrinal positions as well as emotional states of mind.

The following contributions taken together offer a rich and nuanced picture that challenges conceptions that see religious faith and imagination as either contrary positions or conflate them fully. Imagination plays different roles at different levels. We hope this volume will provide further resources for reflection on religion and imagination. It aspires to be a testimony of a phenomenon that cannot be taken lightly when one searches for an understanding of lived religion and its conceptual conditions in the contemporary world.

Perception, Imagination, and the Transfiguration of the Ordinary

Espen Dahl

A first reaction to bringing the notion of imagination into the context of religion might be one of suspicion. There seems to be a clash between how we depict the Christian religion and imagination. Religious discourse, one might assume, must be guided by some authority not at my disposal, perhaps handed over to me, and ultimately referring back to some divine revelation. Imagination, on the other hand, seems to suggest precisely the opposite, that is, my own free invention, completely unrestricted of any authorities, and producing fictive and illusory objects of a fantasy world. However, both the pictures of religion and imagination are, I assume, as common as they are unsophisticated; nevertheless, they are not completely without support in the philosophical literature. What is important to the concern of this article is primarily that such simplified pictures ban perception from playing any significant role in imagination as well as in religion. With such a clean-cut distinction between imagination and religion, perception falls out of the picture. Perception becomes their excluded middle. However, such an exclusion comes at a price, both for the notion of imagination and for its role in religion. It is, therefore, worth asking if the relationship between imagination and perception could be conceived less antagonistically, in order to pave the way for its constructive role in religion. Is it not at least intelligible to understand the world of perception as somehow assuming abilities to imagine, perhaps within a religious register – say, in seeing the world as a gift, or seeing the divine in beauty and wonders? Indeed, this is what I want to propose, by way of suggesting a different notion of imagination: *Imagination*, I will claim, *designates our ability to perceive more or differently – drawing on possibilities in what is perceived that potentially transfigure our otherwise ordinary reality.*

Starting with the problematic conception of imagination, I will in the first part give a short presentation of Jean-Paul Sartre's almost classical account, and in order to put Sartre's position in relief, I will draw on observations made by Paul Ricoeur. In the second part, I turn to Ludwig Wittgenstein and what he calls seeing aspects, in order to relate imagination to perception. To see aspects means to see more and potentially differently, I will argue. The third part will exemplify how such seeing and imagining are relevant to religious contexts in terms of wonders as accounted for by Wittgenstein and particularly Augustine. The fourth and final part elaborates the interweaving of the ordinary and the extraordinary in order to show, more broadly, how imagination in perception is connected to what I will call the transfiguration of the ordinary.

Imagination and perception

Within phenomenology, there has been a tendency to operate with the mentioned divide between imagination and perception. Edmund Husserl notes that whereas every perception entails that we posit the perceived as real, imagination does not.[1] Still, imagination has the same basic structure as perception, the same intentionality toward an object, which means that the imagined is not located in the mind – say, some kind of mental picture or idea as empiricism has it – but directed beyond the mind, toward an imagined object. It is, however, the young Sartre who elaborates the first sustained phenomenological account of imagination. In order to flesh out the distinctive nature of imagination, Sartre draws on Husserl's critique of psychological reductionism and follows up the distinctions between imagination, perception, and thinking. Perception is, Sartre holds, characterised by positing its object as real and existing, but it proceeds stepwise: We can only see a few sides of an object at a time, while the others must be gradually synthesised as we move around the object. Thinking, on the other hand, does not have to synthesise an object with hidden sides but grasps its object instantaneously by means of concepts.[2] Now, imagination differs from both, Sartre holds, for even if the image to which imagination is directed is given in a particular profile, we need not move around it to gather further aspects of it, as in perception, for the image is given without remainder. Nevertheless, images are marked by a certain "poverty" over against perception; they lack the richness that can be explored by perception: since there is nothing hidden here, there are essentially no discoveries to be made.[3]

Sartre argues that the imagined object, say his absent friend Pierre, is not derived from the world of perception. Sartre strongly emphasises that its objects are given to imagination *sui generis*, according to its own terms, and as such, it does not work in tandem with other powers of our consciousness.[4] We realise this if we recall what Husserl calls the doxic modes. Whereas perception posits its object as existing, imagination posits its object differently – either as nonexistent, as absent, or as existing somewhere else. Sartre admits that we presuppose that there are perceptual elements in images, so when I imagine the absent Pierre, I do imagine him as I otherwise would see, hear or touch him.

---

[1] Edmund Husserl, *Ideas for Pure Phenomenology and Phenomenological Philosophy: First Book*, trans. D.O. Dahlstrom (Indianapolis: Hacket Publishing 2014), 215-17.

[2] Jean-Paul, *The Imaginary: A Phenomenological Psychology of the Imagination*, trans. J. Webber (London: Routledge 2004), 8-9.

[3] Ibid., 10, 15.

[4] Ibid., 12.

But this does not make the absent Pierre into an object of perception, for what is constitutive of Pierre-as-imagined is that he is given to me, not existing here and now, but precisely *as absent*. This is not an empty intuition that awaits fulfilling, but, in Sartre's words, an "image wrapped within a certain nothingness."[5]

What does this nothingness mean? What does it tell us about imagination and the imagined object? First, it means that when I imagine something, I do not receive anything given from the world, but I give it spontaneously to myself, as an imagined object cut off from the world that I annihilate. Nothingness pertains both to the object and the world – both are negated in the imagination. "To posit an image," Sartre writes,

> is to constitute an object in the margins of the totality of the real, it is therefore to hold the real at a distance, to be freed from it, in a word, to deny it. Or, if one prefers, to deny that an object belongs to the real is to deny the real in positing the object; the two negations are complementary and the latter is the condition of the former.[6]

As the quote suggests, it is the imagination that first makes possible the denial or annihilation of the world; it is indeed an act of freedom as it surpasses the given world. It is clear that Sartre's appeal to nothingness paves the way for understanding how consciousness has the power to both constitute and deny the world, and by having such double power, imagination manifests my freedom, which becomes a central trope in Sartre's subsequent works.[7]

The focal point for now, however, is Sartre's conception of the relation between perception and imagination. It is hard to deny that we entertain imagined objects that we do not posit as existing in the way we do in perception: think of fairies, unicorns, or absent friends. Sartre's basic conception of the heterogeneity and non-coincidence of imagination and perception seems to be the case: "It follows," he says, "that they exclude one another."[8] Yet, the problem with such a conception lies, I think, in the purification of the two poles of the mutual exclusion. On the imaginative pole, the imagined object is cut off from the perceived world and thus suggests a parallel dimension on top of or besides the lifeworld. On the other pole, we are offered an impoverished understanding of perception, basically confirming the reality at hand. Sartre argues that he cannot imagine Pierre as long as he looks at a table; the image only occurs as he annihilates the table. But I will hold that the excluded middle – I mean, the impure blending of imagination and perception – is not only possible but, indeed, in some cases, a vital element of our

---

[5] Ibid., 14.

[6] Ibid., 183

[7] Ibid., 184-85. Cf. *Being and Nothingness*, trans. H.E. Barnes (London: Routledge 2003), 455-57.

[8] Sartre, *The Imaginary*, 120. Cf. Kearney, *Poetcis of Imaginations* (New York: Fordham University Press, 1998), 59-62.

experience. If a child is looking at the table, couldn't she take the table as a house, sheltering both her and her dolls? In this case, imagination seems to blend with perception, say, in the way we make connections or reorganise experiences, say by taking the desk as a roof of a house and the legs as the walls.

I take Ricoeur to provide a first step toward a richer understanding of the relation between imagination and perception. Ricoeur concedes that Sartre is right in referring to some form of nothingness or "distanciation," as Ricoeur prefers. Yet, Ricoeur finds Sartre's concept of imagination unduly restricted. Fair or not, Ricoeur holds that Sartre never fully frees himself from the traditional Platonic understanding of imagination as reproductive, that is, imagination as modelled on representation of an absent original.[9] Ricoeur argues that Sartre's example betrays him: to imagine the absent Pierre is still a form of reproduction of the absent Pierre.[10] In taking leave of the model of reproductive imagination, Ricoeur suggests a retrieval of the Kantian notion of the "productive imagination," which is a way of conceiving images, poetic expressions, metaphors, or myths as not so much as annihilating reality, but rather adding something to reality and eventually altering the way we perceive the world.

In turning from reproductive to productive imagination, the philosophical focus shifts away from the ontological status of the content and toward its function. Discussing the relation between our two roots of knowledge, intuition, and concept, Kant invokes the imagination's capacity to bridge their heterogeneity, synthesising them according to a schema that enables their mutual integration. Only thus can we, for instance, apply a general concept of a chair to a vast range of different individual instances given to intuition. According to Ricoeur, Kant's essential insight is that imagination is not only, or even primarily, a capacity to create a sphere of its own beyond existence, but the capacity we have to creatively synthesise or reorganise elements into unities that are otherwise different and disparate.

While the Kantian model makes imagination relevant for both language and perception, Ricoeur's exploration of imagination is primarily carried out with respect to linguistic figures, such as myths and poetic utterances. It is particularly proposed over against the phenomenological tendency to treat imagination as a modified perception.[11] Most rewarding to my concern is Ricoeur's exploration of the metaphor, where he explicitly draws on Aristotle, for

---

[9] Salius Guniasus, "Against the Sartrean Background: Ricoeur's *Lectures on Imagination*," Research in Phenomenology 46 (2016):101. For a critical discussion of Ricoeur's claim, see especially pp. 103-105.

[10] George Taylor, "Ricoeur's Philosophy of Imagination," *Journal of French Philosophy* 16 (2006), 96.

[11] Kearney, *Poetics of Imagination*, 128-30.

whom metaphors rely on our ability to recognise similarities in dissimilarities and to bring them vividly before our eyes. According to Ricoeur, a metaphor is an utterance that plays itself out on two semantic levels simultaneously. Take Shakespeare's "Juliet is the sun." The two levels do not literally match – that of the person Juliet and that of the celestial body, the sun – but together, they produce a shock of non-convergence that causes the clash between two semantic fields, which in turn opens up a third sense of imagined unity.[12] Unsurprisingly, Ricoeur finds the contribution of imagination to be as Kant argued, namely, the ability to unite the dissimilar. Imagination can be so vital to metaphors because, contrary to Sartre's conviction, it is never disconnected from neither perception nor thinking in the first place. Or, as Ricoeur puts it: "This insight into likeness is both a thinking and a seeing."[13] Importantly, the unity produced by imagination is, however, not one that effaces differences or swallows them into a totality; rather, the difference is preserved in the assimilation. Ricoeur writes: "Imagination, accordingly, is the *ability* to produce new kinds by assimilation and to produce them not *above* the differences, as in the concept, but in spite of and through the differences."[14]

However, what ontological status does the imagined have for Ricoeur? Does it refer us to the world, or must he, with Sartre, admit that it is "wrapped within a certain nothingness"? Ricoeur claims that it does both: imagination both negates the world and nevertheless refers us to a world. According to such dialectic, Sartre only fulfils the first of several steps. Ricoeur thinks it is true that the imagined object does imply distanciation – otherwise, it would be indistinguishable from perceptions of real states of affairs. Sartre draws the conclusion that imagination is a spontaneous power and that the image contains nothing more than we create, and therefore, as he puts it, "one can never learn from an image what one does not know already."[15] Yet, if, as Ricoeur suggests, the new imagined field is not a reproduction of an absent perception but is a truly novel production, it might also teach us something new, new possibilities proposed by a text. "Because fictions don't reproduce a previous reality," Ricoeur says, "they may produce a new reality. They are not bound by an original that precedes them."[16] Thus, after the first, negative step, Ricoeur proposes a second, in which the imagined world unfolds in front of the text. And from this, a third possible step follows, in which the imagined world refers back to the perception of our life-world, certainly not as an annihilation of that world, but as an augmentation of the life-world. Such augmentation can come about in various ways: in poetics as the constellation of a metaphor, in political

[12] Paul Ricoeur, *From Text to Action: Essays in Hermeneutics II*, 172.
[13] Ricoeur, *The Rule of the Metaphor*, trans. R. Czerny (London: Routledge, 1986), 148.
[14] Ibid., 148.
[15] Sartre, *The Imaginary*, 10
[16] Taylor, "Ricoeur's Philosophy of Imagination," 97.

thinking as the image of a utopia, or in art as the invention of a new painterly style. The first step of suspending the world paves the way for an imaginative reorganisation of the world, even to produce a new reality, and as such, metaphors, utopia, or paintings open new possibilities that surpass previous realities. In this way, imagination is the model for "changing our way of looking at things, of perceiving the world."[17]

Seeing aspects and imagination

Initially, I said that I wanted to explore imagination as our ability to perceive more or differently, and surely, Ricoeur has paved the way for such a productive understanding of imagination. I will now, in my second part, be concerned more directly with the question of perception and imagination's role in it. There are gestures towards the role of perception in Ricoeur's thinking, and as such, it is valuable as a first approach to imagination in perception. Yet, it is also merely a first approach, for Ricoeur tends to explore imagination within the confines of his hermeneutics that unfolds within the verbal or textual dimensions of symbolisation. In what follows, I want to preserve Ricoeur's lessons of the productive imagination but broaden, or at least change, the scope in order to explore imagination, not only as understanding of text and speech but as a power that is operative *in* perception.

Ricoeur refers briefly to Wittgenstein's notion of "seeing as" or "seeing aspects," not in order to bring out its relevance for perception as such, but rather to draw on its relevance for structures of the sensual component of metaphors. As Ricoeur takes it, Wittgenstein has outlined how similarities and dissimilarities can be synthesised into new ways of seeing, precisely by means of what Kant calls productive imagination.[18] Turning to the second part of his *Philosophical Investigations*, in which Wittgenstein treats seeing aspects, let me start where Wittgenstein himself starts. He initiates his investigations by distinguishing between two different objects of sight: "The one: 'What do you see there?' – 'I see *this*' (and then a description, a drawing, a copy). The other: 'I see a likeness in these two faces.'"[19] The first sense of seeing is a trivial sense of a perceptual report where what is seen can be known by anyone once the report, drawing, or copy is given: this is a fork, that is a red apple. The second example, seeing a likeness, is more complex because one cannot presume that everyone will see the likeness the same way – or at all. If I can see the likeness between two faces, what I see is not in the sensual impressions or the fact to which it refers. I can give a report of a face, but it does not capture what I am after, namely a striking likeness between this face and another –

[17] Ricoeur, *The Rule of the Metaphor*, 152.

[18] Ibid., 212-13.

[19] Ludwig Wittgenstein, *Philosophical Investigations*, trans. G.E.M. Anscombe, P.M.S. Hacker, J. Schulte (Oxford: Wiley-Blackwell2009), part II, § 111.

which perhaps does not strike my interlocutor at all. More importantly, however, is that the object of sight implies a *relation* that you actually both see and yet do not see in the first sense of seeing. It seems to have some kind of surplus that begs for further explanations, especially because it is both seen, and in another sense, not seen. A little later on, Wittgenstein makes a variation of the second response: "I observe a face, and then suddenly notice its likeness to another. I *see* that it has not changed, and yet I see it differently."[20] Again, a relation is part of the face actually seen, a relation that cannot be reduced to visual impressions; it entails both recognising the permanence and change in what I see.

The examples may seem trivial, but the consequences might nevertheless be pervasive. Is it not the case that often we do not merely see and register things, but see things and persons in the way they are deeply intertwined with our lives and practices? When I see a familiar face, there are sedimentations of entire fields of experiences, past and present, perceived *in* the face itself. I visit a friend I haven't seen for years. I do not see contours, shapes, colours; I unhesitatingly notice that he has grown older, but still, I recognise his familiarity to me – our past is all there, our former conversations, our adventures, or common engagements. Just as faces can awaken networks of relations, so can also simple things be loaded with perceptual meaning – drawings, gestures, and words can absorb our life with them and thus acquire, using Wittgenstein's notion, a familiar *physiognomy*.[21] Not only do things have physiognomy, we can also paint with words and hear the complaint in music – which is both very common and yet quite astonishing once we think about it.[22]

Interestingly, the quote in which Wittgenstein speaks about seeing a new likeness in a familiar face brings up another important observation, namely the *suddenness* of what you see when being struck by something. This is where Wittgenstein famously appeals to Jastrow's duck-rabbit-drawing. Many have felt the fascinating and paradoxical experience of a simple drawing that changes before our very eyes: no changes of sensation or information, but still the ways we see and relate to the picture abruptly alters.[23] This sudden switch from a rabbit aspect to a duck aspect is what Wittgenstein designates "an aspect's lighting up," or "dawning of an aspect."[24] Of course, such sudden lighting up presupposes that we are willing to see the drawing as *already* either only a rabbit or only a duck; otherwise, it would not contain a radical switch. Wittgenstein calls this presupposed seeing "continuous seeing of an aspect." It takes a particular effort to see the drawing as just lines and dots on a paper; we

---

[20] Ibid., II, §§ 111, 113.
[21] Ibid., II, § 238.
[22] Ibid., II §§ 229, 267.
[23] Ibid., II, § 129
[24] Ibid., II, § 118.

immediately take it as a particularly meaningful figure. Arguably, the lighting up of an aspect is important to Wittgenstein because the sudden irruption discloses the already presupposed willingness to see aspects continuously. Hence, the lighting up discloses that we normally have always taken the familiar physiognomy of things as integral to what we see. As in Heidegger's famous break-down of the hammer, the silent presuppositions first light up in the interruptions: we first acknowledge the underlying web of our world-relation as we are disturbed and interrupted, or perhaps confronted by something we take for granted in an altered way.[25]

In the case of a sudden lighting up of an aspect, we might be filled with wonder. As a response to such a simple yet puzzling fact, Wittgenstein explores its complex conceptual relations, some of which are central to my present concern. Where Sartre carefully distinguishes between perception and thinking, Wittgenstein instead investigates the intimate relation between conceptual thinking and seeing. Let us say that someone is looking at a crowd and suddenly recognises an acquaintance. Wittgenstein then asks: "Is it a case of both seeing and thinking? Or a fusion of the two – as I would almost like to say?" Arguably, it is a fusion in so far as the seeing is also a drawing of connections between what is seen and the conception of an old friend, with all that goes with it. As such, seeing aspects is one way of spelling out the unifying or synthesising power of what Kant calls imagination. Not only does it tie conceptual thinking and perception together, but it also makes non-actual perceptions, say some past event, spring to life as amalgamated with a present perception.[26]

Interestingly, Wittgenstein also turns explicitly to imagination. In other places, such as in *Zettel*, he can, however, stress the distinction between seeing and imagining. In the latter book, he states that imagination can be distinguished from perception, for imagination does not deal with what is true or false, seeing is not a matter of will as imagination is, and so forth. And yet, he points out, there is also an intimate connection between imagination and perception.[27] This connection is picked up as Wittgenstein investigates seeing aspects, where he invites us to look at a drawing of a cube: it might be seen as a glass cube, an upturned box, or boards forming a solid angle.[28] Or you can think of a drawing of a triangle, now seen as standing, now as laying down,

[25] Stephen Mulhall, *On Being in the World. Wittgenstein and Heidegger on Seeing Aspects* (London: Routledge 1993), 121.

[26] P.F.Strawson, "Imagination and Perception," in R.C. Sutherland Walker (ed.), *Kant on Pure Reason* (Oxford: Oxford University Press, 1982), 88-89.

[27] Wittgenstein, *Zettel*, trans. G.E.M. Anscombe, G.H. von Wright (Oxford: Wiley Blackwell 1981), §§ 621, 625, 268. Cf. E. Casey's reading stresses the distinctness of imagination as a condition for its occasional continuation with perception. *Imagining: A Phenomenological Study* (Bloomington: Indiana University Press 2000), 142-45.

[28] Wittgenstein, *Philosophical Investigations*, II § 116.

now as hanging from its apex, or perhaps as a mountain, a wedge, or an arrow pointing.[29] There is little doubt that imagination that allows us to see multiple aspects of such simple figures. Wittgenstein writes:

> The concept of an aspect is related to the concept of imagination. In other words, the concept 'Now I see it as…' is related to 'Now I am imagining that'. Doesn't it take imagination to hear something as a variation of a theme? And yet one does perceive something in so hearing.[30]

To hear a variation of a musical theme, one has to employ imagination to realise how the subtle differences relate to the already presented theme. But importantly, this does not draw our awareness away from perception. Imagination does not cloud the variation in nothingness or distanciation, and it does not produce a separate world because it is what we actually hear that is the point of this game. My ability to see things in new ways or hear a theme altered in its variation depends on the capacity to bring similarities and dissimilarities into play by imagination in perception.

The interest Wittgenstein takes in the sudden lighting up of a new aspect, I argued, is connected to the way it reveals structures that already are at work in our underlying continuous aspect perception that we tend to take for granted. What we take for granted, however, is far from trivial. Wittgenstein, at one place, pauses and observes: "We find certain things about seeing puzzling because we do not find the whole business puzzling enough."[31] In other words, what we take for granted and do not find puzzling is the ordinary life, in which our world-relation implies the kind of intimate familiarity that is displayed in seeing aspects. Moreover, this observation is written in a passage where Wittgenstein treats imagination. It suggests that if we find the sudden change of a drawing puzzling because it is simultaneously implying both perception and imagination, it is because we have not yet realised that imagination is already operative in the continuous aspect perceptions all the time.

From the relatively simple examples of drawings and faces, Wittgenstein soon widens the scope of seeing aspects to the field of pictorial aesthetics, poetics, bodily expressiveness, and the acknowledgement of others. However, I will argue that it also has clear implications that bear directly on *religious* perceptions. There is no doubt that Wittgenstein took religion seriously, and also that his notion of "pictures" plays a central role, both in his early thinking but also in his later, and especially in his lectures on religion. Pictures are interesting here because they somehow seem to imply both imagination and perception, even as the notion of pictures is stretched beyond visual presentations. Now, pictures can play very different roles in our lives, from

[29] Ibid., II § 205

[30] Ibid., II § 254.

[31] Ibid., II § 251.

relatively insignificant gestalt-figures to pictures related to life and death. We may have pictures by means of which we direct ourselves to God, Wittgenstein says, to the final judgment, or to the idea of meeting one another in the afterlife, and so on.[32] But pictures can also keep us as prisoners by preventing us from seeing redeeming solutions to problems.[33] In these cases, the imaginative pictures are obviously not meant as a spontaneous product of consciousness in relation to nothingness, as Sartre will have it, or poetically sketching out possible worlds, following Ricoeur. The more significant pictures, such as religious ones, are not even tied to one or a cluster of specific language games but serve to guide and control many games in an overall way of seeing life as such. As Wittgenstein puts it: "a picture lies at the base of all thinking, it is to be respected and not treated as a superstition."[34] Playing such an important role, pictures must be embraced in the right way. You can hold one religious picture, whereas your neighbour denies it; there is no special data or empirical evidence that generates the difference, no rules of a game can fix the positions. To hold a picture is, I will suggest, a matter of seeing different aspects of life and the world: taking words, deeds, events that occur in games in a particular way. Religiously, they are taken as part of a system of reference that guides life.[35] The seeing of life and world under this aspect requires imagination; to see what is before me as a gift, my life and my world as pointing toward a particular end, entails locating what we see into a particular network of meaning. Thus, life and picture, perception and imagination, cross one another in such a Wittgensteinian view of religion.

Wittgenstein points out that seeing aspects in a simple drawing is often subject to will: I can choose to see the triangle as an arrow or a mountain. Perception of particular things, however, cannot be subjected to will in this manner because it is always restrained by what is given to us. If seeing aspects is both imagination and perception – is it then a matter of will or not? There is probably room for both, depending on the context. By my will, I can look out my window and choose to consider the landscape as God's wonderful creation, in the sense that my will and imagination inform my seeing. In many religiously relevant cases, however, seeing aspects is decisively not experienced as an act of our will, but rather as imposing itself on us – as it were, from what is seen toward what is conceived. In some cases, things can be revealed to us in this way. Still, also here, there is room for lighting up aspects that we, with Cora Diamond, may call "conversions." She starts with a

---

[32] Wittgenstein, *Lectures and Conversations on Aesthetics, Psychology and Religious*, ed. Belief, Cyril Barrett (Oxford: Blackwell 1996), 58-59, 62.

[33] Wittgenstein, *Philosophical Investigations*, § 115.

[34] Wittgenstein, *Culture and Value*, trans. P. Winch, ed. G.H. von Wright (Chicago: University of Chicago Press 1980), 83e.

[35] Ibid., 64e.

rather trivial example. Let us say you encounter a person that is not what we normally would regard as beautiful. But then her personality makes such an impression on you, so that you need to revise the prior concept of beauty. In this case, Diamond claims, the word of beauty has undergone a conversion; the word is the same, but it has been turned around by the experience itself.[36] In an analogous way, Diamond suggests that whereas some prefer to speak generically of "divinity," there may occur encounters with God that force on us a personal name. This idea, borrowed from Franz Rozenzweig, entails that one learns to know God through his doings, which in turn enforces a radical change of the previous understanding of God. The lighting up of the aspect of God's doing imposes on us new ways of understanding the meaning of God. As Diamond writes, it is a matter of a "conversion of our concepts through God revealing himself."[37]

Let me take another example, which is less about sudden changes of aspects than a gradual extension of different aspects. There are legends of the Irish hermit, St. Kevin, staying in a small cave that he had carved out with his hands. Thus, Kevin, we must assume, could see his hands as anyone else can: not *as* something particular, just the human hands used for carving, for cooking, for turning pages, and so on. But he can also stretch them toward heaven in prayer – in which the hands become, as it were, the vessels of religious contact, in relating the human body and soul upwards to the Creator. There is a particular legend that takes the seeing of the hands one step further, especially as we find it in some stanzas from Seamus Heaney's poem "St. Kevin and the Blackbird."

And then there was St Kevin and the blackbird.
The saint is kneeling, arms stretched out, inside
His cell, but the cell is narrow, so

One turned-up palm is out the window, stiff
As a crossbeam, when a blackbird lands
And lays in it and settles down to nest.

Kevin feels the warm eggs, the small breast, the tucked
Neat head and claws and, finding himself linked
Into the network of eternal life,

Is moved to pity: now he must hold his hand
Like a branch out in the sun and rain for weeks
Until the young are hatched and fledged and flown.[38]

---

[36] Cora Diamond, "Wittgenstein on Religious Belief: The Gulfs Between Us," in *Religion and Wittgenstein's Legacy*, ed. D.Z. Phillips (London: Ashgate 2005), 125.
[37] Ibid.
[38] Seamus Heaney, *The Spirit Level* (London: Faber and Faber, 1996). Thanks to Anniken Greve for drawing my attention to this poem.

First, the hand stretched out through the window, and next, the turning of the hand into a nest. Whatever else is going on in this poem, it suggests, I think, a very rich way in which we can see aspects. There is, however, further conversion of our seeing these otherwise bare hands when the blackbird lays her eggs in the praying hands. It is as though the divine addresses itself through a happening in the creation, turns the hand into the response to the miracle of received life. Thus, one simple gesture by a hand becomes, according to this way of seeing it, a nodal point of what the poem calls "the network of eternal life." It takes seeing, but also stories, language, experience, and related practices to see such things. The work of imagination is indeed, as Ricoeur has claimed, the capacity to bring such a complicated network together, with similarities and affinities, and thus make us see these hands in new and different ways.

Wonder and ordinariness

In the next part of this article, I will try to elaborate further the religious significance of such imagination in perception. Again, I will follow a lead from Ricoeur. Speaking of the revelations of the Bible, he asks: "Does not this new being make its way through the world of ordinary experience, despite the closedness of this experience?"[39] I want to pursue this question further, with special attention to how wonders might be seen to make their way through ordinary experience.

In one sense, the everyday seems, at first sight, to be as Ricoeur repeatedly proposes, namely a closed sphere of practicalities and trivialities. And yet, in another sense, these trivialities can easily appear mysterious, perhaps as a thin net over a territory that remains strangely unknown to us, or as being the very inexhaustible condition for so much of what we take to be significant, perhaps strange and mysterious despite its familiarity. In *Culture and Value*, Wittgenstein invites us to consider the following scene:

> Let us imagine a theater: the curtain goes up and we see a man alone in a room, walking up and down, lighting a cigarette, sitting down, etc. so that suddenly we are observing a human being from outside in a way that ordinarily we can never observe ourselves; it would be like watching a chapter of our biography with our own eyes, – surely this would be uncanny and wonderful at the same time. We should be observing something more wonderful than anything a playwright could arrange to be acted or spoken on the stage: life itself. – But then we do see this everyday without its making the slightest impression on us! True enough, but we do not see it from *that* point of view.[40]

Interestingly, what Wittgenstein regards as most uncanny and wonderful is not something that breaks into our experience from another sphere, but rather

[39] Ricoeur, *From Text to Action*, 97

[40] Wittgenstein, *Culture and Value*, 4e.

seeing the most trivial scene in a particular way. Just as it is possible to simply state that there is a drawing, for instance, of a duck-rabbit, one can nevertheless be struck by the strange experience of the lighting up of a new aspect. Correspondingly, where one person can be filled with the strange experience of the extraordinariness of the ordinary scene, Wittgenstein admits, another might just as well look at it "coldly." There is no difference in input or information between the two, but they see the scene differently, or as Wittgenstein puts it here, they see it from different "points of view." In the following note, Wittgenstein goes on to discuss life, birth, sickness, and dreams. There is something very trivial about such things: they happen all the time, repeatedly, all around us. And yet, we can come to see them *as if* for the first time. Wittgenstein continues: "though not that they become aware of these things for the first time but that they do suddenly start to wonder at them," upon which he concludes: "Man has to waken to wonder."[41] Such wonder is, I suggest, the way in which we let imagination draw connections and differences into a new way of seeing what is there.

The wonders that occupy Wittgenstein are those playing themselves out every day, right in front of our eyes. This not only holds for religious experiences but also lies at the heart of his later philosophy. He can say: "If you want to go down deep, you do not need to travel far; indeed, you don't have to leave your most immediate and familiar surroundings."[42] Perhaps this is an echo of one of Wittgenstein's favourite books, Augustine's *Confessions*, where Augustine says this about God: "One does not go far away or return to you by walking or by any movement through space."[43] The travelling metaphor clearly wants to reorient our interests from the remote and foreign, toward another sense of journey, returning us home, toward the near and familiar.

Augustine is the first thinker in the Western tradition that subjects miracles and wonders to any sustained scrutiny. In one of his early accounts, the question he asks himself is why miracles have, as it seems, ceased to happen. One answer he gives is that what once made us wonder has now become familiar and does not strike us anymore. Augustine exemplifies: "Take the alteration of day and night, the unvarying order of the heavenly bodies, the annual return of the four seasons, the leaves falling and returning to the trees, the endless vitality of seeds, the beauty of light, colour, sounds, odours, the varieties of flavours."[44] Given the context, the upshot seems to be: the time for wonders to strike us has ceased. However, this passage is ambiguous because

[41] Ibid., 5e

[42] Ibid, 50e

[43] Augustine, *Confessions*, trans. H. Chadwick (Oxford: Oxford University Press 1992), I, xviii, 28.

[44] Augustine, "The usefulness of Belief," in *Augustine: Earlier Writing*, ed. J.H.S. Burleigh (London: Westminster John Knox Press 2006), 320.

there remains a possibility of awakening us to wonders in the face of the ordinary. Augustine continuous: "If we could speak to someone who saw and sensed these things for the first time, we should find that he was overwhelmed and dizzy at such miracles. But we take light of such things, not because they are easy to understand – for what is more obscure than their causes – but because we are continually aware of them."[45] There are striking similarities to Wittgenstein's strange scene of the ordinary man: not only their common invocation of seeing "as if for the first time." But they are also strikingly similar in the way they portray the ordinary: on the one hand, it tends to turn everything into trivialities we take for granted, and on the other hand, the ordinary is also that which can be seen as the location of wonders. In any case, it will take imagination, I would say, to wrest the seeing from its usual grip and finding new connections and relations in what is seen.[46]

In a later and less ambiguous passage, this time from the commentary of the Gospel of John, Augustine is careful to point out that the miracles witnessed in the Bible should not lead us to marvel at its supernatural character. In introducing the miracle of Canaan, where Jesus turns water into wine, Augustine observes that for those who know God, turning water into wine is hardly marvellous at all. For all wine is made from water drops, nourishing the grapes that in turn are cultivated into wine, and God makes this happen every year. The uncommon is not more important than the common. The point with the uncommon miracles is that God wants to awaken us from our sleep in order to let us see. The strange hiddenness of all of that which is in front of our eyes is certainly important to Wittgenstein's struggle with the ordinary; we are, he says, "unable to notice something – because it is always before our eyes."[47] Augustine thinks of the interconnectedness between the ordinary and the extraordinary in terms of constant recurrence and sudden presence:

> For He is the same God who, throughout the whole creation, worketh miracles every day, which become lightly esteemed by men, not because of the ease with which they are wrought, but by reason of their constant recurrence. Those uncommon works, however, which were done by the same Lord, … occasioned greater astonishment to men, not because these which happens every day are accomplished as it were in the course of nature; but the other appears exhibited to the eyes of men, … as it were, immediately present.[48]

---

[45] Ibid.

[46] I have elaborated the relation between Augustine and Wittgenstein on this point with some greater detail in «Wittgenstein and Augustin eon Seeing Miracles» in *Augustine and Wittgenstein*, ed. J. Doody, A.R. Eodice, K. Paffenroth (Lanham: Lexington Books 2018), 95-112.

[47] Wittgenstein, *Philosophical Investigations*, §129.

[48] *Homilies on the Gospel of St. John*¸ ed. P.A. Böer (Dublin: Veritas Splendor Publications 2012), IX, ii, 1.

No doubt, the uncommon miracles have another impact on us, and yet, as Augustine repeatedly stresses, that does not mean that their significance is greater or different from the common wonders. The whole point is that those uncommon miracles are like a lightening up of a new aspect that turns us toward the continuous seeing of aspects, albeit in new ways. The wonders are all there, all of the time, but we are poor receivers.

Such perspective may lead to a particular understanding of the most famous episode told in his entire authorship: Augustin's own conversion as accounted for in the *Confessions*. One should notice that this life-changing event is strikingly unremarkable in its outer occurrence: no lightning and thunder, miraculous phenomena, no voice from above, but simply a man sitting in his garden, plagued by inner tensions. He reports: "I heard a voice from the nearby house chanting as if it might be a boy or a girl (I do not know which), saying and repeating over and over again 'Pick up and read, pick up and read.'"[49] Once it calls on his attention, Augustine assumes that this must be some sort of children's game, even if he cannot recall in which game such chant is used. Again, the address comes from the most ordinary of scenes – curiously one favoured by Wittgenstein: a simple language game. But of course, the important thing is the way in which Augustine sees it, or rather, hears it: the children's game is recognised as God's voice, as if the most ordinary suddenly turns into the most extraordinary, indeed, the very pivot of Augustine's self-narration. And again, the randomness of the reading when he picks up and reads underlines the strange crossing of trivialities and ultimate significance: "Not in riots and drunken parties, not in eroticism and indecencies, not in strife and rivalry, but put on the Lord Jesus Christ and make no provision of the flesh in its lusts" (Rom. 13: 13-14). While the text addresses Augustine's previous vices, it also suggests that true Christian life is not to be found in false ecstasies beyond the ordinary but in the embodiment of decent and ordinary life itself.

I quoted Ricoeur, posing the question: "Does not this new being make its way through the world of ordinary experience, despite the closedness of this experience?"[50] What I have been driving at with these passages from Augustine is to answer this question affirmatively. Nothing new is perceived; it is laid out in plain sight before our eyes; day turns to night, winter into spring, seeds grow, a man sitting in the garden surrounded by the noise of children playing. But all of a sudden, everything remains the same, and yet everything has changed. It is like a conversion, Diamond and Augustine would say, a conversion of perception and words at times of life as such. Seeing more and otherwise, I will say, draws on the possibilities of imagination in perception.

---

[49] Augustine, *Confessions*, VIII, xii, 29.
[50] Ricoeur, *From Text to Action*, 97

Transfiguration of the ordinary

In my final part, I will return to my hypothesis, namely that imagination is not only a matter of perceiving more and otherwise but also, I said, "drawing on possibilities in what is seen that potentially transfigure our otherwise ordinary reality." I will now draw together some of the upshots from what I have already said in order to address such transfiguration of the ordinary.

While the ordinary tends to become swamped by habits, repetitions, and drowsiness, wonders move in the opposite direction, awakening us to what is in front of our eyes. But what exactly does it mean to see in new ways, when what is seen remains the ordinary? Here I think Husserl has made a significant contribution: Imagination lets the play of free variation unfold in order for us to intuit the *possibility* of phenomena.[51] Indeed, Husserl (and later Heidegger) deems the possibility higher than actuality since it opens us to the essence of things. Arguably, such is one of the important upshots of the imaginative process he calls "eidetic variation."[52] Furthermore, to imagine possibilities does not only refer us to the essence of what things are but also points toward a not yet redeemed state of things; Husserl here draws on the Aristotelian notion of *telos*.[53] The point is simply that, granted such understanding, it will become hard to stick to the traditional, Platonic view, in which imagination refers backwards, reproducing images from former perceptions. Instead, the notion of possibilities of new constellations and connections points *forward* toward productive employment. Ricoeur has seen this with clarity. Take literary fiction: it does not reproduce a previous reality but produces new realities, at a distance from ordinary reality unfolded in front of the text. Such manifestations of possibilities, in turn, can work back into the sense of our lifeworld.[54]

Ricoeur's dialectical movement means, however, that he does not account for the more immediate ways in which Wittgenstein would argue that we can perceive in accordance with imagination. For Ricoeur, imagination affects our seeing through the detour of the sign.[55] Nevertheless, Ricoeur still

---

[51] Julia Janssen, "On the development of Husserl's transcendental phenomenology of imagination and its use for interdisciplinary research," *Phenomenology and the Cognitive Sciences* 4 (2005): 126-27.

[52] Husserl, *Experience and Judgement*, trans. J.S Churchill, K. Ameriks (Evanston: Northwestern University Press 1973), 340-43.

[53] Husserl, *The Crisis of European Sciences and Transcendental Phenomenology*, trans. D. Carr (Evanston: Northwestern University Press 1970), 299.

[54] Ricoeur, "The metaphorical process," 154.

[55] To Ricoeur, the investigations falls short of any true fruitfulness, since it does not move beyond perception and interpretation of ambiguous shapes is in Jastrow's duck/rabbit drawing. Furthermore, regarded as a theory of imagination, Ricoeur thinks Wittgenstein lapses back into the reproductive model, and shows no resources for productive imagining. Cf. Taylor, "Ricoeur's Philosophy of Imagination,".

acknowledges that fiction does not leave the world untouched: it projects something new and even draws on ontological structures of possibilities that are already implied in our reality. "*Fiction*," Ricoeur writes, "addresses itself to deeply rooted potentialities of reality to the extent that they are absent from the actualities with which we deal in everyday life under the mode of empirical control and manipulation."[56] According to Ricoeur, utopia, the non-place of a possible future, is one of the ways in which imagined worlds open present perception. The same applies to Biblical texts, Ricoeur argues, by proposing a new being, be it a new world, a new covenant, the kingdom of God, or new birth. And what "is thereby opened up in everyday reality is another reality, the reality of the *possible*," Ricoeur says.[57] Alternatively, with particular reference to myths, he can say that myths "are not just nostalgia for some forgotten world. They constitute a disclosure of unprecedented worlds, an opening on to the other *possible* worlds which transcend the established limits of our *actual* world."[58]

From a Wittgensteinian point of view, one may argue that Ricoeur is still stuck in a one-sided notion of the everyday: Ricoeur depicts it as the closed world of manipulation and control, something we must suspend in unfolding our imagination. Yet, if the ordinary is the very *home* of both speaking, acting, thinking, and perceiving, then the synthesising function of the imagination must remain attached to the everyday. Moreover, if the ordinary is also the site of wonders, as Augustine claims, then it cannot be completely closed in on itself either, but rather ambiguous and open. True, the ordinary has this tendency toward trivialisation, but it is also true that it harbours rifts and depths, labyrinths and mysteries that can light up at any moment. If we turn critically to Wittgenstein, however, we might still wish to ask what room he leaves for imagining the future, the possible, the new. What new visions are possible if philosophy, according to Wittgenstein, "must not interfere in any way with the actual use of language"? He can even say: "What has to be accepted, [is] the given."[59] More than one critic has pointed out that such a view commits us philosophically to *status quo*, politically to conservatism, and religiously to fideism immune to criticism.[60]

While it is hard to deny that there are appeals to finding back, returning, finding the everyday our home, acceptance, and so forth within Wittgenstein's thinking, the charge loses sight of the *reason* why he wants to point us towards

---

[56] Ricoeur, "The metaphorical process," 154-55.

[57] Ricoeur, *From Text to Action*, 96-97.

[58] Kearney, *Debates in Continental Philosophy* (New York: Fordham University Press 2004), 124.

[59] Wittgenstein, *Philosophical Investigations*, § 124; cf. II, § 345.

[60] Cf. Kai Nielsen, «Wittgenstein's Fideism,» *Philosophy* 42 (1967): 191-209. Ricoeur comes close to the same criticism in "The Later Wittgenstein and the Later Husserl on Language" *Ricoeur Studies* 5 (2014): 40-41.

the given use of language and the given forms of life. It is precisely because he finds that words and life have become out of touch with each other, that we have deformed the way we think and see ourselves in the world; it is, for this reason, we must leave everything as it is – in the sense of taking leave of it, departing from it, letting it go. Wittgenstein's therapies do not lead us out of the ordinary, bracketing or transcending the everyday. Rather, it suggests a return to it, which is at the same time a turning forward – turning us toward a possible everyday that we have lost sight of, toward a life where we can mean what we say and live accordingly. Thus, it is not a radical change from the outside he proposes, but from the inside. As Stanley Cavell has suggested, Wittgenstein is proposing a possible or eventual everyday in the face of the actual everyday that is presently lived in illusion and loss. Cavell writes:

> His philosophy of the (eventual) everyday is the proposal of a practice that takes on, takes upon itself, precisely (I do not say exclusively) that scene of illusion and loss; approaches it, or let me say reproaches it, intimately enough to turn it or deliver it; as if the actual is the womb, contains the terms of the eventual. The direction out from illusion is not up, at any rate not up to one fixed morning star; but down, at any rate along each chain of a day's denial.[61]

Starting in the state of loss and illusion of the actual everyday, then reforming it by descending more deeply into it, and then leaving it, moving on to the eventual everyday: this is hardly a conservative embrace of *status quo*. It is like realising that what we took as our home was a state of exile, but also that the home to which we turn is never a place for finally settling down. The eventual everyday as our home is more like a project, which goal or telos is never fully attained but still intimate enough to make the everyday change. What I want to add to Cavell's understanding is that such dynamics of the everyday takes the capacity to imagine. Imagination can both help in freeing us from the false chains as well as proposing new possibilities. Ricoeur finds that the Biblical promise of the possible has such power because it speaks "to my imagination, proposing to it the 'figures' of my liberation"[62] – freed, as it were, both from the actual everyday and toward to possible everyday. To come to see the ordinary world as a promise is first and foremost to see – and imagine according to that seeing – the ordinary transfigured.

---

[61] Stanley Cavell, *This New Yet Unapproachable America* (Albuquerque: Living Batch Press 1989), 46.

[62] Ricoeur, *From Text to Action*, 101.

Imagination, Representation, and Abduction
On basic Features in Religion

Jan-Olav Henriksen

Introduction

All religion depends on the semiotic character of experience. In religion, symbols, practices, narratives, rituals, and artefacts are all signs that stand in for and represent something more and other than what actually is present or takes place. Therefore, a likely approach to religion is to see it as practices based on and related to representations of the divine reality. Such representations are present in everything from the readings of scriptures to preaching, the celebration of the sacraments of baptism or the Eucharist, or the festival around the symbolic depiction of the elephant Ganesha. They are unavoidable – not only from the point of view of the philosophy of religion (for which I will use Hegel as an example below) but also if one adopts a more specific theological point of view (given that God or the divine is not part of the empirical reality, but only accessible by means of representations, be it in Scriptures, revelations, or God as manifested in Jesus Christ). Representations engender responses and allow for imaginations that open reality up to us in new and/or different ways that point beyond the present.

This article will argue that all representations, including religious ones, imply imagination. Representations cannot do without imagination, and the content of imagination may depend, to some extent, on concrete representations. Representations are signs, and from a semiotic point of view, the connection between imagination and representation is constituted by the capacity for abduction. Abduction is not necessarily a function of a rational mind but consists of our and every being's ability to experience, respond to, see, or understand something as having significance related to a given context. E.g., when a Christian sees wine and bread, she can abductively posit these elements in a context that make them appear as Eucharist, although there is nothing in these elements themselves that make such an inference necessary. What these elements represent depends on the context in which we imagine them. On its part, the context depends on our abductive inferences – how we establish the context for interpreting the elements.

Even conceptual reasoning depends on our ability to make abductive inferences from representations that imply that we imagine something as something. Thus, we need to take issue with an approach to religion that sees imaginations (*Vorstellungen*) as a temporary stage towards a more full or mature religious consciousness, which is the position that Hegel advocates. In order to develop an argument against Hegel, I will, in the two first sections of this article, present elements in Robert Neville's understanding of how imagination is a necessary mode of relating to the world (including its religious relevance) and then make some remarks about abduction. Against that backdrop, I analyse Hegel's understanding of representation. I argue that it downplays the fundamental role of imagination and abduction in religion. Finally, this will lead to the conclusion that it is necessary to understand all religion from its substantial content in representations (and not only their functional dimension). Accordingly, addressing the concrete imaginations of religion is imperative in order to understand what people do with religion and what it does to them.

Hence, the article will provide arguments for two interrelated claims:

- Religions depend on imagination, and imagination in religion requires an abductive capacity that becomes manifest in the interpretation of human experiences made possible by specific representations. The semiotic repertoire on which such interpretations and their concomitant experiences depend is shaped by religious representations' substantive content.
- Accordingly, religions cannot merely be understood from a functional point of view but must be seen as intrinsically related to substantive contents in imaginations that shape practices of orientation and transformation. These practices, in turn, are the result of pragmatically oriented interpretative concerns that employ religious symbols.

Neville on Imagination

Robert C. Neville's analysis of the role of imagination in human life combines a hermeneutically oriented approach to imagination with a clear view of its pragmatic implications and aspects. Thus, he is interested in understanding imagination and focuses on how it works and what it does to enable human life in its different forms.[1]

Neville sees imagination as "the most primary or primitive organisation of human experience." It is religious, regardless of whether it contains any specifically religious symbols of God or related matters. That is the case, he claims, because "Imagination in this basic function as world-making is always religious because it is world constructing." It is religious insofar as it serves "to frame the dimensions or boundaries of experiential worldliness"[2] This view tacitly implies that a religious dimension in imagination is suggested in the short definition of imagination he offers: "The capacity to experience things

[1] I have developed a more comprehensive interpretation of Neville's understanding of imagination in Jan-Olav Henriksen, *Finitude and Theological Anthropology : An Interdisciplinary Exploration into Theological Dimensions of Finitude* (Leuven: Peeters, 2011).

[2] Robert C. Neville, *The Truth of Broken Symbols*, Albany (SUNY, 1999), 55

with images."[3] Accordingly, Neville sees imagination as that which makes a "difference between experiencing something and merely responding as a response in vector of forces." According to him, imagination establishes a particular kind of causal synthesis between the experienced and the imagined – or, in my words, between the representation and what it represents. "It integrates impinging conditions which might not have experiential form in such a way that they take on experiential form and so become parts of experience and subject to reference in interpretative experience."[4] Against this backdrop, imagination is crucial for human orientation and transformation that build on values. It enables responses that value things in an imagined field related to other values.[5]

From a broader perspective, imagination is of crucial importance because it constitutes the worldliness of the world as we experience it.[6] In this constitution, the connections between the elements of the world are made immediately by abduction. Due to such connections and the way abduction allows us to experience the world, imaginations can guide or orient us – not only in space and time but with regard to what matters and not, in terms of values, preferences, etc.

According to Neville, imagination also singles out the perceptive forms in which we experience the world. The identification of such forms has the effect that the world becomes structured in the foreground and background, and we become able to perceive "things," which, in turn, can be distinguished from other things. Thus, imagination is constitutive for how we understand the world – but it also establishes the world as something that unavoidably appears as it is for us, and from our perspective. This is the reason why Neville expands his analysis of imagination with reference to the notion of representation: "In respect of the variable quality of focal attention, the experiential world is a (possible) representation of the real world, and different from it in certain aspects of imaginative structure," he argues. Therefore, "Perceptible things with their imaginative background have their imaginative form of appearance."[7]

Appearances are thus dependent on imagination. They present themselves as the way real things appear – as relative to us as experiencers. Thus, imagination is constitutive for *that* we experience, *what* we experience, and *how* we experience. Furthermore, "Images, in their perceptive thing-in-background imaginative structures, have the intentional vector quality of real things

---

[3] Ibid., 47.
[4] Ibid, 48.
[5] Cf. ibid., 49.
[6] Cf. ibid., 49.
[7] Ibid., 51.

appearing."[8] Hence, "It is the nature of mental stuff – imagination – to make the world appear."[9] Furthermore, the constitutive role of imagination and its abductive dimension determines how experiences have relations of importance amongst one another. These relations of importance are the reason why things appear to have value relative to one another. "Imaginative forms of appearance make these values appear, as the values would not appear without the imagined thing."[10]

It is now possible to explicate more in detail how Neville's analysis of imagination has relevance for the understanding of religion: it is because some elements in the constitution of the experience of the world, or how it is represented in our perception of it, appear in a specific manner as *shaping the world which has a specific impact on human practices and modes of being in the world.* Neville writes about these as "Paradigmatic orienting appearances that have symbolic value for defining ultimate contours (world-construction elements)." These elements "Function as boundary images that define the dimensions of the world itself."[11]

Although imaginations are formed subjectively, they become projected onto the objective world – and thereby also, as objectified in society, re-appropriated subjectively. Thus, religion becomes part of human culture, shared among a group that employs them and considers them as world-important elements. Especially important in this regard is – contrary to Hegel (see below) that these elements are considered contingent and not the result of some logical necessity. Writes Neville; "Where the experiential organization of the appearances of the world clusters symbols around those boundary conditions, the very form of imagination lends itself to conditions of contingency."[12] The world itself is thus experienced as dependent on these conditions that appear in imagination based on abductive inferences from representation.

Two additional features in Neville's analysis of the religious dimension of imagination must be mentioned. First, it is due to a specific way of imagining it that the world becomes experienced as contingent (concerning God, God's creative act, etc.). Second, the symbols that express contingent conditions mark the boundary between the finite and the infinite.[13] Therefore, everything that can be understood as religious symbols will express the finite/infinite contrast, directly or indirectly. However, the employment of them as such will not only require imagination, but also the ability to make abductive inferences about their character and significance.

---

[8] Ibid.
[9] Ibid.
[10] Ibid., 52-53.
[11] Ibid., 56.
[12] Ibid.
[13] Cf. Ibid., 58.

In conclusion, then, for Neville, imagination is the way by which we engage the world.[14] Hence, one can argue that imagination is necessary for the practices of orientation and transformation that people engage in when they engage religious representations. The practices related to these aims are conditioned by symbols that must express the finite/infinite contrast if such practices are to be defined as religious.

A few comments on abduction

It is possible to link the element of contingency that Neville points to above to the abductive element in world-experience. Abduction is an operation of inference that has no necessity but which nevertheless shapes all types of human experience, including religious ones. Abduction is an element in all perceptions. It moves from something observed or experienced to a context of determination or interpretation that allows for explicating its significance and relevance.[15] Abductions need not be theoretical at all, but they may lead to theoretical assumptions about a phenomenon or to conclusions that are more general. For C.S. Peirce, sound abductive reasoning from P to Q involves not merely a determination that, e.g., Q is sufficient for P, but also that Q is among the most economical explanations for P. Simplification and economy call for the 'leap' of abduction. Moreover, in abductive reasoning, unlike in deductive reasoning, the premises do not guarantee the conclusion. One can understand abductive reasoning as inference to the best explanation.

Abductions are always preliminary and have a hypothetical character. There is no final closure for abductive forms of reasoning. The main advantage of abduction is that such inferences give new or more profound meaning to already known phenomena, as they allow for the redescription or recontextualization of an experience. Hence, the imaginative element with which one meets a representation of something assumed to have religious content or character will always also imply the possibility of it as something that could be otherwise.

It is essential to see abduction as something that regulates our perceptions of the world and not as something fundamentally constitutive of it. If abductions constituted the world, "any abductive representation of the world would *ipso facto* be true, i.e., would perfectly correspond to the world. But nothing guarantees that the world is isomorphic to the representation of it: in abduction, we merely act *as if* our representations of it were isomorphic to the world, without, however, thereby asserting that the world is in fact as it is

[14] Ibid., 59.

[15] A thorough analysis of abduction can be found in G. Schurz, "Patterns of Abduction," *An International Journal for Epistemology, Methodology and Philosophy of Science* 164, no. 2 (2008).

represented to be."[16] Umberto Eco, therefore, argues that abduction in our experience of the world is based on a meta-abduction: our reasoning is based on the assumption that it is justified to act based on abductions (*as if* abduction were a valid form of reasoning). Accordingly, "we proceed as if the meta-abduction that the world represented in our first-level abductions is the same as the world of our experience."[17]

These short remarks suggest that abduction plays several roles in relation to religious imaginaries. It contributes to their *conceptual* constitution, their interpretation, inferences about their implications, and the development of the arguments in which they take part. The following will show how these connections are observable as a tacit dimension in Hegel's philosophy of religion.

Re-reading Hegel's view on representations in light of imagination and abduction

Despite the fact that Hegel treats imagination in relation to the German notions *Einbildungskraft* and *Anschauung* in several paragraphs in his *Enzyclopädie,* this treatise does not appear to have continuing influence when he deals with topics related to religion.[18] To the extent that imagination (as *Einbildungskraft*) plays a role, it is due to its capacity to engender representations (*Vorstellungen*). In such representations, the object becomes determined only through the subjective function of imagination. "So ist sie in jenem in sich *bestimmt* erinnert und ihn diesem ihrem Inhalt einbildend. – *Phantasie*, *symbolisierende*, *allegorisierende*, oder *dichtende* Einbildungskraft."[19] The negative assessment of this function may to some extent be based on the role that fantasy (*Phantasie*) plays in his elaborations of the theme, and it spills over into his assessment of representations in religion because of their subjective origin and their concomitant lack of being – "das Moment des *Seienden* fehlt noch."[20]

Against this backdrop, it is no surprise that imagination does not play a large role in Hegel's philosophy of religion. In the final version of his lectures on that topic, it is mainly addressed in a slightly derogatory way. There he treats imagination mainly as indicating the results of invented fantasies or simply being fantasies. This is the reason why the above analysis via Neville may contribute something positively, also when reading Hegel on representation.

---

[16] This point is developed in Francesco Bellucci, "Eco and Peirce on Abduction," *European Journal of Pragmatism and American Philosophy*, no. X-1 (2018): 12-13.

[17] Ibid., 13.

[18] See Georg Wilhelm Friedrich Hegel, *Werke in Zwanzig Bänden*, Theorie - Werkausgabe (Frankfurt am Main: Suhrkamp, 1976), Vol 10, §§ 455-59.

[19] Ibid., § 456, (p. 266).

[20] Ibid., § 457, (p. 267).

Hegel seems to underrate the role that imagination plays in the constitution of the experience of the world.

As is well known, Hegel distinguishes between three modes in which religious consciousness expresses itself:

- In immediate feeling (subjective religion)
- In the concrete representations that allow us to imagine that which is not seen (*Vorstellungen*, (objective religion).[21]
- In conceptual understanding (Begriff, absolute Religion)[22]

In relation to Hegel, I will argue for another approach to representations against the backdrop of Nrville's theory of imagination, representation, and abduction:

1. Even immediate feeling is anchored in some kind of representation that depends on abduction to explicate its religious significance. Perhaps the most prominent examples to illustrate this point is psychological theories such as Kohut's theory of self-objects,[23] but one can also find warrants for similar considerations in William James.[24]
2. The religious stage of (concrete) representations is not to be sublated but is an unavoidable and permanent element in all religious practice and reflection.
3. Even conceptual and rational religious consciousness depends and is working on the basis of representations – since also concepts are representations, albeit not necessarily physical ones.

These claims can be substantiated through a critical analysis of Hegel's insights into the historicity of concepts.[25] He understands the dynamics behind

---

[21] It is worth noting here that "Vorstellungen" in Hegel, from a semiotic point of view, can be seen as overlapping with "imaginations." For further elaborations on "Vorstellungen" in relation to imagination and abductrion, and consequently also the significance for the understanding of (religious) experience in general, see H. Deuser, *Religionsphilosophie,* Berlin: De Gruyter, 2008, § 16.

[22] In the following presentation of Hegel's philosophy of religion, I rely on the edition by Peter C. Hodgson, in Georg Wilhelm Friedrich Hegel, *Lectures on the Philosophy of Religion : The Lectures of 1827*, ed. Robert F. Brown Peter Crafts Hodgson; (Oxford; New York: Clarendon Press; Oxford University Press, 2006).

[23] For Kohut's theory and its significance for religious experience, see Jan-Olav Henriksen, *Relating God and the Self : Dynamic Interplay* (Ashgate, 2013). In the present context, I will not argue further for seeing self-objects as representations that works on similar conditions as imaginations as described by Neville above, but will take that as a given. That it is so, is nevertheless not necessary for the analysis of Hegel that follows in this section.

[24] Cf. William James, *The Varieties of Religious Experience : A Study in Human Nature*, Penguin Classics (New York ; London: Penguin Books, 1985), 27f. (original pagination).

[25] The following analysis of Hegel is a reworking of selected sections in my *Representation and Ultimacy: The Christian Religion as Unfinished Business* (Zürich; Münster: LIT Verlag, 2020). As is obvious from the following, it is not entering into a detailed discussion of Hegel's own views on imagination, although it may deserve a study in itself to discuss the

the development of what he calls the concept (*Begriff*) as the result of processes in which one cannot remain in the immediacy where we originally find ourselves. Concepts are always developed in negation to other concepts. Moreover, the context plays a significant role in how their content is shaped. Hence, already at this stage, it is tacitly suggested that abduction is at play. Abduction leads to the assumptions about which context is the most relevant for constituting the concept and develop it further. Whatever we try to understand is conditioned by contextual and historical processes that involve abductive reasoning. Even when one, like Hegel, claims that understanding starts from and is conditioned by a concept, one cannot ignore that the evolution of a concept is dependent on abductive inferences based on and emerging out of engagement with concrete phenomena.

Furthermore, understanding builds on and is rooted in previous, insufficient forms of thinking that attempted to come to terms with the object that constitutes their content. Because the concept is the basis for the understanding of a phenomenon in Hegel's view, the development of understanding (of religion) is based on the concept's content, and it is the concept that allows for further understanding.[26] However, Hegel downplays the role that representations and imagination continue to play for the content of the concept.[27] At this point, I think Neville's analysis of imagination in experience adds to the foundations of Hegel's reasoning because Neville underscores the continuous role imagination plays.

In both Hegel and his contemporary, Schleiermacher, "conceptualization of religion depends upon their accounts of human feeling, cognition, and action."[28] Hence, both of them address issues that are important to understand how concrete religion depends on abductive modes of inference. They make explicit what remains merely implicit in a great deal of theorizing of religion

potential role that his early writings' view on imagination might be relevant to his lectures on philosophy of religion – or not. On Hegel's views on imagination and ist background in Romanticism, see John Sallis, "Commentary on "Imagination and Presentation" in Hegel's Philosophy of Spirit," in *Hegel's Philosophy of Spirit*, ed. Peter G. Stillman (Albany: State University of New York Press, 1987). and Jennifer Ann Bates, *Hegel's Theory of Imagination* (New York: State University of New York Press, 2004). In general, Hegel's notion of imagination seems to be linked mainly to his views on aesthetics.

[26] Hegel, *Enzyclopädie* I, 307 (Vol 8); Wissenchaft der Logik II, 264 (Vol 6) in Hegel, *Werke in Zwanzig Bänden*.

[27] That is, in the *Lectures on Philosophy of religion*. In the *Encyclopädie,* imaginations plays a certain role when it comes to the formation of signs, and thereby, indirectly also have some bearings on the formation of universal concepts. See See Georg Wilhelm Friedrich Hegel, *Werke in Zwanzig Bänden,* Theorie - Werkausgabe (Frankfurt am Main: Suhrkamp, 1976), Vol 10, § 457 (pp 268-269).

[28] Cf. Thomas A. Lewis, *Why Philosophy Matters for the Study of Religion-and Vice Versa* (New York, NY: Oxford University Press, 2015), 76.

and point to features that must be addressed to explicate more fully what is at stake in religious phenomena. Accordingly, T.A. Lewis claims that,

> Conceptions of the human subject – of our cognition as well as the relation between our practical and theoretical activity, for instance – are integral to conceptions of religion. In this respect, even theorizing of religion that seeks to abstain from these philosophical questions will draw upon particular sets of answers to them, whether conscious of doing so or not. Philosophy is thus unavoidable in the conceptualization of religion.[29]

Even though Lewis is right in pointing to this, one could also argue the opposite: that concrete experience that presupposes both imagination and abduction (cf. Neville, above) is necessary for conceptualisation. Both experience and conceptualization build on historical processes and their outcome and on abductive processes.

In the quoted passage, Thomas Lewis also argues implicitly for highlighting that religion is about more than it articulates when we understand it merely on its own premises, as is the case in immediate beliefs and practices, and in theologies that take for granted the reality to which these relate. This point is what philosophy and reasoning that addresses pragmatic and transcendental preconditions for human life can bring to the fore. One crucial consequence that follows is that philosophical reflection can explicate why religion is not only about a world beyond or about belief in supernatural entities. Hegel illustrates this well, in Lewis' opinion:

> As much as Hegel's project seeks to validate inherited religious claims, it does so by justifying them as representations. Their genuine significance lies not in their relation to particular historical events or literalistic readings of the representational claims but in their representational expression of the truths treated most adequately in philosophy. In perhaps the most important example, Hegel preserves much traditional language about God, validating and justifying it; yet, over the course of his philosophical system, he argues that this absolute is to be understood in terms of the social practices of the human community rather than the superhuman being frequently presented in religious representations.[30]

To understand religions this way, however, implies that what one identifies as religious features can become articulated in the self-conscious and critical reflection where philosophy offers the chances for identifying something as *representations*. The character of such reflection is tied closely to how Hegel understands the pragmatic conditions for the concept – in this case, the concept of religion and how it works for a specific community.

Against this backdrop, philosophical insight into religion cannot be the starting point for what we know about religion. Actual, practised, empirical religion is "a necessary stage in our learning and appropriation of these

---

[29] Ibid.

[30] Ibid., 77.

insights."[31] Nevertheless, one cannot remain by immediate appearances of religion if one is to understand what it is. Religious practices, images, narratives, etc., must be understood as ways to represent a deeper dimension of reality that always brings forth something new. It is most likely here the capacity for abduction is at work in the most apparent way. Thus, by necessity, philosophy as the reflective response to these representations will not be able to round up and bring to closure religions' dealing with the open-ended character of human life. Instead, there are important reasons for thinking, against Hegel, that philosophy itself in its dealing with and reflection on religion will need to explicate why it is not its task to bring about such closure. This points back to what Neville claimed about the role of imagination in our experience of the world and to the role of abduction in the same.

Paul Ricoeur is perhaps the one who has articulated the point about the impossibility of a final sublation of religion into philosophy most clearly. In his famous dictum about how "the symbol gives rise to thought, and thought returns to the symbol,"[32] he develops an understanding of religious representations that seems to acknowledge their continuous role in keeping open a religious attitude towards the world. Religious representations in terms of "[p]arables, paradoxes, hyperboles, and extreme commandments all *dis*orient only in order to *re*orient us," but not so much in terms of our will as in terms of our imagination.[33] But where Ricoeur points to the continuous role of imagination for religion, Hegel's approach concentrates on the conditions for developing the concept.

Hegel's notion of the *concept* implies that all understanding of finite phenomena is insufficient. However, for him, this is not a reason for "returning to the symbol," with all it entails with regard to imagination and abduction. Instead, this insufficiency is the main reason he is critical to a merely empirical approach to religion. It eliminates the chance for seeing the empirical as conditioned by the absolute or the infinite, i.e., God. Hence, his philosophy is not concerned with empirical realities as such. For Hegel, they serve as immediate instances that one needs to overcome in order to develop an understanding that allows for the appearance and the conceptualisation of the absolute. This appearance and its result are still outstanding or deferred, though. Nevertheless, some elements in this approach can prove relevant for the understanding of *religion* and call us back to concrete experience as the basis on which understanding of religion has to build:

---

[31] Ibid.

[32] Paul Ricoeur, *The Symbolism of Evil*, Religious Perspectives (New York: Harper & Row, 1967), 347ff.

[33] *Figuring the Sacred : Religion, Narrative, and Imagination* trans. David Pellauer (Minneapolis: Augsburg Fortress, 1995), 281.

The concept 'religion' is itself an abstraction based on a limited number of experiences and cases that have contributed to the development of what we hitherto have been able to grasp as 'religion.' This limited access to the full phenomenon has implications for the concept of religion as well. However, instead of abstracting from the historical and empirical to develop a concept of religion, one must consider its concrete historical forms and functions within a given context to further understand and conceptualize it.[34] In this process, abduction is at play because merely inductive or deductive approaches will not be able to expand our knowledge of religion, neither as a phenomenon nor the concept itself. A generic and ahistorical notion of religion forbids itself.

Hegel's insistence on overcoming immediacy means that we cannot remain by the phenomenon as it appears. We need to assume, with him, that we do not know what religion is only from what we observe in front of us. Not only do we need to know something about its historical development and origin, but we also need to know something about its present contribution to human life – how it works and, thus, what it *represents* in a given life context. This latter, pragmatic element, is necessary to address in its concreteness, but it is also essential to make the abductions (and sometimes, generalizations) necessary for shaping an adequate concept of religion. Otherwise, our understanding of religion would not be possible to develop. The concept of religion that informs the interpretation of what is at hand is of vital significance: without it, we would neither understand what religion is in the first place nor be able to develop and adjust our understanding of it. Not only is religion itself a contextual and historical phenomenon, so are the preconditions for our understanding of it as well.

Hegel uses the term 'religion' for elements that refer "to the representations and other practices through which we come to know the absolute."[35] Hegel focuses on *knowing*. However, we need to expand this approach because religions also are about *engaging* the absolute. The finite/infinite contrast in symbols suggested by Neville points in this direction, but so does, in fact, also the crucial *pedagogical* role that religion plays in Hegel's thinking. He "develops a vision in which religion plays a central role in shaping our deep

---

[34] These remarks can be substantiated further by the following insights by Thomas A. Lewis: "[H]istorical and social scientific studies of religion necessarily presuppose responses to the kinds of philosophical questions about the nature of reason, belief, and practice that lie at the heart of much work in philosophy of religion. Any attempt to theorize religion depends upon prior commitments— implicit or explicit— about how to construct the object that needs investigation. And these commitments involve non-trivial claims about the nature of reason and its relation to other, related forms of human sensibility. There is nothing wrong with such reliance, but it should be more than implicit. Lewis, *Why Philosophy Matters for the Study of Religion-and Vice Versa*, 81-82.

[35] Ibid., 77.

intuitions about social and political life."[36] This role seems to problematise or contradict contemporary approaches to religion that argue that it should be separated from the political sphere in principle. It is not possible because of its rootedness in the deep psyche of the human. The value commitments from which we orient ourselves are not something we can bracket or ignore in parts of our lives without severe consequences.[37] Neville, as well, underscores this point clearly in his analysis of imagination.

Of course, the fact that value commitments are rooted deeply in our personal feelings, judgments, and psychological dispositions does not mean that they cannot be altered or revised. Philosophical reflection may criticize or offer justifications for them, and thereby make them more transparent. However, such later reflective practices can lead to different results. "Depending on circumstances, the result may be a reformation of habits or a divided self split between deeply ingrained habits and pre-reflective responses, on the one hand, and explicit, theoretical commitments, on the other," writes Lewis.[38] In both cases, an element of transformation is required, and religious practices of formation and reflection may provide the means for it. But such practices cannot exist independent of imaginations and representations.

As we saw, according to Hegel, religion is not directed toward a transcendent, superhuman subject. Religion works to express and shape our self-understanding. Hence, it is a "set of practices through which we reflect upon and express our essence, spirit."[39] Therefore, religion relates to more than the cognitive dimension in human life and practice: religion is "an interrelated set of feelings, representations, rituals, and other social practices that mould and express a consciousness of our own essence."[40] To realise the significance of such experiences and bind them together in a coherent whole, though, we need imagination and abduction.

Moreover, when Hegel focuses on religious practices, he does not exclude belief because "religious practices cannot be understood without reference to the *content* of religious representations – and vice versa. Hegel thus challenges the reduction of religion to either belief or practice."[41] Hence, he opens up to a

---

[36] Ibid.

[37] Ibid. "Because religion shares philosophy's content but is more closely connected to feeling, religion— particularly a child's early religious formation – frequently powerfully informs the subject's most firmly held commitments about our relations to others – how we depend on them, what we owe them, how we ought to act toward them, and so forth. While these commitments can in principle be revised, they are often deeply habitual and pre-reflective. They constitute what we take for granted (and do not articulate) as much as or more than views we espouse in words."

[38] Ibid.

[39] Cf. Ibid., 215.

[40] Cf. Ibid.

[41] Ibid., 209-10. My italics.

broader space for considering what religion is all about than the case is when one focuses on religion as primarily about peoples' beliefs. In this way, he seems to combine a pragmatic and a transcendental approach to religion – since it implies that he then can focus on the effects religious practices has on peoples' lives and self-understanding as the presupposition for their agency.

As is well known, Hegel's *Lectures on Philosophy of Religion* identify *representation* as the form of cognition most closely connected to religion. For him, however, it is the type of cognition for which representations provide the basis that is of interest and not their actual or immediate presence. Thus, he provides a chance for demythologizing religious representations, including doctrine, by sublating their content into his system. This move makes it possible to account for the transformation of representations into thought. For him, this is the highest way of relating to the ultimate. However, despite his preference for thought, Hegel holds, probably very realistically, that most of humanity understands religion's content through representations.[42] It points back to my initial point, that religion depends on and is conditioned by the semiotic potentiality of representations. However, I argue that what Hegel presupposes here as an empirical fact is also a philosophical necessity: religion cannot do without imagination, representation, and the abductive inferences on which they depend.

As indicated at the start of this section, for Hegel, the subjective aspect concerning the certainty of God is established in *feeling*, whereas the objective dimension is established through *representation*. As he says, "For human beings, God *is* primarily in the form of representation."[43] Several things are worth commenting on against this backdrop: Firstly, that there is a relationship between subjective experience in feeling and the object of representation. Secondly, the 'objective' representation is precisely that; of a God who is only possible to experience through representation. Finally, this entails a complicated conclusion: That God is represented by an objective representation that stirs the experience of God in feeling does not exclude that the feeling should also be understood as a mode in which God is represented. Hegel does not address this by his notion of representation because he sees representation as something only present in the objective world. Hence, he

---

[42] Cf. T. A Lewis, Thomas A. Lewis, *Religion, Modernity, and Politics in Hegel* (Oxford ; New York: Oxford University Press, 2011), 151. Cf also the short, but precise presentation nf the role of representation in (Christian) religion in Walter Jaescke, "Absolute Spirit: Art, Religion and Philosophy," in *Bloomsbury Companion to Hegel*, ed. Allegra de Laurentiis; Jeffery Edwards (London: Bloomsbury, 2013), 193.

[43] Hegel, *Lectures on the Philosophy of Religion : The Lectures of 1827*, 291f. He shares this position with Ricoeur. See Paul Ricoeur, *The Conflict of Interpretations*, Essays in Hermeneutics (Evanston: Northwestern University Press, 1974), 481.

overlooks or ignores crucial elements in the role that representations and imagination play for the subjective experience of God.[44]

The valid point Hegel nevertheless makes is that God is never immediately present. Even in so-called mystical experiences, which may have an immediate character, God is only present by the way God is mediated in the experience, and therefore, experienced as God *by means of* the experience. The inference we can make from this fact is that the semiotic element that characterises every experience of God representations (because experience is always an experience of something for someone) suggests that one has to move beyond the immediate and sensual or intuitive experience of something towards an interpretation that could be otherwise. There is no way to secure the experience of God as a secure experience of God – it will always depend on the capacity for interpretation in the subject that relates to the one she *thinks* is God. However, to think that something represents an experience of God cannot be done through induction or deduction – it requires abduction.

Accordingly, against Hegel, we have to say that the "outward" (*für mich*) representation is not a transitory phase or element in the way humans develop their understanding of God (and themselves). The main element in religion is not the concept but the actual experience of God and the world as it appears mediated by imagination and representation. Experience of the world is illuminated or made possible to explore in depth with the help of imagination, and not only through the concept. Hence, neither the reification of the symbol/representation or the literal reading of the Scriptures as such is adequate, but nor is mere philosophical speculation that only uses representation or the scriptures as a stepping-stone towards the philosophy of the absolute.[45]

Therefore, the challenge is to maintain that representations are not merely indices of something else – they are also expanding our experience of the present reality without leaving it behind. To say, like Hegel, that "they are only metaphors"[46] is thus misleading, insofar as it only makes the world a mere appearance, *Schein.* However, important is the insistence that all intuitions we may have about God and which can be formulated in language cannot be taken in a literal sense in the same ways as is the case with objects. God is not wrathful like humans, and even God's love is not like that of humans. However, there are some analogies, which are important to maintain.

In his analysis of Hegel, T.A. Lewis points to representation as what stretches between intuition and thought. "It begins with the sensible content that characterizes intuition and moves from finding itself determined in this manner toward the free self-determination of the most developed forms of

[44] Cf. Hegel, *Lectures on the Philosophy of Religion : The Lectures of 1827.*

[45] Hegel is likely to be read thus, cf. his comments on the historical, ibid., 293f.

[46] Ibid., 293.

thought."[47] It is likely to see such free self-determination as relying on inferences that are not externally determined but abductive. Thus, representations imply the "combination of heteronymous givenness and self-determination," which entails a continuous transformation toward greater determination by the subject, without these connections being determined fully by the subject.[48] In light of Neville's understanding of imagination, however, the heteronymous givenness that conditions thought is nevertheless not independent of imagination. Accordingly, representations simply initiate religious reflection by engendering not only intuition but also imagination.[49]

A representation, as a placeholder for the ultimate, thus has a threefold function in religion. It contributes to the initiation of religious reflection via imagination. Moreover, it provides some of the content and the boundaries for what is possible in the actual development of such reflection, and it delivers opportunities for abductive reflection that goes beyond the immediate present in the representation itself. Thus, one can say that God, who is dependent on representations to come to (the believer's) mind, is potentially present in representations. The opposite would be to misunderstand their function as representations: "Representation misleads if it is taken literally. Taking them literally both leads us to think that religious doctrines are making (indefensible) claims that they are not and, no less importantly, causes us to overlook their genuine meanings."[50] This is why one cannot remain by what is possible to observe from a merely empirical point of view if one is to understand anything about religion. Or, to put it otherwise: A theoretical approach to religion that excludes God as the possible origin and object of representations is not able to grasp how religion, by means of representations, provides chances for orienting oneself on the basis of ultimates that are conceived as transcendental and/or transcendent. By inference, the God notion is a challenge to any approach to the world that exclusively wants to remain by the empirical.

The fact that God is represented in the world and that religious faith identifies God in the signs observable or possible to experience in this world means that the semiotic processes that cause thinking to occur and define the world as related to God do not themselves produce God but must be seen as produced by the divine reality. Imagination and thinking are grounded in God. We know about God based on how God has revealed Godself in the world –

[47] Lewis, *Religion, Modernity, and Politics in Hegel*, 151.
[48] Ibid.
[49] Cf. my reference to Ricoeur's famous dictum about thought and symbol above.
[50] Lewis, *Religion, Modernity, and Politics in Hegel*, 152.

and such revelation cannot occur without either imagination, representations, or the semiotic processes that thinking manifests.[51]

What I previously called Hegel's realistic approach to representations implies that the religious consciousness that develops notions of God based on the experience of the world must build on the natural intentionality of immediate, sensible consciousness and the imagination it engenders. Nevertheless, "the constitution of religious consciousness occurs through a movement of thought out of the confines of immediate consciousness's natural field of awareness."[52] Therefore, this consciousness is not directed towards something in the world as such, but towards the unity of object and thinking. Hegel shows that religion is dependent upon thinking and aims at the unity of the thinking subject with God.[53] Or, in other words: a consciousness that thinks based on religious symbols but does so in a way that excludes God or the ultimate cannot contribute to the unity he describes and is therefore not religious consciousness in any qualified sense. However, based on the above analysis of imagination via Neville, I would argue that religion is just as much dependent on our capacities for abduction and imagination as on our conceptually articulated cognitive capacities.

It is at this point that another problem presents itself to Hegel. Although thinking is necessary to perform or carry out the semiotic processes that result in the experience of something like the experience of God by someone, this cannot possibly mean that Godself is dependent on thinking. That would imply that God only exists because someone is thinking. To avoid this problem, it is necessary to see thinking as a response to how the world presents itself to the subject who thinks. We should understand thinking (and imagination) against the backdrop of Hegel's emphasis on the intermediary role of representation. The reason is simple: If God is dependent on thinking, the thinking subject is God because it is this subject who is the all-determining reality. This is probably the reason why Hegel says that God thinks Godself through human consciousness.[54] However, if thinking is based on, and response to,

---

[51] Cf. Philip M. Merklinger, *Philosophy, Theology, and Hegel's Berlin Philosophy of Religion, 1821-1827* (Albany: State University of New York Press, 1993), 4.:. "Hegel noted that all thinking, including both the Classical philosophy of religion and Enlightenment theology, is grounded in a common object, God. All that proceeds from thought – all the distinctions of the arts and sciences and of the eternal interweavings of human relationships, habits and customs, activities, skills, and enjoyments – find their ultimate centre in the one thought of God. God is the beginning of all things and the end of all things; [everything] starts from God and returns to God."

[52] Ibid., 25.

[53] Ibid.

[54] The Hegelian reasoning here has several concerns, among them also the intention of avoiding what Hegel sees as mere subjectivism. See, e.g., Paolo Diego Bubbio, "Hegel, the Trinity, and the 'I'," *International Journal for Philosophy of Religion* 76, no. 2 (2014).

representation, it means that thinking – as well as imagination – contributes to revealing God in what God is not. This element of negation is among the constitutive elements that a representation of God entails.

In its generic character, the role of representation is then to lead to explicit knowledge of God because it is a manifestation of the interstice realm between the 'thinking subject' and 'the immediate subject.' Representation brings these two sides in the subject together.[55] Thus, "religious representations" provide the means for another mode of being in the world because they manifest a way of experiencing the world that goes beyond the immediate. It also shapes the cognition of the difference between the immediate empirical world's finite character and the infinite character of the universal context that consciousness becomes aware of by engaging representations. Representations are gestures towards the infinite horizon that encompasses their finite character. Their task is to engender our imaginations of what our world is like within such a horizon.

In conclusion: The content of representations matters and should not be sublated into concepts

Representations work in contexts of significance that entail abductions that make connections and thus constitute what we experience. Moreover, Neville argued that imagination is constitutive for all our experience of the world. Hence, imagination and abduction are both elements at work in our dealings with religious representations. These representations are never abstract but allow us to experience the world in a specific way. They have a fundamental and non-reducible role in religion and cannot be seen as mere transitory – *pace* Hegel. Their role is not merely functional – because they constitute our experience.

Kevin Schilbrack has argued convincingly for overcoming the impasse in studies of religion constituted by having to choose between substantive and functional definitions of religion. Instead of choosing one of these options, he argues that we need both of them. The former identifies "certain beliefs, practices, institutions, and communities as religious in terms of what such phenomena do for the participants," whereas the latter "define certain beliefs, practices, institutions, and communities as religious in terms of their focal object."[56]

As a conclusion to the previous discussion, I think Schilbrack makes an important point. How we imagine the divine or religious reality and how it shapes us cannot be determined sufficiently without considering the substantive content which religious imaginaries express. Imagination does not

[55] Merklinger, *Philosophy, Theology, and Hegel's Berlin Philosophy of Religion, 1821-1827*, 33.

[56] Kevin Schilbrack, *Philosophy and the Study of Religions : A Manifesto*, Wiley Blackwell Manifestos (Chichester, West Sussex: Wiley Blackwell, 2014), 116-17.

emerge out of thin air but depends on the experienced reality that engenders it and on how these experiences are represented in both our subjective and our objective world. A mere functionalist approach to religion tends to ignore the individual shape that religion takes on, as well as the substantial diversities in practices of orientation and transformation we find in religious traditions. Schilbrack articulates the basis for this point well when he writes:

> If one does not insist on a pure functionalist or a pure substantive definition, then one can see that the two can overlap, in the sense that a belief or a practice or an institution can be both functionally religious (providing certain kinds of benefits) and also substantively religious (concerning certain kinds of realities). The best definition for the future of philosophy of religion, in my view, is, therefore, a mixed one.[57]

Accordingly, neither the functionalist nor the substantive definition of religion should ignore the role that imagination plays in the overall activities on which religious semiotic practices depend. All religious representations involve our ability to make abductions that may expand not only our knowledge but our imaginations and our reality as well. In turn, religions depend on imagination and imagination, requiring an abductive capacity that expresses itself in interpreting how the world shows itself as human experience. A functionalist approach to religion, or a generic one like Hegel's, which sublates religion into thought, ignores how the semiotic character manifest in the substantive content in religious representations with necessity cannot be exhausted in thought. Hence, Hegel could learn from Ricoeur's famous dictum, which has been an underlying presupposition for the critical analysis presented above: the symbol gives rise to thought – and thought returns to the symbol.[58] Accordingly, as long as imagination, representation, and abduction are involved in religious practices, religion, and the content of experiences with religion, cannot be brought to closure in totalizing thought systems.

---

[57] Ibid., 120-21.

[58] Ricoeur, *The Symbolism of Evil*, 247ff.

The Interruption of Myth in Contemporary French Philosophy

Mads Peter Karlsen

Introduction

As a discipline, philosophy of religion arose from classical philosophical theology after a crisis best crystallized in Kant's devastating critique of the tradition's proofs of God's existence. In a sense, this emergence replays the primal scene of philosophy, commencing with a philosophical revolt against religion, only for religion to return within and through philosophy itself, as a remainder – an apparently recurrrent problem. Hegel, whose *Vorlesungen über die Philosophie der Religion* may be the very starting point of modern philosophy of religion, stages this problem in terms of the dialectic of representation (*Vorstellung*) and concept (*Begriff*), a dialectic that culminates in the concept's sublation of representation, as Hegel claims from the outset of the *Phenomenology*, which nonetheless itself ends with a poetic-religious image.[1] Commenting on this dialectic, French philosopher Paul Ricoeur hits the nail on its head: "Religion," he says, "is the place within philosophical discourse where the necessity to transcend images, representations, and symbols may be contemplated, at the same time as is the impossibility of dispensing with them."[2] Such contemplation of the intimate, critical, and yet fruitful, indispensable tension between philosophy and religion – a tension so pivotal to the philosophy of religion – is also at the core of a recent exchange in French philosophy centred on questioning the myth. The following is an initial attempt to shed some light on the various positions taken in this discussion, as well as on its broader philosophical context and some of its stakes.

*

Let us begin with the beginning, or perhaps, with what has ultimately become the beginning. Let us begin with philosophy, philosophy as a beginning, and

---

[1] Georg Wilhelm Friedrich Hegel, *Phenomenology of Spirit*, trans. A. V. Miller (Oxford: Oxford University Press, 1977), 17-22 and 493 (Hegel (mis)quotes Schiller's poem *Die Freundschaft*).

[2] Paul Ricoeur, "Doing Philosophy after Kierkegaard" in *Kierkegaard's Truth: The Disclosure of the Self*, ed. J. H. Smith (New Haven: Yale University Press, 1983), 340. For an elaboration on this issue in Hegel, see Paul Ricoeur, "The Status of *Vorstellung* in Hegel's Philosophy of Religion," in *Meaning Truth, God*, ed. Leroy S. Rouner, (Indiana: Notre Dame Press, 1982), 70-90.

with the beginning of philosophy, even the beginning of philosophy as the beginning of the end. "Philosophy has begun," as Alain Badiou declares at the beginning of his *Manifeste pour la philosophie* (*Manifesto for Philosophy*) from 1989, continuing, "[I]t does not exist within all historical configurations: its way of being is discontinuity in time as in space."[3] Unsurprisingly, Badiou names this refractive beginning of philosophy at a certain time and place in history – "Plato."

After all, Plato was, as the story goes, the first to pit reason against superstition, to progress from mythos to logos, thus inaugurating not only philosophy but also science, metaphysics, and technology, indeed, perhaps even the idea of what has come to be called "Europe," or "the West." As Plato himself puts it, in the words of Protagoras: "I shall give you argument [logon] instead of fable [mython]."[4] Badiou presents this revolution in thought, of thought, by thought in the following way:

> If Greece saw the birth of philosophy, it is certainly not because it held the Sacred within the mythical resource of the poem, nor because the veiling of Presence was familiar to it in the guise of an esoteric statement about being. Many other ancient Civilizations proceeded to the sacral depositing of being within poetic utterance. The singularity of Greece is much rather to have *interrupted* the narrative about origins [d'avoir *interrompu* le récit des origines] through secularized and abstract statements [...].[5]

I will return to this *interruption*, italicized in Badiou's text, of "the narrative about origins," which he elsewhere describes as mathematics having

---

[3] Alain Badiou, *Manifesto for Philosophy*, trans. Norman Madarasz (Albany: State University of New York Press, 1999), 33.

[4] Plato, "Protagoras", *Plato in Twelve Volumes*, Vol. 3, trans. Walter Rangeley Maitland Lamb (Cambridge: Harvard University Press, 1967), 324d ("τούτου δὴ πέρι [...] οὐκέτι μῦθόν σοι ἐρῶ ἀλλὰ λόγον"). A reading of Plato clearly shows that his understanding and use of myths (and their relation to philosophy) are much more ambiguous and complex than this detached quotation suggests. Unsurprisingly, therefore, Plato scholars have long since problematized the (modern retrospective) identification of a stark opposition between mythos and logos with Plato, paradigmatically expressed in Wilhelm Nestle's classic *Vom Mythos zum Logos* (see e.g., Robert L. Fowler, "Mythos and Logos", *The Journal of Hellenic Studies*, Vol. 131, 2011, 45-66).

[5] Badiou, *Manifesto for Philosophy*, 34 / Alain Badiou, *Manifest pour la philosophie* (Paris: Éditions du Seuil), 14. In *Conditions* Badiou also puts it like this: "Philosophy began in Greece because it was the only place where the matheme warranted the interruption of the sacral exercise of validation by narrative (or as Lacoue-Labarthe would say, by the mytheme). Parmenides names the pre-moment – the moment still internal to sacred narrative and its poetic capture – of this interruption. It is well known that Plato names this interruption himself, pushing reflection to a systematic distrust of anything reminiscent of the poem" (Alain Badiou, *Conditions*, trans. Steven Corcoran [London: Continuum 2008], 34). See also Alain Badiou, *Being and Event*, trans. Oliver Feltham [London: Continuum 2006], 126).

interrupted the sovereignty of the myth.[6] However, let us first pause to linger on the unmistakably polemic tone of Badiou's account. One may not immediately recognize the referent of Badiou's pointed remarks about "the Sacred within the mythical resource of the poem" and "the veiling of Presence familiar in the guise of an esoteric statement about being," but it becomes abundantly clear in the fourth chapter of his manifesto "Heidegger Viewed as Commonplace." In this chapter, Badiou gives the following characterization of how Heidegger interprets Plato's inauguration of philosophy:

> The Platonic interruption of the poetic and metaphoric narrative by the paradigmatic ideal of the matheme Heidegger interprets this as the inaugural orientation of the destiny of Being toward the forgetting of its unconcealedness, the relinquishing of its initial appropriateness to the Greeks' poetic language.[7]

According to Badiou, Heidegger interprets the Platonic beginning as a symptom of what he in his *Manifeste pour la philosophie* describes as modern (post-Kantian) philosophy's "suturing" to poetry,[8] a process that has also led to the disentanglement (*désintrication*) of Plato's original entanglement (*intrication*) of philosophy and mathematics.[9] Whether or not Badiou is right

---

[6] Alain Badiou, *Conditions*, 94. The only definition of *myth* that Badiou provides is that implied by the first quotation, that is, a "poetic narrative about origins." However, this determination (partly) conforms to more elaborate definitions such as the following by Paul Ricoeur: "Myth will here be taken to mean [...] not a false explanation by means of images and fables, but a traditional narration which relates to events that happened at the beginning of time and which has the purpose of providing grounds for the ritual actions of men of today and in a general manner, establishing all the forms of action and thought by which man understands himself in his world" (Paul Ricoeur, *The Symbolism of Evil*, trans. Emerson Buchanan [Boston: Beacon Press, 1967], 5). Both parts of this definition indicate the intimate relation between myth and imagination, if by *imagination* one understands something like a distinct figurative and linguistic (creative) capacity to produce images, from former perceptions or even when there is no perception (e.g. *origins* of the world, mankind, or evil), which can thus be both false and true. (Aristotle, *De Anima*, trans. C. D. C. Reeve [Indianapolis: Hackett Publishing Company, 2017], III 3 427b-429b; Immanuel Kant, *Critique of Pure Reason*, trans. Allen W. Wood [Cambridge: Cambridge University Press, 1999], A 118-124, B 150-152). Ricoeur sums up the creative function of imagination in myth as the "disclosure of unprecedented worlds, an opening onto possible worlds which transcend the limits of our actual world." Indicating the ambiguity of the transcending function of imagination in myths, he furthermore stresses that myths "are not just nostalgia for some forgotten world" (Paul Ricoeur, "Myth as the Bearer of Possible Worlds" in *Dialogues with Contemporary Continental Thinkers*, ed. Richard Kearney [Manchester: Manchester University Press, 1984, 45]). In contrast, Badiou seems precisely to identify the myth with a nostalgia for origins, ignoring its utopian potential.

[7] Badiou, *Manifesto for Philosophy*, 50-51.

[8] Ibid., 61-77.

[9] Badiou, *Conditions*, 93-112. For a further discussion of these issues by Badiou, see also his seminar on Heidegger (Alain Badiou, *Heidegger. L'être 3 – Figure du retrait 1986-1987* [Paris: Fayard, 2015]).

in his characterization and diagnosis of Heidegger is, of course, debatable. Thus, it seems only fair to break off briefly and listen to what Heidegger himself has to say about the Greek beginning of philosophy and how the relationship between logos and mythos functions in this beginning. I will quote a passage from Heidegger's lecture course *Was heißt Denken?* (*What is Called Thinking?*):

> Myth means the telling word [das sagende Wort]. ... Logos says the same [λόγος sagt das Selbe]; Mythos and logos are not, as our current historians of philosophy claim, placed into opposition by philosophy as such [durch die Philosophie als solche]; on the contrary, the early Greek thinkers are precisely the ones to use mythos and logos in the same sense [die frühen Denker der Griechen gebrauchen λόγος und μυθος derselben Bedeutung]. Mythos and logos become separated and opposed only at the point where neither mythos nor logos can keep to its original nature. In Plato's work, this separation has already taken place. Historians and philologists, by virtue of a prejudice which modern rationalism adopted from Platonism, imagine that mythos was destroyed by logos. But nothing religious is ever destroyed by logic; it is destroyed only by the God's withdrawal [der Gott sich entzieht].[10]

Although several significant things are going on in this passage, for now suffice it to say that Heidegger's main claim appears to be that the commonplace notion that philosophy began by opposing logos to mythos, by parting with myth, is itself, one might say, a myth. A myth of the beginning, beginning with Plato, a myth inaugurating not philosophy as such (*die Philosophie als solche*), but rather the metaphysical forgetting of Being, or philosophy as this very forgetfulness. The separation of logos and mythos is a myth, not because it never took place, but because with its origin narrative it conceals how mythos and logos were initially unopposed, how for the Greeks "logos says the same" (*λόγος sagt das Selbe*) as mythos, as Heidegger notes.[11]

Against this backdrop, one might ask whether Badiou is not precisely guilty of endorsing and reproducing this myth of logos' parting from mythos, and thus of substantiating the forgetfulness of the question of Being? And does this not confirm that Badiou and Heidegger are in absolute opposition on this matter, as Badiou himself seems to suggest? Perhaps. Yet, care should be taken not to let Badiou's proclivity for polemics lure one into too simplistic an understanding of Badiou's conception of these matters.[12]

Thus, in the above-quoted passage from his *Manifeste pour la philosophie*, Badiou notably does not, in fact, claim that mythos, or "the narrative about origins," as he puts it, is "separated from" or "opposed to" logos, or in Badiou's

---

[10] Martin Heidegger, *What Is Called Thinking?*, trans. Fred D. Wieck and J. Glenn Gray (New York: Harper & Row), 10 / Martin Heidegger, *Was heißt Denken?* (Tübingen: Maw Niemeyer Verlag, 1954), 6-7.

[11] Heidegger, *What Is Called Thinking?*, 10 / Heidegger, *Was heißt Denken?*, 7.

[12] Badiou is, for instance, well aware of the ambiguity in Plato concerning the relationships between mythos and logos and between philosophy and poetry (see Alain Badiou, *Handbook of Inaesthetics*, trans. Alberto Toscano [Stanford: Stanford University Press, 2005], 16-27).

terms mathematics. More precisely, he instead claims that mathematics has interrupted, in French *interrompu*, myth. Several similar expressions appear elsewhere in Badiou's oeuvre, for instance, in his 1988 masterpiece *L'être et l'événement* (*Being and Event*), contained in a meditation on Heidegger entitled "Nature: Poem or matheme?" where Badiou writes: "The Greeks did not invent the poem. Rather, they *interrupted* the poem with the matheme."[13] Here, "interrupted" is once again in italics. But what precisely is meant by this? Badiou frequently uses the terms *interruption* and *interrompu* throughout both his manifesto and *L'être et l'événement*, but never elaborates on what exactly he means by these terms.

One might speculate that Badiou is using "interruption" synonymously with his key concept of the "event." In other words, he intends the word to designate an utterly unpredictable and incalculable occurrence that opens up the possibility of something, which previously seemed impossible, and thus beginning the creation of something entirely new that Badiou calls a truth-procedure.[14] Yet, this cannot be the case with regard to the beginning of philosophy, for, as Badiou has often emphasized, philosophy is conditioned by the truths produced from scientific, artistic, political, and amorous events, but produces no truths of its own,[15] for which reason the beginning of philosophy cannot itself be an event. Rather, philosophy begins precisely because of and on the conditions of the events that inaugurated the truth-procedures of art, politics, and love, but above all mathematics, which enabled myth to be interrupted. So, again: What does Badiou mean by this term "interruption"? Is it to be understood in merely its lexical sense, as a "stopping," a "discontinuity," a "pausing," a "suspension," a "breaking" into and in between? Or could it also have a more philosophical and technical meaning?

Myth interrupted

I would like to try to shed some light on Badiou's claim that mathematics interrupts myth and to indicate that perhaps Badiou's conception of the relation between myth, mathematics, and philosophy is neither as unambiguous nor as oppositional to Heidegger's understanding of mythos and logos as it might first appear. To this end, I would like to introduce another contemporary French philosopher, Jean-Luc Nancy, who is both one of the most attentive contemporary readers of Heidegger and an important interlocutor to Badiou. Badiou and Nancy initiated their dialogue in the early 1980s when Badiou was invited to attend some seminars and gave two lectures at the Centre for Philosophical Research on the Political, which Nancy co-directed with Philippe

---

13 Alain Badiou, *Being and Event*, 126. See also *Conditions*, 34.

14 Badiou, *Manifesto for Philosophy*, 33-39.

15 E.g., Badiou, *Manifesto for Philosophy*, 35.

Lacoue-Labarthe.[16] A revised version of Badiou's lectures was published in 1985 in his book *Peut-on penser la politique?* (*Can Politics be Thought?*).[17] The following year, in 1986, two years before the release of Badiou's *L'être et l'événement*, Nancy published a highly influential collection of essays entitled *La communauté désoeuvrée* (*The Inoperative Community*). In one of these essays, *Le mythe interrompu* (*Myth interrupted*), Nancy takes up "the indispensable task" of thinking through what it means to be living in a world marked by what he calls "the interruption of myth."[18] Although he does not connect this interruption with the theme of the beginning of philosophy in this essay, he does so elsewhere.

One occasion on which Nancy discusses the beginning of philosophy is actually in a paper first presented at a 1999 conference devoted to Badiou[19]

---

[16] Alain Badiou, "Can change be thought? A dialogue with Alain Badiou" in *Alain Badiou – Philosophy and Its Conditions*, ed. Gabriel Riera (Albany: State University of New York Press, 2005), 239. The interchange between Badiou and Nancy that has been ongoing since the mid-1980s is quite complex and often implicit or tucked away in footnotes. Even trying to map out the references between them is a rather arduous task, so the following is merely a fragmentary list of the main posts. Badiou has written on Nancy in the following texts: *Manifesto for Philosophy*, *Conditions*, "The Caesura of Nihilism" and "The Reserved Offering" (the last two of which are specifically about Nancy's work). Nancy has written on Badiou in: *The Sense of the World*, *The Creation of the World* and "Philosophy without Conditions." The most extensive discussion of Badiou's relationship with Nancy is probably Christopher Watkin's *Difficult Atheism*.

[17] For more on the context of Badiou's lectures at the Centre for Philosophical Research on the Political, see Bruno Bosteels, "Translator's Introduction" in Alain Badiou, *Can Politics Be Thought?*, trans. Bruno Bosteels (Durham: Duke University Press, 2019), 16-21.

[18] Jean-Luc Nancy, *The Inoperative Community*, trans. Peter Connor, Lisa Garbus, Michael Holland, and Simona Sawhney (Minneapolis: University of Minnesota Press, 1991), 47. Nancy's close collaborator Lacoue-Labarthe uses a similar expression in his 1986 monography on Celan and Heidegger, namely "Poetry is the interruption of art" (Philippe Lacoue-Labarthe, *Poetry as experience*, trans. Andrea Tarnowski (Stanford: Stanford University Press, 1999), 67. Lacoue-Labarthe himself confirms this similarity (with reference to Nancy): "[…] the theme of the 'interruption of myth' […] is also for me, via Celan, that of the interruption of art" (Philippe Lacoue-Labarthe, *Heidegger, Art and Politics*, trans. Chris Turner [Cambridge: Basil Blackwell, 1990], 91). Moreover, in his discussion of Celan as the poet who breaks with poetry's suture to philosophy, Badiou refers explicitly to Lacoue-Labarthe and this expression (Badiou, *Manifesto for philosophy*, 86). As I will refer to later, Lacoue-Labarthe and Badiou had a series of exchanges on the issue of how to think about the relationship between poetry, politics, and philosophy, and the role myth plays in this relationship.

[19] Jean-Luc Nancy, "Philosophy without Conditions," in *Think Again. Alain Badiou and the Future of Philosophy*, ed. Peter Hallward (London: Continuum, 2004), 39-49. See also Jean-Luc Nancy, *The Creation of the World or Globalization*, trans. François Raffoul and David Pettigrew (Albany: State University of New York Press, 2007), 123. The chapter "Creation as Denaturation: Metaphysical Technology," which reflects on the beginning of philosophy, is an elaboration of a part of "Philosophy without conditions."

where he offers a complex reading that brings Badiou in close contact with the deconstructionist tradition from which he usually distances himself. In two passages about halfway into the paper, Nancy makes an assertion rather similar to Badiou's claim that philosophy begins with an interruption of myth, stating: "From the outset [...] philosophy was a deconstruction of [...] the mythico-religious world of given meaning [...]." A few pages later, he writes: "[...] philosophy as such begins [...] when meaning or sense is [...] de-mythified."[20] Nancy makes a parallel statement in his short book "*Un jour les dieux se retirent...* " ("*One Day the Gods Withdrew...*") published in 2001, the same year as his essay on Badiou. "Philosophizing," Nancy writes here, "begins precisely where meaning is interrupted."[21] While Nancy thus agrees with Badiou's notion that philosophy begins with an interruption of myth, his account of what makes this interruption possible fundamentally differs from Badiou's. According to Nancy, mathematics does not condition the beginning of philosophy, at least not initially. Instead, as he formulates it in his Badiou paper, it is conditioned by "a breaking-out, a departure: namely, the departure of the gods (a departure whose initial name in the West is monotheism, already pregnant with 'the death of God')."[22]

This quote from Nancy seems to echo the end of the passage from *Was heißt Denken?* that I earlier recalled. The one in which Heidegger states that "historians and philologists, by virtue of a prejudice which modern rationalism adopted from Platonism, imagine that *mythos* was destroyed by *logos*. But nothing religious is ever destroyed by logic; it is destroyed only by the God's withdrawal [der Gott sich entzieht]."[23] This resonance with Heidegger's *Was heißt Denken?* brings me back to Nancy's essay on the interruption of myth – if in no other way than its link to an apparent reference in Nancy's essay on the same text by Heidegger.

We find this apparent reference to Heidegger in a section of the essay where Nancy discusses "what myth ended up becoming," as he puts it. He explains

---

[20] Jean-Luc Nancy, "Philosophy without Conditions," 45, 48. For a short exchange between Badiou and Nancy on this matter, see also: Alain Badiou & Jean-Luc Nancy, *German Philosophy: A dialogue*, trans. Richard Lambert (Cambridge: MIT Press 2018), 41-47.

[21] Jean-Luc Nancy, "*Un jour les dieux se retirent...*" (Bordeaux: William Blake, 2001), 13 (my translation).

[22] Nancy, "Philosophy without Conditions," 46. This withdrawal – which is at once a closure and an opening and gave rise to tragedy (art), politics, mathematics, and philosophy – emerges from what Nancy terms a "force of denaturation" originating from a set of techniques such as iron-making, writing, accounting, navigation, and town planning (ibid. 46). See also Nancy, *The Creation of the World*, 84-85, and Badiou & Nancy, *German Philosophy*, 42-43, where Nancy describes the contrast between himself and Badiou: "[Y]ou take the Greek precisely as already given – as given all at once – whereas I'm always haunted by the fact that there are first of all a number of conditions at work [...]," 43.

[23] Heidegger, *What Is Called Thinking?*, 10 / Heidegger, *Was heißt Denken?*, 7.

that "The Greek *mythos* – Homer's *mythos*, that is, speech, spoken expression – becomes 'myth' when it takes on a whole series of values that amplify, fill, and enable this speech, giving it the dimensions of a narrative of origins and an explanation of destinies."[24] And then a few lines later, he adds: "The greatness of the Greeks – according to the modern age of mythology – is to have lived in intimacy with such speech and to have founded their logos in it: they are the ones for whom *mythos* and *logos* are 'the same' [Ils sont ceux pour qui *muthos* et *logos* 'sont le même']."[25] Now here are the passages from Heidegger that Nancy seems to be referring to at the end of the quote: "The early Greek thinkers are precisely the ones to use *mythos* and *logos* in the same sense," or as he also puts it, "Myth means the telling word [das sagende Wort]. … *Logos* says the same [λόγος sagt das Selbe]."[26] Thus, although Nancy agrees in a certain sense with Heidegger's notion that God must withdraw for philosophy to begin, if the passage I quoted indeed alludes to Heidegger, as I suggest, Nancy nevertheless equally distances himself from Heidegger in so far as this allusion places Heidegger within the category "the modern age of mythology," which celebrates the Greek overlapping of mythos and logos. Philippe Lacoue-Labarthe offers an implicit explanation for why Nancy tacitly includes Heidegger in this category, describing what he calls Heidegger's "remythologization": "We know the sequence: The essence of art is *Dichtung,* the essence of *Dichtung* is *Sprache* […], the essence of *Sprache* is *Sage* – which is *muthos.*"[27] The opposition between mythos and logos – inaugurated by and inaugurating philosophy – might be a myth, as Heidegger implies, but apparently so is the notion of their pre-Platonic indistinguishability. Philosophy is inaugurated not

[24] Jean-Luc Nancy, *The Inoperative Community*, 48.

[25] Nancy, *The Inoperative Community*, 49 / Jean-Luc Nancy, *La communauté désoeuvrée* (Paris: Christian Bourgois Éditeur, 1986), 123. In the footnote to the French text, Nancy makes no reference to *Was heißt Denken?* or any other text. However, this footnote contains two other references to Heidegger (to the French translations of *Vorträge und Aufsätze,* without page number, and to *Holzwege,* with page number), but these are references for two quotations in the footnote and not for the passage quoted in the body text. In the English translation the references are simply omitted. In the French edition of *Was heißt Denken?,* the passage to which I suggest Nancy might be alluding is translated as "et précisément les premiers penseurs parmi les Grecs emploient Mythos et Logos dans le même sens" (Martin Heidegger, *Qu'appelle-t-on penser?,* trad. G. Granel [Paris: PUF, 1957], 29). It is perhaps worth mentioning that in his book *L'imitation des Modernes*, also published in 1986, Philippe Lacoue-Labarthe quotes the exact same passage from *Was heißt Denken?* when discussing Heidegger's understanding of the relationship between mythos and logos (Philippe Lacoue-Labarthe, *L'imitation des Modernes. Typograpies 2* (Paris: Éditions Galilée, 1986), 196-197).

[26] Heidegger, *What Is Called Thinking?*, 10 / Heidegger, *Was heißt Denken?,* 7.

[27] Philippe Lacoue-Labarthe, *Heidegger and the Politics of Poetry*, trans. Jeff Fort (Chicago: University of Illinois Press, 2007), 33. See also Lacoue-Labarthe, *L'imitation des Modernes*, 196.

through its opposition of mythos and logos, whether this inauguration is conceived as a progress or a decline, but through "the interruption of myth." So, let us now return to the question of what Nancy means by this expression.

It appears to have at least two meanings. First of all, Nancy uses it to designate a certain feature of the present, namely, that we live, as Nancy puts it "in a world in which mythic resources are profoundly lacking."[28] This confronts us with a state that Georges Bataille, as Nancy reminds us, has called "the absence of myth." Nancy elaborates:

> For reasons that I shall explain later, I will substitute this expression [the absence of myth] with *the interruption* of myth. It is nonetheless true that 'the absence of myth' [...] defines what it is we have arrived at, and what we are confronted with. What is at stake in this confrontation is not simply an alternative between the absence of myth and its presence. If we suppose that "myth" designates, beyond the myths themselves, even beyond myth, something that cannot simply disappear [quelque chose qui ne peut pas simplement disparaître], the stakes would then consist in myth's passage to a limit and onto a limit where myth itself would be not so much suppressed as suspended or interrupted.[29]

Let us try to unpack some of the things that Nancy is saying here. What does it mean that what is at stake in the interruption of myth is not simply an alternative between the absence of myth and its presence? I will suggest two things: First, even when we are confronted with its absence, myth does not disappear; it is still present, namely in the form of new mythologies, including the myth of the absence of myth. Moreover, the absence of myth is present as an awareness of myth as myth, that is, an awareness that "myth is a myth." Accordingly, even if myth – despite, or perhaps due to, its absence – is still present, still a possibility, it can no longer be the basis for new mythologies. This is why, as Nancy puts it, "myth designates something that cannot simply disappear," and since myth can neither simply disappear nor be surpassed, nor produce new mythologies, what is at stake is rather its passage to a limit-point in which it is interrupted. This is what constitutes its interruption, in that, as Nancy writes, "[...] *'myth' is cut off from its own meaning, on its own meaning, by its own meaning*."[30] In other words, in passing to its limit-point myth is interrupted, interrupted in a certain sense by itself, or more precisely by its own repetition, although not as the repetition of itself as the self-same. Thus, the thought that myth interrupts itself or is cut off from its own meaning by its own meaning, as expressed in the statement "myth is myth," is already a consequence of the equivocal meaning of the word "myth" (also present in the above-quoted definition by Ricoeur). In Nancy's words: "In order to say that myth is a myth (that myth is *a myth,* or that 'myth' is a myth), it has been necessary to play on two quite distinct and opposite meanings of the word

[28] Nancy, *The Inoperative Community*, 47.

[29] Ibid.

[30] Ibid., 52.

'myth.' The phrase 'myth is a myth' means in effect that [1] myth, as inauguration or as foundation, is a [2] myth, in other words, a fiction, a simple invention."[31] This is the second sense in which Nancy understands the phrase "interruption of myth" – as something that happens with myth within myth by virtue of myth. In a key passage of the essay, Nancy provides us with a helpful illustration of this notion of interruption of myth by using the acoustic metaphors of the voice and music. He writes:

> [T]he interruption of myth is not a silence [...]. In the interruption of myth something makes itself heard, namely, what remains of myth [ce qui reste du mythe] when it is interrupted – and which is nothing if not the very voice of interruption, if we can say this. [...] This voice seems to play back the declarations of myth, for in the interruption there is nothing new to be heard, there is no new myth breaking through; it is the old story one seems to hear. When a voice, or music, is suddenly interrupted, one hears just at that instant something else, a mixture of various silences and noises that had been covered over by the sound, but in this something else one hears again the voice or the music that has become in a way the voice or the music of its own interruption: a kind of echo, but one that does not repeat that of which it is the reverberation. [...]. A name has been given to this voice of interruption: literature (or writing [écriture], if we adopt the acceptation of this word that coincides with literature).[32]

Not wishing to provide a detailed exposition of this quote, I will simply make two notes. First, Nancy affirms that something remains (*reste*) when myth is interrupted, which, as he stated earlier in the text, is to say that "myth designates something that cannot simply disappear."[33] He further clarifies that what remains of the myth is, more precisely, the very voice of interruption (myth's interruption of itself), and that this voice remains as an echo (a repetition, but not of the self-same). Next, I want to emphasize Nancy's final point, whereby he says that the interruption of myth should be understood as a transition from myth to literature or writing – or, perhaps better, as a transition from myth as myth to the echo of myth as literature-writing – *écriture*.

Demythologization

Philosophers of religion might find a familiar ring to this notion of interruption of myth, which Nancy scholars have compared to Derrida's deconstruction,[34]

---

[31] Ibid.

[32] Ibid., 61-63.

[33] A more detailed explanation of what precisely *remains* (*reste*) in the interruption of myth could be given through a detour on Derrida's account (e.g. in *Glas*) of the remainder (*le reste*) understood along the lines of what he calls the *trace* (see Jacques Derrida, *Paper Machine*, trans. Rachel Bowlby [Stanford: Stanford University Press, 2005], 151-152). However, such an exposition is beyond the scope of this paper.

[34] Marie-Eve Morin, "Putting Community under Erasure: Derrida and Nancy on the Plurality of Singularities," *Culture Machine* 8, (2006), accessed November 15, 2020, https://culturemachine.net/community/putting-community-under-erasure/.

and which is clearly inspired as much by – a critical encounter with – Heidegger as by Bataille and Blanchot. Indeed, one might have been struck by the thought that Nancy's proposition with this notion resembles that made by Rudolf Bultmann and others under the heading "demythologization." Apparently, this too has crossed Nancy's mind, as he mentions it in a short passage at the beginning of his essay, though only to reject the idea. This is how he formulates it:

> [T]he interruption of myth [...] is not the same thing as what has been called 'demythologizing,' an activity that distinguishes between 'myth' and 'faith' and that depends, moreover, on the possibility of positing something like 'faith,' while it leaves intact the essence of myth itself [tandis que par ailleurs il laisse intacte, en elle-même, l'essence du mythe]. The notion of interruption proceeds quite differently.[35]

At the core of this quote lies Nancy's claim that demythologization leaves the essence of myth itself intact. Nancy does not specify what he means by "the essence of myth itself," but in a footnote to the above passage, he provides two comments, the second of which offers a lead. To begin with, Nancy notes that "It remains nonetheless eloquent, and memorable, that one of the most acute thinkers of 'demythologization,' Dietrich Bonhoeffer, was killed by the Nazis."[36] In other words, even if demythologization leaves the essence of myth intact, Nancy nevertheless clearly grants it a certain critical potential. He then adds: "Furthermore, what remains intact of myth [ce qui demeure intact du mythe] even within the thinking of demythologization is brought to light perfectly in the opposition drawn by Paul Ricoeur between 'demythologization' and 'demythization'."[37] Nancy elaborates no further on this opposition, nor does the footnote provide a reference to any text by Ricoeur, who has written about demythologization on several occasions. However, one text in which Ricoeur addresses the opposition to which Nancy refers is an essay entitled "Démythiser l'accusation" ("The Demythization of Accusation") in *Le conflit des interpretations* (*The Conflict of Interpretations*).

---

[35] Nancy, *The Inoperative Community*, 47 / Nancy, *La communauté désoeuvrée*, 120 (translation modified). It is worth mentioning that Lacoue-Labarthe proposes a similar distinction in his critical remark that the demythologization proposed by Adorno and Benjamin, which is the main inspiration for his own notion of "interruption of art," "[...] must not be confused with the slogan of the Protestant theology inspired by Heidegger (or inspired in Heidegger by Bultmann) [...]." (Lacoue-Labarthe, *Heidegger and the Politics of Poetry*, 50).

[36] Ibid, 60. Nancy does not name Bultmann, whose work on demythologization was also a countermove against the new mythology of the Nazi regime. However, elsewhere Nancy groups Bultmann with Bonhoeffer and Barth as representatives of a part of Christianity that deconstructs itself and breaks with itself as religion (Jean-Luc Nancy, *Adoration. The Deconstruction of Christianity II*, trans. John McKeane [New York: Fordham University Press, 2013], 34).

[37] Nancy, *The Inoperative Community*, 60 / Nancy, *La communauté désoeuvrée*, 120.

On the opening pages of this essay, Ricoeur explains how he wants to distinguish between two functions of "demythization," writing:

> On the one hand, demythization recognizes myth as myth but with the purpose of renouncing it. In this sense we must speak of demystification. The result of this renunciation is the gaining of a thought and a will which are no longer alienated. The positive side of this destruction [cette destruction] is the manifestation of man as maker of his own human existence. On the other hand, demythization is recognizing myth as myth but with the purpose of freeing its symbolic basis. In this sense we must speak of demythologization. What is deconstructed here [Ce que l'on défaire ici] is not so much myth as the secondary rationalization [le rationalisation seconde] that holds it captive, the pseudo-logos of myth [le pseudo-logos du mythe]. The result of this discovery is the gaining of the revealing power that myth conceals under the mask of objectification. The positive side of this destruction [cette destruction] is the establishing of human existence on the basis of an origin which it does not have at its command but which is announced to it symbolically in a word which founds it.[38]

Demystification (that is, demythization in the former sense) differs from demythologization (demythization in the latter sense) in several ways. First of all, demystification serves to renounce and destroy myth, which suggests that nothing of myth remains after this process. Second, when man is thus freed from the alienating effects of myth, demystification will simultaneously disclose man as his own maker. Demythologization, on the other hand, results in not the destruction (*déstruction*) of myth, but its deconstruction (*défaire*), more precisely the deconstruction of "the secondary rationalization that holds it captive, the pseudo-logos of myth." As such, something "remains of myth," to use Nancy's term, namely, as Ricoeur puts it, "its symbolic basis", which he also describes as the "revealing power of myth" (concealed under the mask of objectification). Once demythologized, myth reveals that human existence is based on "an origin which it does not have at its command."[39] So how does demythologization thus differ from Nancy's notion of the interruption of myth?

Nancy's main complaint with demythologization is, as already mentioned, that something "remains intact of the myth [demeure intact du mythe]"; "it leaves untouched the essence of myth itself [il laisse intacte, en elle-même, l'essence du mythe]."[40] It is certainly true, as Ricoeur indicates, that something of myth remains with demythologization, but this is also true of Nancy's interruption of myth. What remains in each case, however, apparently differs. In the case of demythologization, what remains of myth is, as emphasized by Ricoeur, the symbolic basis revealing to man that his existence is embedded in something of which he cannot be the master. In other words, the symbolic basis

---

[38] Paul Ricoeur, *The Conflict of Interpretations. Essays in Hermeneutics*, trans. Peter McCormick (London: Continuum, 2004), 335-336 / Paul Ricoeur, *Le conflit des interpretations. Essais d'herméneutique* (Paris: Points, 2017), 330-331.

[39] Ricoeur, *The Conflict of Interpretations*, 336.

[40] Nancy, *The Inoperative Community*, 47 / Nancy, *La communauté désoeuvrée*, 120.

of myth confronts man with a limit, a limit to his power over, and knowledge of, his own existence. In contrast, what remains of myth, according to Nancy, is the voice of interruption, an echo of myth, which he calls literature-writing (*écriture*). Thus, in demythologization what remains of myth – that is, its symbolic basis – seems to be something that *precedes* the demythologization and is disclosed precisely as its basis though this demythologization, whereas what remains of myth in its interruption – that is, literature-writing – seems to be something existing only *after* the myth is interrupted, an echo, as Nancy writes. Thus, two different ways, or modes, of remaining appear to be at stake here. In the first case, something remains that has been there all along, as the *basis* of myth. In the second case, something comes to remain only after that which it becomes a remainder of has disappeared, as an *echo* of myth. Perhaps it is this difference between a *preceding* "basis" and a *succeeding* "echo" that Nancy has in mind when he claims that demythologization leaves the essences of myth untouched?

However, there are a couple of other noteworthy differences between Nancy's notion of the interruption of myth and the notion of demythologization sketched by Ricoeur, which might help explain Nancy's statement. First, there is the issue of revelation. Both demythologization and interruption of myth will enable something to be revealed. Demythologization functions to make the revealing power of myth accessible, and what is revealed through this power is that human existence is based on "an origin which it does not have at its command," as Ricoeur puts it.[41] According to Nancy, literature writing also reveals something, but "literature's revelation, unlike myth's, does not reveal a completed reality, nor the reality of a completion." What literature reveals is rather "that it is itself [...] essentially interrupted."[42] Perhaps it is Ricoeur's reference to "an origin" that Nancy makes the target of his complaint that demythologization leaves the essence of myth untouched in so far as the concept of origin seemingly implies a notion of a complete reality? However, here one should of course bear in mind that what characterizes the origin revealed by demythologization is that man does not have this origin at his command. It is, in other words, an origin that limits human reality, thus making it precisely incomplete (finite).

Second, both demythologization and the interruption of myth involve the respective critical elements of interruption and deconstruction. However, demythologization serves to deconstruct (*défaire*) the "secondary rationalization" or, as Ricoeur also puts it, "the pseudo-logos," that holds the revealing power of myth captive, whereas what is interrupted in the

[41] Ricoeur, *The Conflict of Interpretations*, 331.
[42] Nancy, *The Inoperative Community*, 63.

interruption of myth by myth is myth itself.[43] So what does Nancy understand by myth? In the opening pages of his essay, he describes myths as narratives of origins and beginnings – of the beginning of the world, of our societies and communities – the function of which he later summarizes in this concise formula: "Myth [...] is fiction that founds."[44] Elsewhere, in *Le mythe Nazi* (*The Nazi Myth*), an essay co-written with Philippe Lacoue-Labarthe, Nancy and Lacoue-Labarthe define myth as "an instrument of identification," and specifying this definition, they state: "Myth is a fiction [...] whose role is to propose, if not to impose, models or types [...] in imitation of which an individual, or a city, or an entire people, can grasp themselves and identify themselves."[45] Could it be this mechanism of identification that Nancy suggests demythologization leave untouched? Or, put slightly differently, if the essence of myth is identification, as Nancy suggests, then does demythologization actually leave this untouched? These are crucial questions.

Deconstruction and hermeneutics

Because demythologization concerns human self-understanding,[46] it also involves the issue of identity. As such, one could see Nancy's critique of demythologization as a version of a familiar objection against existential and philosophical hermeneutics. In short, this objection states that any form of understanding and self-understanding always tends, if not to appropriate, then to disregard or diminish the otherness of the other as well as of oneself, thus upholding the idea of self-identity, self-transparency, and self-presence.[47] This critique was raised by, among others, Derrida in 1981 during the famous Paris

---

[43] This is a crucial difference, even if the notions of "interruption of myth" and "demythologization" may be similar in terms of the idea that myth interrupts itself, since the process of demythologization, as Bultmann emphasizes, is initiated in the New Testament texts themselves by their kerygmatic core (Rudolf Bultmann, *Jesus Christ and Mythology*, trans. Schubert M. Ogden [New York: Charles Scribner's Sons, 1958], 33-34). See also Ricoeur's preface to the French translation of Bultmann's book (Ricoeur, *The Conflict of Interpretations*, 387-388).

[44] Nancy, *The Inoperative Community*, 56.

[45] Philippe Lacoue-Labarthe and Jean-Luc Nancy, "The Nazi Myth," *Critical Inquiry*, 16, No. 2 (Winter, 1990), 297, 298-299.

[46] Ricoeur, *The Conflict of Interpretation*, 387. See also Bultmann, *Jesus Christ and Mythology*, 73-76.

[47] Jacques Derrida, "Three Questions to Hans-Georg Gadamer," in *Dialogue and Deconstruction: The Gadamer-Derrida Encounter*, eds. Diane P. Michelfelder and Richard E. Palmer (Albany: State University of New York Press, 1989), 53. For Gadamer's response to Derrida, see the same volume: Hans-Georg Gademer , "Reply to Jacques Derrida" (while this reply is critical of Derrida, Gadamer nevertheless "[...] agree[s] with him on this point about a 'breach' [...]", 56), Hans-Georg Gadamer, "Hermeneutics and Logocentrism," 119, and Hans-Georg Gadamer, "Letter to Dallmayr," 97.

encounter between himself and Gadamer. On that occasion, Derrida posed the following rhetorical question to Gadamer: "Whether one speaks of consensus or of misunderstanding [...], one needs to ask whether the precondition for *Verstehen,* far from being the continuity of *rapport* [...], is not rather the interruption of *rapport,* a certain *rapport* of interruption, the suspending of all mediation?"[48] So, Derrida is saying that in order to understand – the other as well as oneself – one must, if not understand, then perhaps experience, that there is something – about the other and oneself – that one cannot understand. In my reading, this hardly means one should stop understanding, quite the contrary: One should try to understand what it means that one cannot understand, and, indeed, what it means that one cannot understand without this element of not-understanding.[49]

Although not explicitly discussing hermeneutics in his essay on myth, Nancy nevertheless reflects briefly on the issue of self-understanding and literature-writing (*écriture*), stating:

> In a sense, we understand ourselves and the world by sharing this writing [*en partageant cette écriture*], just as the group understood itself by listening to the myth. Nonetheless, we understand only that there is no common understanding of community, that sharing does not constitute an understanding [...], and that it gives no one, including community itself, mastery over being-in-common.[50]

In sharing the literature-writing that interrupts the mimetic identification of myth, one understands that no common understanding exists, or, more precisely, that no common understanding exists other than or beyond the common understanding of this. Although it may sound more radical, I think

---

[48] Jacques Derrida, "Three Questions to Hans-Georg Gadamer," 53. See also Jacques Derrida, *A Taste for the Secret*, trans. Giacomo Donis (Cambridge: Polity Press), 30-31.

[49] One could argue that this is precisely what Derrida attempts to do when gesturing to Gadamer in a lecture held on Celan in 2003 and honouring Gadamer, noteworthily entitled "Rams: The *Uninterrupted Dialogue* between Two Infinities, the Poem" (my italics). Here Derrida rejects the idea that his 1981 meeting with Gadamer was simply a missed encounter. Rather, as Derrida clarifies, with reference to the question quoted above: "This question marked at once the test, if not the confirmation, of the misunderstanding, the apparent interruption of the dialogue, but also the beginning of an interior dialogue in each of us, a dialogue virtually without end and nearly continuous. At that time, indeed, I called for a certain *interruption.* Far from signifying the failure of the dialogue, such an interruption could become the condition of comprehension and understanding" (Jacques Derrida, *Sovereignties in Question. The Poetics of Paul Celan*, trans. Thomas Dutoit and Outi Pasanen [New York: Fordham University Press, 2005], 139).

[50] Nancy, *The Inoperative Community* 69 / Nancy, *La communauté désoeuvrée*, 171. For a complex discussion of hermeneutics by Nancy that critically considers both Bultmann and Ricoeur, see "Sharing Voices" in *Transforming the Hermeneutic Context: From Nietzsche to Nancy*, eds. Gayle Ormiston & Alan Schrift (Albany: Suny Press, 1990).

that Nancy's point is basically the same as Derrida's, namely that the precondition for understanding is an interruption of understanding.

Against the objection that the hermeneutical concept of self-understanding implies leaving self-identity intact, to play on Nancy's wording, one could reply that the self-understanding that demythologization aims at engendering is a self-understanding in which we precisely come to understand that there is something about our world and ourselves that we can never fully understand. This is to say that there is a limit to understanding, or, in other words, that we will never be able to absolutely identify who we are. Moreover, the precondition for this kind of self-understanding is precisely that our self-understanding is challenged by the revelation of something other. In a text from 1984 where Gadamer reflects on his Paris encounter with Derrida, he says something along these lines:

> The basis of this disagreement, it seems to me, is a misconception of what self-understanding is. "Self-understanding" is perhaps a misleading term that I have used and in which I found a natural connection with modem protestant theology and also with Heidegger's own linguistic tradition. However that may be, this word actually does not refer at all to the unshakable certainty of self-consciousness [*Selbstbewusstsein*]. Rather, *Selbstverständnis* has a pietistic undertone suggesting precisely that one cannot succeed in understanding oneself and that this foundering of one's self-understanding and self-certainty should lead one to the path of faith. *Mutatis mutandis,* this applies to the hermeneutical usage of this same term. For who we are is something unfulfillable, an ever new undertaking and an ever new defeat.[51]

The point that I am trying to make here is not that Nancy is wrong to object that demythologization leaves the essence of myth untouched or to claim that the notion of the interruption of myth proceeds quite differently than demythologization. Rather, I am seeking to understand this objection and claim more precisely. As such, I may have brought Ricoeur's demythologization and Nancy's interruption of myth, hermeneutics, and deconstruction, as well as Derrida and Gadamer, closer to each other than perhaps they really are. If so, then at least I am not the only one. In his reply to Derrida in 1981, Gadamer ends on the following evangelic note: "One must lose oneself in order to find oneself. I believe I am not very far from Derrida when I stress that one never knows in advance what one will find oneself to be."[52] Let us now return to

---

[51] Hans-Georg Gadamer, "Letter to Dallmayr", 97. Here, Gadamer mentions modern protestant theology and Heidegger in the same sentence while discussing the concept of self-understanding (as something both conditioned and challenged by the encounter or dialogue with the other [ibid. 95]). This naturally leads one to think of Bultmann, with whom Gadamer also studied when participating in Heidegger's lectures in Marburg. On this issue, see also Gadamer's essay on Bultmann: "On the Problem of Self-Understanding" (in Hans-Georg Gadamer, *Philosophical Hermeneutics*, trans. David E. Linge [Berkeley: University of California Press, 1977], 44-58).

[52] Hans-Georg Gadamer, "Reply to Jacques Derrida", 57.

Alain Badiou and the question of how we might understand his notion that mathematics interrupts myth in light of the discussion on Nancy's interruption of myth.

Closing remarks

I began this contribution with the statement Badiou made about the beginning of philosophy in his book *Manifeste pour la philosophie*. This book title is itself a certain statement about and a call for the beginning, or perhaps more aptly, re-beginning of philosophy. It is a statement directed against a prevailing claim in contemporary philosophy, proposed by philosophers themselves, that philosophy is at its end, or as Badiou puts it "that philosophy is impossible, completed, assigned to something other than itself."[53] Against this claim, Badiou proposes the following counter-statement: "I postulate not only that philosophy is possible today, but that this possibility does not take the form of a final stage. On the contrary. The crux of the matter is to know what the following means: taking one more step."[54] Philosophy did not begin as its own end, so it is possible to take another step, to begin again. As Badiou explains later in the book, however, to do this means precisely to repeat mathematics' Platonic interruption of the myth (narratives of origin), an interruption that would relieve philosophy from poetry, to which, according to Badiou, it has been sutured since the early 19th century, since Romanticism, paradigmatically expressed in Nietzsche and Heidegger.[55]

So, once more, how should we more clearly understand this interruption that Badiou proposes? As a cut that completely separates poetry from philosophy? As an absolute discontinuity between poetry and mathematics? Or is the answer actually far more complicated? Philippe Lacoue-Labarthe thinks so. In a fascinating paper published in 1991, he discusses the thesis Badiou presents in his *Manifeste pour la philosophie*, criticizing Badiou for failing to properly differentiate between myth and poetry. Lacoue-Labarthe puts it like this: "it seems to me that the suturing of philosophy to the Poem, as Badiou analyzes it [...] does not exactly concern poetry, and especially not poetry in its properly modern exigency. There is a sort of misunderstanding at work here [...] which can be designated with one word: myth. It may be that, in reality, this suturing

[53] Badiou, *Manifesto for Philosophy*, 27.

[54] Ibid., 32. Badiou also retrospectively summarizes his manifesto's concern as follows: "[T]he philosophical position I combated twenty years ago was principally the Heideggerian position in its French variants (Derrida, Lacoue-Labarthe, Nancy, but also Lyotard), which consisted in announcing the irremediable end of philosophy in its metaphysical form and considering the arts, poetry, painting and theatre as proffering the supreme recourse for thought. My 'Platonic gesture' was to reaffirm the possibility of philosophy in its original sense [...]" (Alain Badiou, *Second Manifesto for Philosophy*, trans. Louise Burchill [Cambridge: Polity Press, 2011], 117.

[55] Ibid., 66-77, 98. See also Badiou, *Conditions*, 93-112.

did not happen to, or was not imposed upon, the Poem, but rather the Mytheme."[56] His point is not merely that Badiou misses some nuance by not distinguishing between myth and poetry, but that he misses something crucial when he collapses them: Namely, not only mathematics, perhaps not even primarily mathematics, has the capacity to interrupt myth; poetry can do it as well. Thus, later in his paper – concluding a reading of Walter Benjamin's interpretation of Romanticism (in contrast to Heidegger's) as being characterized by an idea of "poetry as prose" (*poésie comme prose / der Poesie als der Prosa*) that anticipates a modernist conception of art as mechanical and the artist as a manufacturer – Lacoue-Labarthe writes: "We are thus on the verge of the Matheme, as Badiou would say, who in fact does not fail to use similar declarations from Rimbaud or Mallarme as a backdrop: 'O, rigorous mathematics.' But the Matheme, if we follow Benjamin, is not the 'mathematical.' It is the Poem itself, that is, prose."[57] In short, when the poem becomes prose, it has the same interruptive capacity as what Lacoue-Labarthe calls the Matheme, which Badiou ascribes solely to mathematics – or at least this seems to be the implicit claim. Lacoue-Labarthe's paper was published as part of his book *Heidegger – La politique du poème* (*Heidegger and the Politics of Poetry*). In another chapter of this book, where he discusses Heidegger's and Benjamin's readings of Hölderlin, he briefly returns to Badiou's thesis about the suturing of contemporary philosophy to poetry. At the end of the chapter in a section entitled "Postscript," he reproduces a long passage from a letter from Badiou in which the latter seems to not only accept Lacoue-Labarthe's critique, but also to affirm his suggestion that poetry itself contains the resources for interrupting myth. Badiou writes:

---

[56] Lacoue-Labarthe, *Heidegger and the Politics of Poetry*, 23. Moreover, according to Lacoue-Labarthe the issue concerns not merely the suturing of philosophy to the poem from Romanticism to Heidegger, but also the *political* nature of philosophy's suturing to the poem (ibid.).

[57] Ibid., 37. An exploration of the theme of Romanticism – and the different ways in which Badiou, Lacoue-Labarthe and Nancy understand it – would undoubtedly be relevant to the present discussion, particularly, perhaps, because Nancy, drawing on Blanchot, understands the *interruptive* nature of the fragment as a defining characteristic of the Romantics' conception of literature (*écriture*) (Philippe Lacoue-Labarthe and Jean Nancy, *The Literary Absolute. The Theory of Literature in German Romanticism*, trans. Philip Barnard and Cheryl Lester [Albany: State University of New York Press, 1988], 57). Space constrictions prevent an examination of this issue here, but let me note that Badiou's conception of Romanticism seems to be closer to that which Lacoue-Labarte ascribes to Heidegger than the one he construes from Benjamin's texts (Lacoue-Labarthe, *Heidegger and the Politics of Poetry*, 34-37). One could ask whether Badiou's criticism of Romanticism would not need to take this differentiation of Romanticism into account, and especially Lacoue-Labarthe's reiteration of Benjamin's reading of Romanticism as implying an idea of poetry as prose (ibid., 20-21, 37, 58, 78).

> If it turns out that the immanent operation of the poem, already – or even especially – for Hölderlin, is in no way the establishment of the sovereignty of myth (or of sacred names), but on the contrary their erasure, and therefore a becoming prose; *then* the mytheme is not an intrinsic given properly located in the poem, but, already, a speculative appropriation that does violence to the poem. In that case, are you not calling 'mytheme' the very thing that I am calling 'suture'?[58]

Thus, contrary to what he sometimes seems to be saying, Badiou ultimately actually rejects any absolute opposition between the poem and the matheme, affirming that "one of the peculiar characteristics of my own project is that it requires both the reference to poetry and a basis in mathematics."[59] Thus, even if Badiou calls for a repetition of the Platonic gesture as philosophy's disentanglement (*désintrication*) from poetry and its re-entanglement (*réintrication*) with mathematics in contemporary philosophy, as he describes it, this seems to be a question of maintaining a tension between mathematics and poetry within philosophy, rather than excluding the one over the other. While Plato ended up banishing the poets from the polis, and Heidegger in his return to the pre-Socratics sought to exclude mathematics from philosophy, Badiou wants to follow Fernando Pessoa's example and take a path between: "Pessoa's modernity lies in casting doubt on the pertinence of the Platonism/anti-Platonism opposition: The task of the thought-poem is neither allegiance to Platonism nor its reversal."[60] This seems to leave Badiou in a position not that far from Nancy's notion of "the interruption of myth as literature [écriture]" as well as Lacoue-Labarthe's notion of "poetry as prose."[61]

So, where does all this leave us with regard to the relation between mythos and logos, representation and concept, religion and philosophy? Clearly, this

---

[58] Lacoue-Labarthe, *Heidegger and the Politics of Poetry*, 81. While in this passage Badiou clearly indicates that the suturing of philosophy to the poem – its speculative appropriation – is something that philosophy does to the poem, in *Manifesto for Philosophy* his explanation is less clear-cut, suggesting that poetry itself also plays a part in forming this suture (Badiou, *Manifesto for Philosophy*, 69-70).

[59] Badiou, *Theoretical Writings*, trans. Alberto Toscano and Ray Brassier (London: Continuum, 2004), xvi.

[60] Badiou, *Handbook of Inaesthetics*, trans. Alberto Toscano (Stanford: Stanford University Press, 2004), 44. See also Badiou, *Manifesto for Philosophy*, 74-77.

[61] For a more thorough discussion of the complex dialogue between Badiou and Lacoue-Labarthe on these matters, see Tom Betteridge, *Badiou, Poem and Subject* (London: Bloomsbury Academic, 2020), 89-103. Badiou's interchange with Lacoue-Labarthe is no less complicated to unravel than the one with Nancy. Badiou has written briefly on Lacoue-Labarthe in two books (*Manifesto for Philosophy* and *Conditions*) as well as more extensively in his essays "Philippe Lacoue-Labarthe," "The anti-Wagnerian position of Philippe Lacoue-Labarthe," and "In Search of Lost Prose." On the other hand, Lacoue-Labarthe has written on Badiou in the following texts: "Liminaire sur l'ouvrage d'Alain Badiou, L'etre et l'evenement," "Poetry, Philosophy, Politics," "The Courage of Poetry," and *Musica Ficta: Figures of Wagner* (the two first specifically concern Badiou's work).

question has no simple answer, for, as we have seen, what often presents itself as a clear-cut opposition is, in fact, an ambiguous and extremely complex relationship. Of course, this hardly makes it any less pertinent a matter for the philosophy of religion to consider. On the contrary.

Envisioning good actions:
On Aristotelian *phantasia* and the Appearance of Ethical Principles

Jonas Holst

Introduction

Imagine a world in which the highest good, in so far as it exists, does not appear. It would not be present in the actions of those, who inhabit this sombre place, nor in their minds. One might think that these people could imagine what it would be like to act ethically well and know what constitutes goodness, but this would be a mere appearance, a ghostly shadow of what is really good, which would remain outside the whole realm of fleeting and delusory phenomena. Only somebody who had ventured to go beyond the world of appearances, would have a chance of knowing if the supreme good exists and realise what its true nature is.

Although this may sound like a late modern dystopia, anyone well-versed in ancient philosophy will know that a similar tale was first told by Socrates in Book 7 of Plato's *Republic*: In the allegory of the cave, Socrates describes a subterranean place in which the sun, symbolising the supreme good, does not appear. Not even a ray of sunlight reaches the cave-dwellers, who are enchained without being able to move and turn their gaze to look beyond the wall against which they lean part of their back and head. They only see images, thanks to a fire behind them, and hear sounds echoing off the wall situated in front of them, and as they have never seen or heard anything else, they take this to be everything there is.[1]

In so far as the cave-dwellers do not have it in them to move beyond this subterranean world which they are stuck in, a way out will not appear or become imaginable, until somebody enters from the outside, releases one or more prisoners and leads them towards the exit. However, if these are the conditions that every reader of Plato's allegory will have to accept in order to understand its meaning and implications, one might ask how the first prisoner escaped from the cave. If he or she also received help to get out, then it raises the same question again, which will repeat itself, until we stop and think about the miserable conditions in the cave. Contrary to what some interpreters of the

[1] Plato, *Republic (Der Staat)*, transl. F. Scleiermacher (Darmstadt: WBG, 2001), 514a-515c.

allegory have asserted,[2] nobody can get out alone, which again implies that the one who enters the cave, must be somebody who *is* from the outside.

This being from the outside, who has descended into the cave to release somebody, is of a higher ontological order. Given that Plato holds the reality and the visions one may have outside the cave to be "divine", there also seems to be something divine about the being who has descended, but whose exact abode we do not know. This is the metaphysical significance of Plato's allegory, which contains explicit references to Socrates' own examined life. In the *Republic*, the good is god-like and can only be known through theoretical insight, carried out by the eye of the soul. The reason for this is that in ordinary perception, according to the metaphysical hierarchy established in the *Republic*, nothing of the higher reality, governed by the good, shines through. This does not necessarily mean that everything is bad down in the cave. The prisoners do, at least, not seem to experience it like that. However, emptying the cave of resources to get access to reality and making the dwellers completely ignorant, as Plato does, has another unfortunate consequence: It is only by using force or even violence that a cave-dweller can be obliged to move towards the exit.[3]

Apart from being philosophically unsatisfactory that Plato in his thought experiment does not explain how the liberation of a prisoner exactly comes about and who is behind it, it is even more unfortunate, seen from an ethical point of view, that in an allegory on education, described as a movement towards knowing the good, force or violence is presented as the only means to reach that goal.[4] Would it be possible to open another more ethical way towards the good, according to which humans have a chance of acting well as a result of how the good appears to them?

Following Aristotle, who criticised Plato for elevating the good too high above the desires and deliberations of human beings in their everyday efforts

---

[2] In *The Human Condition* (Chicago & London: The University of Chicago Press, 1998/1958), Hannah Arendt misreads Plato's allegory, when she declares that "the philosopher, having liberated himself from the fetters that bound him to his fellow men, leaves the cave in perfect 'singularity' [...]" Nobody frees him or herself in Plato's cave, but the one who escapes is liberated by someone else, who accompanies or rather forces the cavedweller towards the exit. Other commentators center exclusively on the epistemological parallels between the analogies of the Line and the Cave without considering the pedagogical and political role of force needed to liberate a prisoner. For a summary of this discussion, see John Malcolm, "The Cave Revisited," *The Classical Quarterly*, Vol. 31, No. 1, (1981): 60-68.

[3] Plato, *Republic* 515e-519a.

[4] It should be remarked that Plato in other dialogues, such as the *Gorgias* and the *Phaedrus*, does seem to let the good appear in this world, for example through virtue and beauty, whose nature is, according to Socrates' enigmatic phrase in the *Philebus* (Darmstadt: WBG, 2001), the place where the good takes refuge (*Philebus*, 64e).

to live well, the present article will adopt a phenomenological approach which explores how something that appears good is correlated with human imagination or *phantasia*.[5] Contrary to the Platonic vision of the good in the allegory of the cave, Aristotle argues that what is good for us humans does appear in this world and that the appearance of the good, the so-called apparent good, corresponds to a more or less clear vision of certain ethical principles and goals. Seen from this perspective, it is because Plato cuts off the cave-dwellers from reality, which they cannot reach through ordinary perception or imagination, that they need to be pushed forcefully to exit the cave. If it could be shown that imagination and its close connection to appearances do play a role for humans' access to a shared reality, then force may not be necessary and imagination could prove to take on an ethical significance.

The present article is meant as a contribution to a phenomenological field within the philosophy of religion which conceptualises moral action as aiming at the realisation of the good in relation to others. Despite being a field and an endeavour that has been taken up by modern thinkers, among others Gabriel Marcel, Emmanuel Levinas, Martin Buber and K. E. Løgstrup, it is not foreign to the ancient religious scriptures. The aim of reinterpreting the ethical significance of the Aristotelian conception of *phantasia* in the first part is to put it to the test in the second part and see how far it may help shedding new light on a biblical text, namely the parable of the Good Samaritan, in which the man, who has come from outside this world to save humankind from sin, namely Jesus Christ, directs our attention to the love of our neighbour as a manifestation of inheriting eternal life and loving God.

Considering that Aristotelian ethics does not make room for the stranger or for love in a Christian sense, it may seem remarkable or even awkward to draw on Aristotle in the suggested reading of a key text in the *New Testament*. However, it will be argued, in a critical discussion of the Danish theologian K. E. Løgstrup's interpretation of the parable of the Good Samaritan, that the Aristotelian concept of *phantasia* is not narrowly limited to his virtue ethics but can serve to uncover a meaning of envisioning good action, as well as the opposite, which traverses the divide between ancient Greek philosophy and Christian theology.

On the link between appearance and imagination

In ancient Greek, the words for appearance (*phainesthai*) and imagination (*phantasia*) are closely linked etymologically; a link which Plato seems to take advantage of in the *Theaetetus* and the *Sophist*, where *phantasia*, the few times

[5] Although imagination remains the best translation of *phantasia*, which is intimately linked with visual perception, the Greek term can, according to Aristotle, refer to any lasting perception through the five senses and its subsequent reproduction. *Phantasia* will therefore be left untranslated throughout the article.

it is employed, refers to appearances, most often false appearances.[6] Yet, it is Aristotle who, possibly inspired by Plato, develops this link between the two concepts further and takes it in a new direction. In contrast to his great predecessor, Aristotle dissociates *phantasia* from being primarily a false image of reality and gives it a significant role to play in the dynamic process of acquiring knowledge halfway between perception and thinking. Although he recognises that some of the images generated by *phantasia* may be misleading or even false, Aristotle maintains that human action and thinking do not come about without *phantasia* and that even though one has a false impression of reality, it is still possible to grasp something as true, for instance when the sun appears to be one foot wide. However, one firmly believes that it is bigger than the entire inhabited earth.[7]

As *phantasia* is the generator of impressions (*phantasmata*) which originate from sense perception (*aisthêsis*), it is not identical to perception, but neither can it exist without perception. *Phantasmata* are, according to Aristotle, lasting impressions that remain stored in the body and the soul, manifesting themselves as memories, dreams and illusions.[8] *Phantasia* can, contrary to perception, reproduce these stored impressions seemingly at will and combine them in novel ways that either represent or misrepresent reality. Yet, before anyone actively reproduces a picture of something and sets it before his or her eyes, as Aristotle puts it,[9] this "something" has already made an impression on the soul and aroused a physiological reaction in the body. Aristotle is well aware that things make a different impression on different people, depending on who they are and how they are disposed. For the following reflections on the ethical significance of *phantasia*, this is an important claim that Aristotle makes in *The Nicomachean Ethics*, where *phantasia* becomes tied up with one's ethical disposition and ability to envision good actions:

> Suppose that someone were to say that everyone seeks the apparent good (*tou phainomenou agathou*), but that we do not control its appearance (*phantasia*). Instead, whatever sort of person each of us happens to be also determines the sort of end that appears (*phainetai*) to him.[10]

---

[6] Plato, *Theaitetos* 152c, *Sophistes* 264a (Darmstadt: WBG, 2001); see also Krisanna M. Scheiter, "Images, Appearances, and Phantasia in Aristotle," *Phronesis* 57 (2012): 267.

[7] Aristotle, *De anima* (*Über die Seele*), transl. W. Theiler (Hamburg: Felix Meiner Verlag, 1995), 3.3.428a-b.

[8] Aristotle, *De anima*, 3.3.428a-b; see also Jakob Leth Fink, "Aristotle on deliberative Phantasia and Phronêsis," in *Phantasia in Aristotle's Ethics* , ed. J. L. Fink (London and New York: Bloomsbury Academic, 2019), 128-129.

[9] Aristotle, *De anima*, 3.3.427b.

[10] Aristotle, *The Nicomachean Ethics* (Indianapolis/Cambridge: Hackett, 2014) 3.5, 1114a-1114b. The original text used: *Ethica Nicomachea* (Oxford: Clarendon Press, 1963).

From this passage on the appearance of the good, it becomes clear how closely *phantasia* and *phainetai* are linked for Aristotle, who not only contends that it is thanks to *phantasia* that goals appear and can be pursued in the first place, but, even more important, that depending on who somebody happens to be, certain ends will appear, whereas others will not, or they may be distorted or stay in the background. In the context of the quotation, Aristotle argues against the view that who somebody is should be determined by his or her nature, as if the person in question had nothing to do with how things appear to him or her. If that were the case, there would be no difference between the vicious and the virtuous, who would not have any influence on how things appear to them, and we would be back in Plato's cave. The cave-dwellers in Plato's allegory are not free to change their perspective on things. They are not even free to move around and can, therefore, not really be held accountable for their ineptitude and ignorance. For Aristotle, this goes against everything on which ethics, politics and human societies are built.

In Aristotle's treatise on the soul, the so-called deliberative form of *phantasia* is connected to the specific form of practical reasoning which distinguishes humans from other living beings, whose perception of the world does not seem to be combined with reflections and judgments, at least not to the same degree as human beings.[11] Seen in this light, Plato's cave-dwellers, who do not deliberate rationally about any kind of common good, look more like animals or perhaps humans living below their best level of existence, in a dark, subterranean cave, instead of rising above it to live off the earth and build a society on it. The cave-dwellers could possess some variety of *phantasia*, but not the deliberate form of which Aristotle speaks, as this presupposes reasoning about what would appear to be the best thing to do in a given situation. The predicament of the cave-dwellers is that they have no critical distance to what they see and hear, which happens to be mere shadows and echoes, but they do not know that, as they are incapable of distinguishing between what something appears to be and what it really is.

Seen in this light, Plato and Aristotle may not be too far away from each other theoretically. The cave-dwellers do not have sufficient imagination to envision anything else than what they passively perceive in front of them, which again means that their perception and imagination are almost indistinguishable. Yet, *phantasia* in humans, who deliberate about the good, is, according to Aristotle, precisely defined by going beyond what is simply given in perception, combining and rearranging simple perceptions to create more complex ones.[12] Still, after having settled that *phantasia* both depends on and transcends perception, there is another danger lurking in the shadows of Plato's allegory: Every human being may be in search of the apparent good, but what

---

[11] Aristotle, *De anima*, 3.3.434a.

[12] Ibid., 3.3.428a-b.

if this is all there is, a mere appearance, and nothing truly good to deliberate about? Aristotle does not raise this question, at least not in this form, but, as we saw, this is the real challenge in Plato's allegory of the cave, leading to another related problem: How can anyone escape from the cave and move beyond mere appearance?

Aristotle's solution to this problem is well known: He changes the whole metaphysical scenario and takes, instead of a cave, society or the *polis* as his starting point, where all people grow up and acquire habits by carrying out certain activities and seeing others do the same in contact with a tangible reality. It lies outside the scope of this article to dig deeper into the many differences between Platonic and Aristotelian metaphysics, but the one question about the appearance of the good in human action has to be dealt with in order to delimit the significant role which *phantasia* plays in practice. For Aristotle, those who act well and do it in a noble way, love what they do and feel joy when they act and also see others act in the same way.[13] This may sound self-indulgent, but according to an Aristotelian outlook, if someone who is virtuous disliked acting virtuously, that person would not really be virtuous, but rather a living contradiction who would go against what he or she were supposed to be, namely virtuous.

Aristotle's assertion that noble and beautiful actions (*tais kalais praxais*) contain their own form of pleasure and joy is not to be understood egoistically, so that a virtuous person would only cherish his or her own actions. Rather the plural form of a specific kind of actions, namely the noble and beautiful ones, indicates that the virtuous person qua virtuous also finds joy in other people acting virtuously. In fact, becoming aligned with other people acting well is, Aristotle claims, one of the primary ways, in which human beings become good friends and this ethical relationship constitutes the most enduring bond that holds societies together.[14] It is not because it is pleasurable that virtuous people act well, but because it is noble, i.e. they act justly and wisely because justice and wisdom together with the other virtues are good enough in themselves to sustain and harmonise human practice.

In this Aristotelian sense, the genuine good appears attractive to those who have become aligned to it through habituation. As Jakob Leth Fink has shown in a recent contribution, it is the function of deliberative *phantasia* to provide both a "framework for deliberation", i.e. a situated view of a given context, and "to facilitate practical thinking with *phantasmata* that might lead to action depending on which *phantasma* is most attractive."[15] Practical thinking is meant to reason about and find the means to good action, but the appearance of ethically salient principles and goals relies on and goes through *phantasia*, whose

[13] Aristotle, *The Nicomachean Ethics*, 1.8.1099a.

[14] Ibid, 8.1.1155a; 9.9.1169b-1170a.

[15] Fink, "Aristotle on deliberative Phantasia and Phronêsis," 134.

configuration in each person depends on how things and situations are perceived: pleasurable, disagreeable, painful, attractive, neutral or unattractive. There are, of course, many ways in which *phantasia* can be mistaken, for instance by taking something which promotes human well-being to be awful or being attracted by something utterly destructive, but this also means that *phantasia* can get it right and draw humans towards the truly good, although this may be difficult to find as a consistent trait in human beings. For Aristotle, much depends on education and the ethical ways in which humans are introduced to and become acquainted with the valuable and virtuous aspects of life.

When the opposite happens, and *phantasia* either fails to offer any guidance or distorts the value of the possibilities at hand, a person can become morally blind: "the principle does not immediately appear (*euthus ou phainetai*) to the person who has been corrupted by pleasure or pain."[16] As Fink observes, it is not due to an intellectual failure of practical reasoning that the person in question does not see what the relevant options and ethically salient goals are in a given situation.[17] It is rather that he or she, by being corrupted by pleasure and pain, is either unaffected by the situation or is affected too little or too much and thus lacks the motivating *phantasma* which could serve as a starting point for virtuous action. Principles and goals are correlated in Aristotelian ethics so that if the principle, which is built up through ongoing perception, imagination, experience and reflection, does not appear, neither does the goal.[18]

Perhaps the principle could appear at some point later, but even if that were the case, it would not be the right one, as long as the agent is corrupted by pleasure and pain which distorts his or her vision of the ethical goal. To the practically wise, who have an enduring disposition and knowledge of what it means to act well, their *phantasia* immediately presents them with the right end, which again implies, in so far as *phantasia* depends on perception, that they clearly sense and feel what has to be done in a given situation without being misled by pleasure and pain. Often they would still have to reason about the means to reach the goal, but Aristotle concedes in another passage that one can be disposed so as to act well without thinking twice or having to decide about which option to take.[19]

The Good Samaritan reread

In the most influential tradition of Western moral philosophy, which is guided by universal rational principles and treats "moral imagination" as an

---

[16] Aristotle, *The Nicomachean Ethics*, 6.5.1140b.

[17] Fink, "Aristotle on deliberative Phantasia and Phronêsis," 141.

[18] Norman Lillegard, "Passion and Reason: Aristotelian Strategies in Kierkegaard's Ethics," *The Journal of Religious Ethics*, Vol. 30, No. 2 (2002): 253.

[19] Aristotle, *The Nicomachean Ethics*, 3.8.1117a.

oxymoron[20], Aristotle's ethical and practical philosophy has often been interpreted as relying on intellectual virtues with *phronêsis* as the cusp of situated human reasoning. Aristotle himself explicitly assigns a privileged place to *phronêsis* in his ethics. However, he also underlines that this intellectual virtue "is not only a rational state."[21] It needs to be guided by virtuous dispositions which perceive the right end. Moreover, as we have seen, there are situations in which people act well out of an immediate sensation and a clear vision of the best end, mediated by *phantasia*.

The question to be raised in the following reading is if Aristotle's account of *phantasia* could cover specific situations of emergency which it may not have been meant to represent, or if it will be faced with challenges that it cannot meet. The parable of the Good Samaritan, which has been handed down to us in the *Gospel of Luke*,[22] seems to present a serious challenge to Aristotelian ethics. The context of the parable is that Jesus Christ has been confronted by a Jew, who wants to know how he can inherit eternal life, to which Jesus answers: "What is written in the Law?". The Jew, who knows the sacred Scriptures by heart, immediately responds in accordance with the orthodox doctrine: to love God with all your heart and your neighbour as yourself. Jesus says that he is right, but he is seemingly unaware of what this form of love entails, as he goes on to ask Jesus who his neighbour is. Instead of answering his interlocutor straight away, Jesus offers the parable of the Samaritan, who stops at the side of a dangerous road leading from Jerusalem to Jericho, to help a man in dire need. The man has been robbed of his belongings and lies half-dead at the roadside.

Right before the Samaritan arrives, a priest and a Levite had passed the man by, apparently indifferent to his suffering, or they were at least not sufficiently affected by his agony to stop at his side. They do see him, Jesus recounts, but without deviating from their course. Now, the Samaritan sees him and is struck by the sort of pain felt in his own flesh when seeing someone suffer. The ancient Greek term employed in the Biblical text is a passive form of the verb *splangchnizomai*, which expresses a gut feeling or a sensation felt in the most vital organs of one's body. The common translation of the verb is to have pity or mercy, which may convey part of what the Samaritan feels, when he sees the man in pain, but it should not be forgotten that what makes the samaritan approach and help the man in need is rooted in and emerges out of a bodily felt sensation which forms part of the whole situation in which the Samaritan finds himself, and tells a story about how it appears to him.

---

[20] Mark Johnson, "Moral Imagination," in *The Routledge Handbook og Philosophy of Imagination*, ed. Amy Kind (New York: Routledge, 2016), 355-367.

[21] Aristotle, *The Nicomachean Ethics*, 6.5.1140b.

[22] Luke 10:25-37, in *Novum Testamentum Graece*, ed. Nestle-Aland (Stuttgart: Deutsche Bibelgesellschaft, 1998).

Yet, does the scene with the man lying almost dead in the ditch not appear in the same way to the three travelers? Following the text, it would be difficult to deny that they see the same thing, namely a man lying at the roadside, but this is not the same as that they all have the same perception of the situation or that it appears in an identical way to the three of them. Did the priest and the Levite see that the man was in agony and thus in need of help? We do not know nor do we know what they were thinking or feeling when they passed the man by, but either his suffering did not appear to them at all, or if it did, it did not strike them as urgent enough to interrupt whatever they were doing. The road from Jerusalem to Jericho was notoriously dangerous in ancient times, and they might be hurrying along out of fear of being ambushed, or perhaps the priest was "moved to feel distrust for the injured man as a possible source of impurity", as two other interpreters suggest, who understand "the appearances of the phenomenal world" as shaped by the subjects' "immediate and ultimate goals, the intensity of their emotional interactions."[23]

The key point in relation to the topic of the present article is that the priest and the Levite do not suffer any significant change like the Samaritan, who immediately deviates from the road, as he becomes aligned to and aware of the man's suffering through his gut-wrenching sight. He is so affected by what he sees that there does not seem to be room or time for any deliberation or decision making before he goes up to the man. His compassion, understood as suffering with the injured man, urges him to care for the man by curing his wounds and taking him to an inn, where he pays for his stay and whatever else may be needed while the man is there. At the end of the story, Jesus not only returns the initial question to the Jew, who posed it, but he turns it around by asking which of the three was a neighbour to the injured man. Without hesitation, the Jew answers what the story makes painstakingly clear: The Samaritan was the one, who got as close as one can get to another human being, by sharing his pain and acting on it in order to alleviate it.

The Danish theologian K. E. Løgstrup interprets the parable as relaying a full enactment of mercy on the part of the Samaritan, in whose mind there is no real distinction to be made between motivation, action and fulfilment: "Mercy only exists as a completed action which is moved by what it wishes to fulfil."[24] The Samaritan's whole attention is drawn to the other, whose agony he does not seem to have any other choice but to alleviate. Løgstrup coins the term "the sovereign expression of life" to designate the selfless and spontaneous way, in which mercy breaks through without the merciful having any

---

[23] Michael G. Lawler and Todd A. Salzman, "Virtue Ethics: Natural and Christian", *Theological Studies* 74 (2013): 446, 452.

[24] K. E. Løgstrup, *Opgør med Kierkegaard* (København: Gyldendal, 1994), 123 (my translation).

control or power over it. The Samaritan does not decide to be merciful, according to Løgstrup, but is overwhelmed by it as a sovereign expression of life.

In a later comment on the Christian love of our neighbour, Løgstrup remarks with reference to the merciful Samaritan that there is an element of "phantasy" (*fantasi*) in the idea that what you wish that the other does onto you, you should do onto the other.[25] This should not be understood as a call to fantasise about what the other might want, but rather in the sense of putting oneself in the place of the other in order to figure out what sort of help one would like to receive if one were in the place of the other. According to Løgstrup, that is the way in which one should fulfil the act of love just like the Samaritan did "out there on the road."

Yet, in the light of our reinterpretation of the Aristotelian conception of *phantasia*, the element of phantasy, which Løgstrup identifies as crucial for the Samaritan's merciful love, calls for a deeper phenomenological grounding in the human body. Considering that both Løgstrup's early and late thinking contains phenomenological reflections on the body that could possibly help uncover the somatic and emotional ground out of which such expressions of life as love and mercy arise, it is remarkable that he does not highlight the literal meaning of the Danish word for mercy, *barmhjertighed*, which is traditionally used about the Samaritan and which denotes showing mercy towards others with one's bosom and heart. Aristotle's insistence that perception through the five senses provokes some physiological change in the body and makes an enduring impression on the human psyche, which is both marked by it and forms it according to the specific configuration of the soul's *ethos*, may allow us to take one more step towards a phenomenological interpretation of the Samaritan's both passive and active approach.

It could come as a surprise that Aristotle's philosophy is considered to be relevant in this context, as he has traditionally been seen, also by Løgstrup, as promoting an ethnocentric vision of the flourishing and self-sufficient form of life, so characteristic of Hellenistic culture which did not consider strangers, slaves and women to have equal status as Greek men. However, in his account of *phantasia*, he offers a broad and neutral explanation of how the human psyche becomes tied to the body through somatic sensations, which are not limited to virtuous action but also entails ethically problematic practices. Thus, pain and pleasure, which Løgstrup does not take into account in his interpretation of the good Samaritan, can have a decisive influence on the *ethos* and *phantasia* of an agent, who can become morally blind or ethically clear-sighted depending on the measure of pain and pleasure felt. Aristotle did not, or only to a very small degree, consider the ethical significance of agents being confronted with agony, but this should not make us refrain from envisioning

---

[25] K.E. Løgstrup, *Etiske begreber og problemer* (Aarhus: Klim, 2018), 44.

what is implied in acting well in situations such as the one described in the parable of the Good Samaritan.

Applying the Aristotelian framework, the principle of good action does not appear to the priest and the Levite, because they do not feel a sufficient amount of pain when seeing the man in agony and so they remain aloof, seemingly indifferent to his suffering. One could speculate that they might have other goals in sight that for them had priority over saving the man, or maybe one or both of them did feel some uneasiness when seeing the man, but it was not enough, for whatever reason, to change their course, and so they did not get to imagine or envision any other way of acting than to continue down the road. Their *phantasia* was not aroused, and, seen from an Aristotelian point of view, it would be because neither of them had a sense perceptual disposition to be sufficiently affected and motivated to approach the stranger lying at the side of the road. Here we do not have to draw the same conclusion as Aristotle. The Samaritan might not, at least not from the beginning, be disposed in the ethically right way either. Regarding the priest and the Levite, it is probably not out of "thoughtlessness" that they do not go any closer. Even Aristotle would agree to this. Rather to the contrary, having one thought too many or being one step ahead of the situation may have obfuscated their vision and be the main reason why they are not fully present and see what other, especially ethical, possibilities lay open to them.

In contrast to the priest and the Levite, what the Samaritan is called to do, namely to help the man in agony, appears immediately to him, and he acts accordingly and spontaneously, as Løgstrup also maintains. However, there does not seem to be any need for the Samaritan, or time for that sake, to put himself in the place of the other, as his gut-wrenching or heart-rending sensation has already established a connection to the man. Before phantasy becomes an activity, supposedly carried out by the Samaritan "to change roles" with the suffering man, as Løgstrup claims,[26] *phantasia* is a *pathos,*[27] according to Aristotle, which makes an agent receptive to certain impressions, often laden with or provoking certain emotions. What concerns Aristotle less, although he does touch upon it, is that *phantasia* also has an accumulative effect on what one perceives so that one may, over the years, become more or less experienced and virtuous in practical affairs.

Conclusion

The above offers an alternative to the phenomenological and ethical implications of Plato's allegory of the cave, in which the truly good does not appear. Neither perception nor *phantasia* allows the cave-dwellers to access

---

[26] Ibid., 44.

[27] Aristotle, *De anima*, 3.3.427b.

any reality beyond the place they are tied to. Only through an external and forced liberation from the shadow world of the cave do they have a chance of going beyond their limitations and get a vision of the good in life.

In the *Nicomachean Ethics* and *On the Soul*, Aristotle develops another approach to reality, in which the good does appear to humans, who do not need to be liberated forcefully from imprisonment in order to envision good actions and act well. This is made possible by the mediating role of *phantasia*, which through a combination of sense perceptions and the highlighting of salient features in a situation may "present" an agent with certain ethical principles and goals.

Although *phantasia*, at its most basic, according to Aristotle, relies on perception to generate lasting impressions, it is not constrained by an actually perceived phenomenon or by conveying veridical information. Through *phantasia* a person can abstract from and combine sense perception in alternative ways which in a context of pursuing practical purposes allows for a wide range of modes of envisioning action. The way people see and act in complex situations depends on how these situations appear to them, i.e., complex combinations of *phantasmata*, and this again tells a story about who they are and how their *ethos* is configurated, according to lived experiences of what is pleasurable and painful, useful and useless, noble and ignoble.

The parable of the Good Samaritan can be read as an example of the vital role that the body may play in envisioning or seeing clearly what is demanded of someone in an urgent situation. Aristotle does usually not reflect on such situations, and his anthropologically biased view of man as being in possession of reason may not do full justice to emergency situations, in which emotions guide humans toward the ethically most salient features and goals. Still, his account of *phantasia* as enabling agents to envision good actions is sensible enough to make plausible that it is through the bodily felt sensation of pain when seeing the man suffering in the ditch that the Samaritan becomes connected to the suffering man's agony and acts immediately on it. In contrast to the priest and the Levite, the situation appears sufficiently painful and urgent for him to approach and help the man in need, who is saved thanks to the *misericordia* of the Samaritan.

Imagination and Givenness

On Michel Henry's Phenomenology of Life as a Contribution to a Christian Philosophical Critique of Scandinavian Creation Theology

Ulrik Nissen

In 2017 an anthology published on Scandinavian creation theology and the post-secular age claimed that there is an identifiable Scandinavian creation theology "movement" with roots in the theologies of K.E. Løgstrup, Regin Prenter, and Gustaf Wingren, beginning from around the mid-twentieth century.[1] According to this anthology, the creation theology movement has been a characteristic trait of Scandinavian theology for at least half a century. The contributors to the anthology also argue that this movement may serve as a model for a reconfiguration of Reformation theology for a post-secular age. Finally, it is one of the claims of the editors and authors that Scandinavian creation theology provides an approach to examining the relation between the "common sense" and the "communal sense" understood as the relation between concerns shared by all and the particular issues raised by particular communities.

The present essay takes this claim about a Scandinavian creation theology as one first step in a reflection on the question about a Nordic understanding of imagination. The leading question of the essay is, if the characteristic Nordic creation theology can be enriched by a broader understanding of creation theology than found in its traditional Nordic representatives and if imagination can be said to play a key role in such a reformulation. It is the *thesis* of the essay – and what I will attempt to argue – that the phenomenological thought of the French philosopher Michel Henry, can enrich this particular Nordic approach and give it a broader understanding of human reality with imagination as a key concept.

A common background for the mentioned Scandinavian theologians is their shared Lutheran heritage. Løgstrup, Prenter, and Wingren are all placed within the Lutheran tradition, and their work must be understood in the light of this theological heritage. Both Prenter and Wingren have large studies on Luther's

[1] Niels Henrik Gregersen, Trygve Wyller, and Bengt Kristensson Uggla, eds., *Reformation Theology for a Post-Secular Age: Løgstrup, Prenter, Wingren, and the Future of Scandinavian Creation Theology*, vol. 24, Research in Contemporary Religion (Göttingen: Vandenhoeck & Ruprecht, 2017).

theology, which have become some of their most known works.[2] Løgstrup has not to the same extent written extensive studies on Luther, but his work is deeply influenced by Luther's theology, as also demonstrated in a recent book.[3] It seems fair to claim that their Lutheran heritage is an important source for their emphasis on creation theology. This emphasis on the creation theology as central for Luther's theology is further sustained both in a relatively recent study by Johanna Schwanke and in Herbert Olsson's classical study from the early 70ies.[4] However, what seems to be missing in this portrait of Luther's theology is the centrality of Christ for his theology (and this may even be a more general shortcoming in Scandinavian theology). As a counterposition, I will argue that in light of Luther's theology, it is central for the Lutheran tradition to argue for a deep Christological understanding of reality. It lies at the core of the Lutheran tradition to maintain an understanding of a saturated concept of reality with a tension between reality as it appears to us and the believed or imagined reality.[5] This may, of course, also be argued with respect to the mysterious presence of God within everyday life, the political order etc. However, as I wish to contend in the present essay, this mysterious presence of an imagined or hidden reality is also closely linked to a Christological understanding of reality.[6]

---

[2] See for example Regin Prenter, *Spiritus creator: Studier i Luthers theologi* (Aarhus: Universitetsforlaget, 1944); Gustaf Wingren, *Luthers lära om kallelsen* (Lund1942); *Skapelsen och lagen* (Lund: Gleerup, 1958).

[3] Svend Andersen, *Løgstrup & Luther*, Løgstrup biblioteket (Aarhus: Klim, 2017).

[4] Herbert Olsson, *Schöpfung, Vernunft und Gesetz in Luthers Theologie*, vol. 10, Acta Universitatis Upsaliensis. Studia Doctrinae Christianae Upsaliensia (Uppsala: Uppsala University, 1971); Johannes Schwanke, *Creatio ex nihilo : Luthers Lehre von der Schöpfung aus dem Nichts in der grossen Genesisvorlesung (1535 - 1545)*, vol. 126, Theologische Bibliothek Töpelmann (Berlin: de Gruyter, 2004). Luther's theology as a source for the Scandinavian creation theology is also shown in Allen G. Jorgenson, "Martin Luther in Scandinavian Creation Theology," in *Reformation Theology for a Post-Secular Age: Løgstrup, Prenter, Wingren, and the Future of Scandinavian Creation Theology*, ed. Niels Henrik Gregersen, Bengt Kristensson Uggla, and Trygve Wyller, Research in Contemporary Religion (Göttingen: Vandenhoeck & Ruprecht, 2017).

[5] In the current essay I argue for a continuity between belief and imagination, as we shall see later.

[6] This understanding of a saturated Christological reality holds parallels to the deep Christology which Niels Henrik Gregersen is also elaborating upon, when he argues for a material and creaturely incarnation, which extends the incarnation to all biological life forms. See for example Niels Henrik Gregersen, "The Extended Body of Christ: Three Dimensions of Deep Incarnation," in *Incarnation: On the Scope and Depth of Christology*, ed. Niels Henrik Gregersen (Minneapolis: Fortress Press, 2015).

The centrality of Christological themes in Luther's theology

Several studies demonstrate the centrality of Christological themes in Luther's ethics, despite their different accentuations (among these are some of the contributions from the Finnish Luther research in recent years).[7] Marc Lienhard follows this observation when he opens his study on Luther's Christology with a quotation from Luther's commentary to the Galatians: "In my heart only one article rules, namely the faith in Christ from whom, by whom and to whom all my theological thoughts flow forth and back day and night. Still, I do not believe to have understood more than a feeble and poor beginning, yes, only a small part of this wisdom's altitude, latitude, and profundity."[8] This is essential in his understanding of justification by faith and in several other crucial debates. One of the sustained characteristics of his theology is the affirmative view on Chalcedonian Christology, which I have shown in a recently published book on *The Polity of Christ*.[9] Several recent Luther-studies demonstrate the centrality of this motif for Luther's ecclesiology, theology, political thought etc., not least with reference to the *communicatio idiomatum*.[10] "The

---

[7] Oswald Bayer, *Freiheit als Antwort: zur theologischen Ethik* (Tübingen: Mohr, 1995); Veli-Matti Kärkkäinen, "'The Christian as Christ to the neighbour': on Luther's theology of love," *International Journal of Systematic Theology* 6, no. 2 (2004); Dietmar Lage, *Martin Luther's Christology and Ethics*, Texts and studies in religion (Lewiston, NY: Edwin Mellen Pr, 1990); Tuomo Mannermaa, *Der im Glauben gegenwärtige Christus. Rechtfertigung und Vergottung. Zum ökumenischen Dialog*, Arbeiten zur Geschichte und Theologie des Luthertums; N.F., Bd. 8 (Hannover: Lutherisches Verlagshaus, 1989); Antti Raunio, *Summe des christlichen Lebens: die "Goldene Regel" als Gesetz der Liebe in der Theologie Martin Luthers von 1510 bis 1527*, vol. 13, Reports from the Department of Systematic Theology (Helsinki: University of Helsinki, 1993); "Faith and Christian living in Luther's Confession concerning Christ's supper (1528)," *Lutherjahrbuch* 76 (2009).

[8] WA 40 I, 33, 7-11 (quoted after Marc Lienhard, *Martin Luthers christologisches Zeugnis: Entwicklung und Grundzüge seiner Christologie* (Göttingen: Vandenhoeck & Ruprecht, 1980), 9 (my translation)).

[9] Ulrik Nissen, *The Polity of Christ. Studies on Dietrich Bonhoeffer's Chalcedonian Christology and Ethics*, ed. Brian Brock and Susan F. Parsons, T&T Clark Enquiries in Theological Ethics (London: T&T Clark Bloomsbury Publishing Plc., 2020).

[10] Oswald Bayer, *Creator est creatura: Luthers Christologie als Lehre von der Idiomenkommunikation*, Theologische Bibliothek Töpelmann, 138 (Berlin: de Gruyter, 2007); Bo Kristian Holm, *Gabe und Geben bei Luther. Das Verhältnis zwischen Reziprozität und reformatorischer Rechtfertigungslehre*, Theologische Bibliothek Töpelmann; 134 (Berlin: Walter de Gruyter, 2006), 190ff; Dennis Ngien, "Chalcedonian Christology and Beyond: Luther's Understanding of the Communicatio Idiomatum," *The Heythrop Journal* 45, no. 1 (2004); Kjell Ove Nilsson, *Simul. Das Miteinander von Götllichem und Menschlichem in Luthers Theologie* (Göttingen: Vandenhoeck & Ruprecht, 1966); Johann Anselm Steiger, "Die communicatio idiomatum als Achse und Motor der Theologie Luthers: Der "fröhliche Wechsel" als hermeneutischer Schlüssel zu Abendmahlslehre, Anthropologie, Seelsorge, Naturtheologie, Rhetorik und Humor," *Neue Zeitschrift für systematische Theologie und Religionsphilosophie* 38, no. 1 (1996).

communicatio idiomatum moves into the centre of Martin Luther's Christology, even his theology as a whole. For him, the communication of idioms becomes a central figure in order to understand the person of Jesus Christ and his fulfilled work – never to isolate one from the other."[11]

What is important to note here, is that the *communicatio idiomatum* is not just central for Luther's Christology but is an underlying mode of thought for his theology as a whole. The German scholar, Anselm Steiger, describes the *communicatio idiomatum* as a hermeneutical vehicle for Luther's theology as a whole.[12] I will not here go further into Luther's understanding of this Christological motif. Suffice it here to state that Luther's theology cannot be rightly understood separate from his Christology. The parts of Scandinavian creation theology that apparently seem to ignore this side of Luther's theology miss out on essential characteristics of this theology. In line with this Christological premise in Luther's theology, I contend in the current essay that without this Christological presupposition, theology is at risk of losing its *proprium.* Thereby, the broader debate with other disciplines and the broader cultural or public debate is at risk of losing the other voice of theology that enriches and broadens the conversation.

The Mystery of Christ as a Believed and Imagined Reality

Luther's emphasis on the centrality of Christ is also found in one of the leading figures of Lutheran theology in the twentieth century – Dietrich Bonhoeffer. This is reflected several places in his theology, to an extent that, in the recently published handbook on Bonhoeffer, it can be formulated accordingly: "It is Christology which stands at the centre of Dietrich Bonhoeffer's theology and which enables him to develop a critical stance towards other theological positions of his time. In Jesus Christ, Bonhoeffer finds the point by which to orient all Christian thinking about God as well as about human beings and the world."[13] Suffice it here to mention his "Lectures on Christology" from 1933. When Bonhoeffer here reflects on the present Christ, and where Christ is present, he refers to Christ as the center of our existence, history, and nature.[14] For Bonhoeffer, it makes no sense to speak of human reality separate from Christ. Also, in his *Ethics,* he returns to this understanding when he reflects on the concepts of reason, culture, humanity, and tolerance as returning to Christ

---

[11] Oswald Bayer, *Martin Luthers Theologie. Eine Vergegenwärtigung* (Tübingen: Mohr Siebeck, 2003), 213 (my translation).

[12] Steiger, "Die communicatio idiomatum," 1 (my translation).

[13] Christiane Tietz, "Christology," in *The Oxford Handbook of Dietrich Bonhoeffer*, ed. Michael Mawson and Philip G. Ziegler (Oxford, UK: Oxford University Press, 2019), 150.

[14] Dietrich Bonhoeffer, "Lectures on Christology (Student Notes)," in *Berlin. 1932-1933*, ed. Larry Rasmussen, Dietrich Bonhoeffer Works (DBWE) (Minneapolis: Fortress Press, 2009 (1933)), 324-27.

when they are threatened. This is due to his understanding of Christ as the origin of these concepts. "Only that which participates in Christ can endure and overcome. Christ is the centre and the power of the Bible, of the church, of theology, but also of humanity, reason, justice, and culture. To Christ, everything must return; only under Christ's protection can it live."[15] As for Luther, it can be argued that this may be understood in the light of a Chalcedonian understanding of a mysterious presence of Christ within human reality – without separation and without confusion. However, as Bonhoeffer also points out in his "Lectures on Christology" – this is also a mystery that can only be grasped in faith. "Thus, the matter itself is left as a mystery, for we cannot enter into it within the parameters of positive thinking. We can only enter in faith."[16] I will contend that we can also say it is an imagined reality.

Hereby we touch on the relation between faith and imagination. In its classical theological sense, faith is "... the assurance of things hoped for, the conviction of things not seen." (Heb. 11:1). It is a deep confidence in the reality of something here and now which is not empirically verifiable and at the same time is to come in the future. For Luther, faith was *fiducia* understood as the trust in Christ, where the believer clings to Christ in order to attain the promised mercy of God.[17] For both the understanding of faith in "The Letter to the Hebrews" and in Luther it may be argued that faith is directed toward an imagined reality. This is not to say that this reality is "merely" imagined (and in that sense an imagined illusion), but it is a reality which is believed and therefore can only be grasped in faith, which is also Bonhoeffer's point. But just as Bonhoeffer argues that although this reality can only be grasped in faith, it is still the ultimate reality toward which he directs all other aspects of reality and in light of which all these other sides of creaturely life must be viewed, maybe we can also say that from a theological perspective we have to reflect upon what it means today that Jesus claims to be the way, the truth, and the life (John 14:6). This reflection also points forward to the next section on the phenomenology of life.

If we hold on to the reality of Christ as a believed reality that is grasped in faith, the immediately following question arises – what implications does this hold for our understanding of imagination with respect to the Christ reality? The concept of imagination is etymologically derived partly from the Anglo-Norman *ymaginacione*, where it describes a faculty of the mind involved in forming images or concepts.[18] It is often associated with the word *phantasia,*

---

[15] *Ethics*, ed. Clifford J. Green, vol. 6 (DBWE 6), Dietrich Bonhoeffer Works (Minneapolis: Fortress Press, 2005), 341.

[16] "Christology," 342.

[17] Markus Mühling, "Fiducia," in *Religion Past and Present* (Brill).

[18] See "imagination, n.," *OED Online* (Oxford: Oxford University Press), https://www-oed-com.ez.statsbiblioteket.dk:12048/view/Entry/91643?redirectedFrom=imagination.

which indicates that the term often refers to a mental state. When we imagine something, it is an activity of our minds, where we envision something that deepens or helps us to better understand reality, our motivations, desires, or feelings. The concept is, however, also contested. There is no consensus on exactly how to understand or define the concept. Consequently, the term is often used intuitively.[19] The relation between belief and imagination has been discussed by various philosophers, ranging from seeing it as a continuum between the two to those arguing for a difference.[20] For a proper assessment of this question, we have to specify also what we mean by belief. In the works of Peter Langland-Hassan, where he reflects, e.g., on the psycho-social formation and role of belief for a child's imagination, belief is a mental state. Belief in this sense is seen as a case of imagining and therefore in continuity with imagination, but belief is here not seen in relation to religious faith.[21] The same applies to Susanna Schellenberg, where belief and desire are seen in relation to imagination, and it is argued that there is a continuum between imagination and belief. The argument is that imaginative immersion makes it possible to imagine something that at the same time leads to believing it. An example could be the scientist imagining the future outcome of an experiment and, at the same time, forming a belief about these results. The functional role of imagining and believing are thereby seen on a continuum.[22] In both Schellenberg and Langland-Hassan, belief and imagination are seen as related, but for both of them, belief is not understood in relation to its religious uses.

When I use belief in the present context, I understand it as synonymous with religious faith. My focus is on the Christian understanding of faith, where it is closely connected to the question of salvation. It is intimately related to the

---

[19] A recent handbook on imagination, its historical and philosophical roots and contemporary uses in aesthetics, cognitive science, ethics, political philosophy, and epistemology shows that the concept is so broad that it is not possible to reach a common understanding of what it means. See Amy Kind, *The Routledge handbook of philosophy of imagination*, Routledge handbooks in philosophy (Routledge, 2016).

[20] For a survey of thinkers who see belief and imagination as fundamentally different, others arguing for intermediate states between the two, and those arguing for a unity with the exception that belies is associated with a normative aim of truth, see Neil Sinhababu, "Imagination and belief," in *The Routledge Handbook of Philosophy of Imagination* (Routledge, 2016). For the sake of the current essay, it may be noted that Sinhababu discusses "belief" as a philosophical concept and as such it has only indirect bearings on its more religious aspects.

[21] See for example Peter Langland-Hassan, *Explaining Imagination* (Oxford: Oxford University Press, 2020); "Pretense, imagination, and belief: the Single Attitude theory," *Philosophical Studies* 159, no. 2 (2012).

[22] Susanna Schellenberg, "Belief and Desire in Imagination and Immersion," *Journal of Philosophy* 110, no. 9 (2013).

justification of the sinner through faith in Jesus Christ (Rom. 3:21-26).[23] Hereby, faith is seen primarily in contrast to justification from works prescribed by the law. As such, it is different from the philosophical use of belief, where it may be seen as an assumption that lacks a proper warrant or maybe even is illusory, as when you imagine that something bad could happen to you if you see a black cat crossing the road close to you. The Christian understanding of faith is a trust in Christ, and yet it is also a comprehensive faith in the triune God as the creator, redeemer, and sanctifier. It is a belief in God as the One who has created life, restored life in Christ, and promises to fulfil life at the end of times.[24] Hereby faith is also comprehensive and an expression of an ultimate conviction about a deep mystery of reality, where faith seeks an understanding of reality, even as it claims that this reality is revealed in Christ.[25] Even if faith here can be seen as holding a resemblance to imagination, it is still faith understood as a conviction about reality. In this sense, faith becomes an interpretative scheme of thought for understanding reality. In other words, we come to an understanding of reality through faith – which moves toward a Bonhoefferian understanding of grasping reality through faith. This connection between faith and imagination is also shown by Eleanor Helms, who argues that there is a resemblance between Søren Kierkegaard's and Maurice Merleau-Ponty's understanding of the teleological structure of experience. Both thinkers argue that there is a believed reality (Kierkegaard) or an "arc of consciousness" (Merleau-Ponty) which implies that the immediate appearances are always more than their immediacy. The arbitrariness of the immediate is overcome by an ordering of the experience within this wider context. For Kierkegaard, it is an argument for faith, for Merleau-Ponty, it is a phenomenological approach to reality. Common for both of them is the understanding of reality as always more than the immediately perceived.[26] This parallel between faith and a phenomenological approach to reality leads us to the next section and one of Merleau-Ponty's followers and critics.

---

[23] See also Alister E. McGrath, "Faith (Chapter 1)," *Theology: The Basics* (John Wiley & Sons, Ltd., 2017), https://doi.org/10.1002/9781119158110.ch1. 1-18.

[24] Grünschloß Andreas et al., "Faith," in *Religion Past and Present*, ed. Hans Dieter Betz, et al. (Brill, 2011).

[25] I have developed some of these themes further in Ulrik Nissen, "The Christological Ontology of Reason," *Neue Zeitschrift für systematische Theologie und Religionsphilosophie* 48, no. 4 (2006).

[26] "Imagination, rather than being an obstacle of faith and deeper selfhood, becomes our link to what is beyond immediate appearances. Kierkegaardian faith depends on this ability to recognize a richness in experience that is not strictly or immediately 'there'. Rather than being a call to will something or feel something, faith may be a call to see something in this richer sense", see Eleanor Helms, "Imagination and Belief," in *The Kierkegaardian Mind*, ed. Adam Buben, Eleanor Helms, and Patrick Stokes (London / New York: Routledge, 2019), 302.

Michel Henry's phenomenology of life

Following the Bonhoefferian claim about a believed and imagined Christological reality, Michel Henry may help us take this reflection a step further. Henry seems only to have been read rather sporadically in a Nordic context with only a few studies on his thought so far.[27] However, this limited attention to his thought calls for a re-assessment, not least from potential theological readers. Henry's thought is part of what has been called a "theological turn" in French phenomenology by both those critical of this turn and its more favourable readers.[28] In the dawn of his academic career in the early 60es, he focused on a critique of Husserlian phenomenology and argued for an immanent pre-intentional form of appearing in his "phenomenology of life."[29] Instead of following Husserl and other phenomenologists in arguing that the appearance of phenomena is linked to the question about how objects are given, i.e., how they are appearing, Henry argues that there is a pre-intentionality given with appearing itself. So, rather than reflect on how things appear to us, we need to ask the question, how does appearing appear? This early approach to self-appearing leads Henry to a critical stance on what he calls "ontological monism" and its subsequent reduction of human subjectivity. In contrast to the inherent risk of reducing the subject to a function of outward directedness, Henry is concerned with the deeper question of intentionality itself and how we ensure the homogeneity of the objects with the intentionality of the subject. Henry's focus on

---

[27] Among studies with an explicit focus on Henry, I have only been able to find the following: Dan Zahavi, "Michel Henry and the Phenomenology of the Invisible," *Continental Philosophy Review* 32, no. 3 (1999); "Subjectivity and Immanence in Michel Henry," in *Subjectivity and Transcendence*, ed. Arne Grøn, Iben Damgaard, and Søren Overgaard (Tübingen, Germany: Mohr Siebeck, 2007). A few articles also discuss Henry in the passing with studies on other phenomenologists, see for example Jonna Bornemark, "Ambiguities of the human body in phenomenology and Christian mysticism," in *The Body Unbound: Philosophical Perspectives on Politics, Embodiment and Religion*, ed. Marius Timmann Mjaaland, Ola Sigurdson, and Sigridur Thorgeirsdottir (Newcastle upon Tyne: Cambridge Scholars, 2010); "Religion at the center of phenomenology: Husserl's analysis of inner time-consciousness," in *Impossible time: Past and future in the philosophy of religion*, ed. Marius Timmann Mjaaland, Ulrik Houlind Rasmussen, and Philipp Stoellger, Religion in philosophy and theology (Tübingen: Mohr Siebeck, 2013); Espen Dahl, "The inner tension of pain and the phenomenology of evil," *International Journal of Philosophy and Theology* 78, no. 4-5 (2017); "Weakness and Passivity: Phenomenology of the Body After Paul," in *Phenomenology of the Broken Body*, ed. Espen Dahl, Cassandra Falke, and Thor Eirik Eriksen (New York: Routledge, 2019).

[28] Bruce Ellis Benson and Norman Wirzba, eds., *Words of life: New theological turns in French phenomenology*, Perspectives in continental philosophy (New York: Fordham Univ Press, 2010); Dominique Janicaud et al., *Phenomenology and the "theological turn": The French debate*, trans. Bernard G. Prusak and Jeffrey L. Kosky, vol. 15ibid. (2000).

[29] Michel Henry, *De la phénoménologie. 1, Phénoménologie de la vie*, Épiméthée (Paris: PUF, 2003); *De la subjectivité. 2, Phénoménologie de la vie*.

appearing in itself and the subsequent self-appearing leads him to argue that there is a non-intentional, or pre-intentional, side to appearing, which in the origin of manifestation refers only to itself. In Henry's early philosophy, he refers to life as a fundamental mode of self-appearing. Viewed as a phenomenon, life is self-appearing and self-affective. It is in this understanding of the phenomenon of life[30] or primacy of life[31] or phenomenology of the invisible[32] that we find Henry's original contribution to French phenomenology in his early writings.

However, this focus on the pre-intentional side to appearing does not set Henry apart from other leading phenomenologists, as Dan Zahavi points out in a critique of Dominique Janicaud. We find this concern with the phenomenology of the invisible also in e.g., Husserl, Heidegger, Merleau-Ponty, and even Derrida and Levinas.[33] However, what sets Henry apart in his interest in the phenomenology of the invisible is his turn to an explicit philosophy of Christianity. This is not least apparent from around the mid 90es in his *C'est moi la vérité. Pour une philosophie du Christianisme* from 1996, his work on the incarnation as a philosophy of the flesh and at the dawn of the new millennium with *Paroles du Christ* from 2002.[34] A central aim in these works is carefully to contemplate what it means in the light of Henry's phenomenology of life that Christ has called himself the truth and the life. For Henry, this self-description is closely connected to an understanding of subjectivity as rooted in life. In continuation of his understanding of life as self-appearing or self-affective, Henry refers to the New Testament understanding of God as life as an expression of this invisible phenomenon of life:

> According to Christianity, there exists only one Life, the unique essence of all that lives. This does not mean an unchanging essence or an ideal archetype, like that of a Circle that is present in all circles, but rather an active essence, deploying itself with an invincible force,

---

[30] *De la phénoménologie. 1, Phénoménologie de la vie*; *De la subjectivité. 2, Phénoménologie de la vie.*

[31] Steven DeLay, *Phenomenology in France: A philosophical and theological introduction* (Abingdon, Oxon: Routledge, 2019), 42-72.

[32] Zahavi, "Michel Henry."

[33] Dan Zahavi, "Michel Henry og det usynliges fænomenologi," *Kritik* 32, no. 137 (1999): 16-17.

[34] Michel Henry, *C'est moi la vérité: pour une philosophie du christianisme* (Paris: Seuil, 1996); *Incarnation: une philosophie de la chair* (Paris: Seuil, 2000); *Paroles du Christ* (Paris: Éditions du seuil, 2002). It is the writings after this turn which I am particularly interested in this essay. All of these works are now translated into English: *I am the truth: toward a philosophy of Christianity* [C'est moi la vérité], Cultural memory in the present (Stanford, Calif.: Stanford University Press, 2003); *Words of Christ*, trans. Christina M. Gschwandtner, Interventions (Grand Rapids, Mich.: William B. Eerdmans Pub., 2012); *Incarnation: A philosophy of flesh*, trans. Hefty Karl, Northwestern University studies in phenomenology and existential philosophy. (Evanston, Illinois: Northwestern University Press, 2015). In the current essay I refer to the English translations.

a source of power, the power of engendering that is immanent in anything that lives and unceasingly gives it life. Inasmuch as this Life is that of God and is identified with Him, the Apostle could write: "One God and Father of us all, who is over all and through all and in all" (Ephesians 4:6).[35]

If God is the self-affective source of life, Christ is understood as the revelation of this God. When Christ refers to himself as the truth and life, it is a claim of being the incarnation of the invisible phenomenon of life. It is in Christ that the self-affectivity of life is revealed to us. Or, as Henry formulates it, it is life's self-revelation:

What is specific to life as self-revelation is, therefore, the fact that it reveals itself. This apparent tautology implies two distinct meanings that we must now separate (…). Self-revelation, when it concerns the essence of Life, means, on the one hand, that it is Life that achieves the revelation, that reveals – but, on the other hand, that *what Life reveals is itself*.[36]

In other words, Life (understood as the primordial essence of life, i.e., God) is revealed in the manifestation of life, the phenomena of life. When Christ in the New Testament refers to himself as the truth and the life, this is, according to Henry, an expression of this self-engendering, self-revelatory expression of life. But when life as an absolute Life is also seen as an expression of God,[37] Christ is thereby also understood in unity with the Father. As Henry puts it in the chapter entitled "The Phenomenology of Christ" in his *I am the Truth* (or *C'est moi la vérité*):

In its absolute self-engendering, Life is the Father of whom Christ is the Son (…) This condition – that of being the Arch-Son co-engendered in the process of Life's coming-into-itself as the essential Ipseity in which Life reveals itself – is co-engendered as the True (for what is more true than that which reveals itself completely in and of itself?), in such a way that Life knows itself in that essential Ipseity that in turn know it, being merely the site of Life's self-revelation …[38]

In the previous section, we briefly touched upon the role of imagination in Merlau-Ponty and thereby upon the broader question of imagination in phenomenological thought. In Henry, the concept of imagination plays an explicit role in his early writings.[39] In his later writings, though, his focus is directed more clearly towards the self-engendering of life itself and the Christian philosophical implications of thats. It is this side of Henry that allows us to pose the question whether we, in the light of Henry's phenomenological thought, can argue that there is a pre-intentional side of life as appearing in itself (a givenness of life), which we can only grasp with our imagination, just as

[35] *I am the truth*, 54.

[36] Ibid., 29.

[37] Ibid., 54, 73.

[38] Ibid., 74.

[39] See for example several passages in Michel Henry, *The essence of manifestation*, trans. Girard Etzkorn (The Hague: Martinus Nijhoff, 1973).

Bonhoeffer can claim that there is a given Christological reality that can only be grasped in faith, We can never become the subjects of this self-engendering of life, or control it. Still, the self-engendering of life can appear to us through our imagination.[40] Following this line of thought, Christ as the revelation of the self-engendering of life, the Christological reality of life can be understood as a given reality, which we grasp through our imagination. Here, imagination is not something that is "only" situated in the mind or "merely" a mental state or activity. Rather, imagination is a pre-conditional arc of consciousness, where the perceiving subject opens herself up for a wholeness of reality beyond the immediately perceived. "The perceiving subject must, without leaving his place or his point of view in the opacity of sensing, tend toward things whose key he does not hold in advance, and whose design [*projet*] he nevertheless carries within himself, he must open up to an absolute Other that he prepares from deeper within himself."[41] Imagination thereby points to the mystery of reality, which from a theological perspective can be claimed to be Christ himself – a mystery which is grasped in faith (Bonhoeffer) or imagination (Henry).

Michel Henry's contribution to Scandinavian Creation Theology

At this point, we can return to our initial engagement with the claim of the recent anthology on Scandinavian creation theology. Despite its merits in portraying leading Scandinavian theologians' emphasis on creation theology during the latter half of the twentieth century, the anthology seems to be susceptible to the same weakness or deficit which is at risk for any creation theology losing sight of the relation to Christ as the defining mark of a Christian theology. It is only in the contribution by Jan-Olav Henriksen that the trinity is treated more substantially.[42] In the index to the book, there are no references

---

[40] In the recent handbook on phenomenology, Julia Jansen writes the chapter on phenomenology and imagination, see Julia Jansen, "Imagination De-Naturalized: Phantasy, the Imaginary, and Imaginative Ontology," in *The Oxford Handbook of the History of Phenomenology*, ed. Dan Zahavi (Oxford: Oxford University Press, 2018). Jansen argues that Edmund Husserl's understanding of imagination entails a "de-naturalization", as the distinctiveness of imagination derives from exactly not being bound to the spatio-temporality of natural objects. Jean-Paul Sartre and Maurice Merleau-Ponty are both inspired by Husserl, but where Sartre develops his thoughts existentially, Merleau-Ponty takes it in a more ontological direction. For Merleau-Ponty there is not such a sharp contrast between the real and the imaginary. It is this dynamic relation between the real and the imagined that we find continued in Henry, even as he focuses his work on the pre-intentional.

[41] Maurice Merleau-Ponty, *Phenomenology of perception*, trans. Donald A. Landes (London: Routledge, 2012), 340 (quoted after Helms, "Imagination," 294).

[42] See Jan-Olav Henriksen, "The Economic Trinity and Creation," in *Reformation Theology for a Post-Secular Age: Løgstrup, Prenter, Wingren, and the Future of Scandinavian Creation Theology*, ed. Niels Henrik Gregersen, Bengt Kristensson Uggla, and Trygve Wyller (Göttingen: Vandenhoeck & Ruprecht, 2017).

to Christ or to the Holy Spirit.[43] In other words – this recent contribution to Scandinavian creation theology apparently sets aside defining hallmarks of a Lutheran theology in its attempt to develop a theology shared by all. Even if this may appear sympathetic (and some might even find it fruitful) from a first reading, the question arises, what is left? If we leave out the defining features of a Christian theology, are we not left with an accommodated form of theology, which is not "post-secular," but rather has secularized itself at its very core? As we have seen, this is fundamentally at odds with the essential features of Luther's theology, just as it ignores pivotal figures in Scandinavian theology who are deeply engaged with Lutheran theology and who approach this with an emphasis on both Christology and pneumatology.[44] It is even more peculiar, as the anthology hereby sets Scandinavian theology apart from a very influential theological line of thought during most of the twentieth century with inspiration from, for example, the theology of Karl Barth. Rather than continuing this attempt to formulate a creation theology with only very limited reference to Christology (or the trinity), maybe Scandinavian theology should instead focus more on the core of Christian theology – i.e., Jesus Christ and what it means that God is revealed to us in Christ? Maybe this would be a more fruitful way forward for developing a Reformation theology for a post-secular age? This is where, e.g., Michel Henry's phenomenology of life holds the potential to enrich a Scandinavian theology. It seems that there is a viable course for a future reshaping of Scandinavian theology, which goes beyond a potentially shallow creation theology and where the phenomenological approach at the same time provides a ground for arguing that this is not to be understood in a narrow sense, but in a deeper and more profound sense about life as such, as the pre-intentional origin of life. Henry's turn to a philosophy of Christianity seems to open up a way to a philosophical understanding of a shared and common reality (and hereby a common concern with creation theology) as ultimately tied to an understanding of Christ as the self-engendering of life (and hereby to a defining characteristic of a Christian theology).

---

[43] Jesus is referred to often, but primarily as the historical Jesus. Admittedly, the index refers to persons and not topics. This may explain the omission of the Holy Spirit. But theologically the trinity is traditionally conceived as a unity of three persons. So it remains strange, also because one of the most significant writings of Regin Prenter focused on the Luther's theology of the Holy Spirit, Prenter, *Spiritus creator: Studier i Luthers theologi.*

[44] Many works could be mentioned, but apart from the Finnish Luther-research and Prenter suffice it for example to mention Anders Nygren, *Den kristna kärlekstanken genom tiderna: Eros och agape. Första delen* (Stockholm: Svenska kyrkans diakonistyrelses bokförlag, 1930); *Den kristna kärlekstanken genom tiderna: Eros och agape. Senare delen* (Stockholm: Svenska Kyrkans Diakonistyrelses Bokförlag, 1936); N. H. Søe, *Kristelig etik*, 5. ed. (København: G. E. C. Gad, 1967); Anna Marie Aagaard, *Helligånden sendt til verden* (Aarhus: Aros, 1973).

The current article carries the title "Imagination and Givenness." I have pointed to Luther's and Bonhoeffer's understanding of the centrality of Christ for a deep and saturated understanding of reality. In Bonhoeffer, we also saw the remark that this is a reality that can only be grasped in faith. This raises the question, whether this is an imagined reality? Is it only a reality that faith imagines? Or maybe faith is interpreting a reality that is already given? In the light of Henry, it seems possible to argue for an understanding of reality, where God can be understood as the absolute life and thereby the invisible phenomenon of life that precedes any appearance. God is thus the self-revealing, self-affective life that is revealed in Christ. If we follow Henry's phenomenology of life, faith does not express an imagined reality in the sense that it is a subjective interpretation of life. Rather, faith is situated in life and is an expression of the givenness of life, when it claims Christ as the truth and the life.

If we take this Christological approach to our interpretation of reality, Christ becomes the key to understanding who we "really" are. It is in Christ and through Christ that we come to know who we are. Bonhoeffer is an example of such an understanding in a Lutheran tradition,[45] and Henry can be read along similar lines in French phenomenology, but equally significant is the recognition that a Christologically saturated concept of reality does not stand in contrast to a creation theology. For a Scandinavian creation theology, it can be an enrichment to include richer Christological motifs and thereby speak more profoundly about a deeper and fuller understanding of life as it is given, imagined, and known in Christ.

[45] Bonhoeffer, "Christology," 324-27.

Plantinga, Schellenberg, and Mental Images at the Heart of Faith

Roomet Jakapi

Introduction

The traditional analytic epistemology of religion has mostly overlooked the role of imagination in faith and religious thinking. This is because the focus has been on the epistemic status of religious *belief*. It has been assumed that belief, understood as a species of propositional attitude, aims at truth, whereas imagination does not and is therefore of less interest and value. Alvin Plantinga's impressive work *Warranted Christian Belief* pays a great deal of attention to the role of imagination in human cognition and also discusses religious imagination.[1] However, like many other epistemologists, Plantinga takes beliefs and imaginings to be entirely distinct from each other and therefore does not see religious imaginings as constituents of religious beliefs and faith. At the same time, Plantinga's book is a powerful expression of an apologetic way of thinking.

The contemporary Anglophone philosophy of religion encompasses several other ways of thinking. For example, various non-doxastic accounts of faith have been proposed, and some of them describe the nature of faith precisely in terms of imagination. Thus J.L. Schellenberg has offered, in *The Will to Imagine*, an account of imaginative faith as opposed to religious belief.[2] He argues that the appropriate attitude in the domain of faith is one of scepticism and, accordingly, proposes to abstain from all currently available "sectarian" beliefs. Instead, he introduces an abstract, "non-sectarian" religious doctrine called simple ultimism and a corresponding imaginative attitude that one should take towards it.

Plantinga's and Schellenberg's motives and positions differ radically from one another, but their accounts of proper religious faith have some important features in common. As both of them are analytically trained philosophers, they start off from the technical concept of belief. While Plantinga construes faith in terms of properly basic beliefs and Schellenberg construes it in terms of imagination, they both take proper faith to be propositional. They also appear to assume that believing and imagining are distinct activities with no gray areas

[1] Alvin Plantinga, *Warranted Christian Belief* (Oxford: Oxford University Press, 2000).

[2] J. L. Schellenberg, *The Will to Imagine: A Justification of Skeptical Religion* (Ithaca and London: Cornell University Press, 2009).

in between. Furthermore, they both think that religious faith can be rational in the absence of evidence.

My aims in this article are to question the existence of a clear line between religious belief and religious imagination, and more specifically, to show the relevance of mental imagery for the epistemology of religion.[3] Throughout the article, I will rely on the widely used distinction between propositional imagination (imagining that something is the case) and imagistic imagination (mental imagery).[4]

In what follows, I shall argue, firstly, that mental images with religious content can have epistemic significance in the domain of religious faith and, therefore, should have a significant role in epistemological models such as Plantinga's. I will show how mental images can be parts of religious beliefs. However, I will not assess the correctness of Plantinga's model as a whole. Secondly, I will examine Schellenberg's project of non-doxastic, imaginative faith regarding simple ultimism. I will show how the ultimistic faith can include mental images with specific and relevant religious content and how, due to such imagistic representations, this faith comes close to belief. Thirdly, I will apply the findings of the aforementioned sections to more ordinary situations to show that mental images can be parts of beliefs and thus can aim at truth. Accordingly, I will claim that the standard conception of beliefs as propositional attitudes is too restrictive and needs revision. Finally, I will discuss two problems regarding the main claims made in the article.

The Aquinas/Calvin Model and Religious Imagination

Philosophical accounts of religious faith may differ significantly on what constitutes the core of faith. It could be trust, belief, hope, affection or something else, or a combination of various elements.[5] Plantinga belongs to those

---

[3] I shall speak of "mental images" in the sense of picture-like mental representations as experienced by humans. For an overview of the history of, and current controversies regarding, the concept of mental imagery, see Nigel J. T. Thomas, "Mental Imagery," in *Stanford Encyclopedia of Philosophy*, edited by Edward N. Zalta (2014), https://plato.stanford.edu/entries/mental-imagery/.

[4] There is a debate on whether imagining always involves mental imagery. A thorough "imagery-based account of the imagination" is offered by Amy Kind, "Putting the Image Back in Imagination," *Philosophy and Phenomenological Research* 62, no. 1 (2001): 85–109. Quite a few philosophers have argued, however, that propositional imagination does not require mental imagery. For overviews of the debate, see Dominic Gregory, "Imagination and Mental Imagery," in *The Routledge Handbook of Philosophy of Imagination*, edited by Amy Kind (London and New York: Routledge, 2016), 97–110, 103–106, and Shen-yi Liao and Tamar Gendler, "Imagination," in *Stanford Encyclopedia of Philosophy*, edited by Edward N. Zalta (2019), https://plato.stanford.edu/entries/imagination/.

[5] See John Bishop, "Faith," in *Stanford Encyclopedia of Philosophy*, edited by Edward N. Zalta (2016), https://plato.stanford.edu/entries/faith/.

philosophers who regard belief as the key concept in this domain, while he also assigns a considerable role to will and affection.[6] For him, the main object of inquiry and justification is Christian belief. This broad concept of Christian belief covers (1) a number of theistic beliefs about the existence and attributes of God, as well as (2) specifically Christian beliefs such as those concerning "trinity, incarnation, Christ's resurrection, atonement, forgiveness of sins, salvation, regeneration, eternal life."[7] The latter beliefs are constitutive of the Christian faith.

Plantinga applies strict epistemic criteria to both of these sets of beliefs to show that they are rational and warranted and, furthermore, under certain circumstances, amount to knowledge. He famously proposes an epistemological model, named the Aquinas/Calvin model, according to which these beliefs are acquired in a basic, immediate way, without relying on argument or propositional evidence. The beliefs in question, he says, are properly basic and warranted insofar as they are produced in us, in certain circumstances, through reliable cognitive processes or mechanisms.

Plantinga's model posits two mechanisms of belief-production that operate in the domain of faith. One is a sense of divinity (*sensus divinitatis*) that humans are naturally equipped and created with. The sense of divinity "is a disposition or set of dispositions to form theistic beliefs" in various situations.[8] It functions, for example, when a belief in God is spontaneously formed upon observing some marvellous objects in nature, feeling guilty for wrongdoing, or asking for help in grave danger.[9]

Theistic beliefs, then, arise in response to certain experiences that trigger the sense of divinity. The relevant experiences may or may not involve "sensuous imagery that typically goes with perception" or include a feeling of "the presence of God."[10] But there is one kind of experience that is always present when beliefs are formed, according to Plantinga, and that is called "*doxastic experience*, the sort of experience one has when entertaining any proposition one believes."[11] When one believes and entertains the proposition that 3 + 2 = 5, one has precisely that kind of experience. When one starts to believe and entertains the proposition that God exists, one also has a doxastic experience.[12]

Theistic beliefs are formed in us, Plantinga claims, in a way similar to how other kinds of basic belief—perceptual and memory beliefs, certain *a priori* beliefs—spontaneously arise in relevant situations.[13] Like our other cognitive

---

[6] Plantinga, *Warranted Christian Belief*, 290–323.
[7] Ibid., 241.
[8] Ibid., 173.
[9] Ibid., 173–174.
[10] Ibid., 182–183.
[11] Ibid., 183; italics original.
[12] Ibid.; see also ibid., 110-112.
[13] See ibid., 175.

faculties, the sense of divinity is aimed at producing *true* beliefs (which it does if it functions properly in a suitable environment).[14]

Plantinga also extends the Aquinas/Calvin model to the specifically Christian beliefs and posits another belief-producing mechanism called the inward or internal instigation of the Holy Spirit. This is a supernatural mechanism that produces true Christian beliefs when one reads or hears the gospel. These beliefs too are formed spontaneously, in a basic way:

> What is said simply seems right; it seems compelling; one finds oneself saying, 'Yes, that's right, that's the truth of the matter; this is indeed the word of the Lord' […] What one hears or reads seems clearly and obviously true and (at any rate in paradigm cases) seems also to be something the Lord is intending to teach.[15]

Thus, upon encountering the gospel, one strongly feels not only that the biblical teachings are true but also that they come from God. Due to the supernatural action of the Holy Spirit upon us, we realize that it is God speaking.[16] This means, in Plantinga's technical language, that God communicates certain *propositions* to us, and these are the objects of faith: "[W]hat one believes are propositions. To have faith, therefore, is (at least) to believe some propositions."[17] The words of the Bible express a vast number of propositions, only some of which are strictly relevant to faith: "[T]he propositional object of faith is the whole magnificent scheme of salvation God has arranged. […] The content of faith is just the central teachings of the gospel; it is contained in the intersection of the great Christian creeds."[18]

Plantinga's model aims to explain how, in suitable circumstances, true religious beliefs arise in a basic way. Now, I presume that most people who have formed, and hold, theistic beliefs, have at some point also formed some mental images concerning God, his characteristics, his relationship with the world and human beings, and so on.[19] The images may be concrete or abstract, clear or fuzzy, in varying degrees. In the context of Plantinga's doxastic model, they could be regarded as by-products of the proper functioning of the sense of divinity. However, these images are unimportant for Plantinga's epistemological purposes. The epistemic virtues of theistic beliefs are gained independently of the question of how we depict God in imagination. Similarly, Christians are likely to form mental images related to "the central teachings of the gospel,"

---

[14] See ibid., 154–156.

[15] Ibid., 250.

[16] Ibid., 251.

[17] Ibid., 248.

[18] Ibid.

[19] For a recent psychological study of the mental images of God among American Christians, see Joshua Conrad Jackson, Neil Hester and Kurt Gray, "The Faces of God in America: Revealing Religious Diversity Across People and Politics," *PLoS ONE* 13(6) (2018), https://doi.org/10.1371/journal.pone.0198745.

but these images are really not a part of the extended Aquinas/Calvin model. The model construes faith in terms of belief—taken in a narrow, technical sense of "belief"—and implies that religious mental images do not have much epistemic value.

Plantinga rejects Kaufman's view that theology should be seen as a work of constructive imagination.[20] Whether this particular criticism is justified is a question that goes beyond the scope of this article. But in any case, Kaufman belongs to those thinkers in contemporary Anglophone theology who have pointed out the importance of imagination in religious thought and behaviour, not only on the theoretical level of theology but also on the practical level of prayer, devotion, and orientation.[21] I believe that religious imagination deserves much more attention than it has thus far received in the context of epistemology as well.

In the rest of this section, I will try to show the relevance of mental imagery for epistemological inquiry in the domain of faith. I will do so by introducing the following thought experiment. Suppose two adult Christians, A and B, go to the same church and sincerely believe everything that is said in the Apostles' Creed, which they regularly read aloud at church services. Among other things, then, they believe in "the resurrection of the body, and the life everlasting." They believe the same propositions. They both *believe that*, at the end of this world, there will be a general resurrection of the dead that, in some sense, is bodily, and in which they will participate. They also *believe that* a blissful post-mortal life will continue forever. However, now suppose that, in relation to these propositions, A and B have formed and retained rather different *images*. A has always pictured the resurrection as a physical event in which our earthly remains would be transformed into shiny, incorruptible bodies. As for eternal life, A has always imagined this to take place on Earth. B, by contrast, has always pictured the resurrection as a purely, or essentially, spiritual event that concerns our souls rather than our bodies. B's images of the resurrection involve some vague and abstract bodily figures but nothing properly and robustly physical. B's images of eternal life are of souls floating in heavenly space. All the images in question were spontaneously formed at one time and have not changed significantly since then. A and B have these different images but no corresponding, specific propositional thoughts. They have not specifically discussed or carefully thought about the doctrines in question or do not remember having done so. Nor have they propositionally *imagined that* the dead will rise

[20] Plantinga, *Warranted Christian Belief*, 32–42.

[21] See Gordon D. Kaufman, *The Theological Imagination: Constructing the Concept of God* (Philadelphia: Westminster, 1981), 21–32. See also Garrett Green, *Imagining God: Theology and the Religious Imagination* (Grand Rapids, MI, and Cambridge, UK: Eerdmans, 1989) and Paul Avis, *God and the Creative Imagination: Metaphor, Symbol and Myth in Religion and Theology* (London and New York: Routledge, 1999).

and there will be everlasting life. The teachings of their church do not determine how to picture those supernatural things. But they both believe wholeheartedly.

Do A and B have the same beliefs about bodily resurrection and eternal life? Proposition-wise, yes; image-wise, no. The propositional content of their beliefs is the same, but the imaginative contents are different. Perhaps the images in question are not directly relevant for the epistemic evaluation of the rationality and justifiability of A's and B's beliefs. Perhaps the images are not part of the meaning of the relevant phrases in the Creed. But the images are present and seem to be parts of A's and B's beliefs.

Now suppose it turns out that the general resurrection will indeed involve a transformation of human remains into more refined bodies, that the eternal life will take place on Earth, and that this is how we shall experience those things. It would seem that, while the propositional content of A's and B's beliefs was the same, A's images represented the resurrection and eternal life more closely and more correctly than B's images. The correctness of the images in question is determined by how things will be in the afterlife.

Finally, suppose there is a third devout Christian, C, who goes to the same church as A and B. Unlike A and B, C has *only* propositional thoughts, and *no* mental images at all, in relation to the bodily resurrection and eternal life. C just *believes that* these things will take place after death, without ever picturing them. Now it would seem that A's and B's beliefs are more specific and have more content than those of C, and this extra content is provided by imagination. It turns out, at the end of this world, that all three individuals correctly believed *that* there would be a bodily resurrection and eternal life. However, due to their different images, A was right, and B was wrong about *how* these things would occur and be experienced. C did not imagine those details and so did not believe anything about them.

One way to interpret this situation is to say that, in addition to the identical propositional content, A's and B's beliefs have different imaginative contents. We could also describe their images as correct or incorrect depictions of reality.[22] C's beliefs, however, had only propositional content but lacked imaginative content. It seems that, in certain cases, mental images can be regarded as parts or components of beliefs, and thus, they can aim at truth.[23]

---

[22] For the view that imagistic imagination is, in certain situations, "reality-oriented," see Timothy Williamson, "Knowing by Imagining," in *Knowledge Through Imagination*, edited by Amy Kind and Peter Kung (Oxford: Oxford University Press, 2016), 113–123.

[23] Susanna Schellenberg holds that imaginings and beliefs are on a continuum. See Susanna Schellenberg, "Belief and Desire in Imagination and Immersion," *Journal of Philosophy* 110, no. 9 (2013): 497–517. For a critical response to her view, see Neil Sinhababu, "Imagination and Belief," in *The Routledge Handbook of Philosophy of Imagination*, edited by Amy Kind (London and New York: Routledge, 2016), 111–123, 116–118.

In light of these considerations, I would argue, in opposition to Plantinga, that what we believe are not just propositions. The content of belief can be, at least in part, imaginative. Therefore, epistemological accounts and models of religious belief should explicitly address and examine the relationship between religious beliefs and imaginings. That, of course, concerns not only the beliefs regarding bodily resurrection and eternal life, but also many other beliefs, Christian and non-Christian.

Ultimism, Imagination, and the Return of Belief

Schellenberg's non-doxastic conception of faith, in connection with his abstract description of the ultimate reality, stands in stark contrast with Plantinga's Calvinistically minded defence of Christian belief. However, their views on the nature and workings of proper faith, as they understand it, have certain features and starting points in common. For one thing, both thinkers hold that religious faith can be rational in the absence of evidence. What Plantinga offers, instead of evidence, is a foundationalist description of the emergence of the religious beliefs that constitute the Christian faith, whereas Schellenberg embraces skepticism regarding all religious beliefs that are currently available and proposes a sort of abstract, imaginative faith. Furthermore, although very different from each other, both of these accounts are about *propositional* faith. Finally, both philosophers seem to assume that belief and imagination are distinct categories exclusive of each other.

As Schellenberg explains in an earlier book, *Prolegomena*, he holds that there is no "evidence causally sufficient to produce" religious *beliefs*, but we can rationally exercise a weaker attitude towards religious propositions, namely, *propositional faith* involving *voluntary assent*.[24] The conception of religious faith without belief, along with Schellenberg's own religious doctrine, called ultimism, is further developed in *The Will to Imagine*.

Ultimism is a doctrine about fundamental, transcendent reality and our relation to it. To be precise, Schellenberg distinguishes between *simple ultimism*, or *ultimism itself*, which constitutes the universal and abstract core of all religions, and *qualified versions of ultimism*, that is, specific, "sectarian" religious claims. He defines simple ultimism as "the claim that there is (metaphysically and axiologically) an ultimate reality in relation to which an ultimate good can be attained."[25] Thus the doctrine has two explicit components: the metaphysical and the axiological one. As it turns out, however, the doctrine is also "salvific" insofar as it entails "that there will be some sort of afterlife for at least some of us."[26] The qualified versions of ultimism "are all those claims—often large

[24] J. L. Schellenberg, *Prolegomena to a Philosophy of Religion* (Ithaca and London: Cornell University Press, 2005), 132, 138–139.

[25] Schellenberg, *The Will to Imagine*, 15.

[26] Ibid., 32.

conjunctive claims—that entail simple ultimism but add religious content to what it says about ultimates, filling that out in some way."[27] The traditional Christian doctrine of God would be an example of qualified ultimism.[28]

"Simple ultimism alone," says Schellenberg, is "the proper object of propositional religious faith."[29] It is a doctrine suitable for a contemporary religious sceptic. Due to its abstract, undetailed, and general form, simple ultimism is open to a vast number of "actual and possible religious claims."[30] However, according to Schellenberg, our ignorance in religious matters is presently so big that faith regarding any traditional, specific religious claims cannot be justified.[31] He thinks that humanity is at a very early stage of its "intellectual and spiritual development" and that "new religious possibilities" may unfold in the future.[32]

The religious sceptic can adopt and practice simple ultimism without *believing that* the ultimate reality exists or has certain specific features rather than others. Instead, the sceptic *imagines that* the world is such that the propositions constituting this doctrine are true and gives her *assent* to what she imagines:

> Someone who comes to have faith with respect to simple ultimism finds herself without evidence sufficient to cause belief of these propositions (recognizing that they may be false or perhaps even in some hidden way incoherent), but positively evaluating the states of affairs they report, she nonetheless tenaciously pictures or imagines the world to herself as a world in which they are true and committedly gives her assent to what is thus held before the mind…[33]

The assent in question is not just a single act of consent. Rather, it becomes a regular practice or policy.[34] Faith regarding simple ultimism is propositional ("faith that") *and* imaginative.[35] In the absence of sufficient evidence, one optimistically chooses to *imagine that* the ultimate reality exists and also *that* things will be fine, or even great, in the afterlife. As illustrated in the *Prolegomena*, the same attitude can be exercised in various life situations. For example, in a situation where a person does not yet know whether or not her friend went to the World Trade Center on September 11, 2001, and, accordingly, died in the terror attack or escaped harm, she can optimistically focus "on the idea that her friend has indeed escaped harm."[36]

---

[27] Ibid., 15.
[28] Ibid., 16.
[29] Ibid., 19.
[30] Ibid., 23.
[31] Ibid., 21–25.
[32] Ibid., 14, 21.
[33] Ibid., 35.
[34] See ibid., 35–47; cf. Schellenberg, *Prolegomena*, 129–139.
[35] See Schellenberg, *The Will to Imagine*, xiii, 3.
[36] Schellenberg, *Prolegomena*, 130.

In *The Will to Imagine*, Schellenberg explains, in a footnote, that the kind of imagination he talks about in these contexts and takes to be essential for religious faith, is *propositional imagination*.[37] When he explains how faith regarding simple ultimism can be exercised in a continuous manner, the imaginative content of faith becomes more pictorial:

> Perhaps there is some "tag" standing for the whole conjunction of ideas, such as "All shall be well," or some symbol, such as—choosing one possible example at random—the Greek letter omega, which the individual teaches herself to bring to mind at regular intervals and especially when relevant matters arise; or perhaps our person of faith recurrently imagines the universe flooded with light, sweeping darkness away. There are indeed many ways in which, and through which, one might rightly be said to be thinking of the content of the propositions concerned.[38]

Thus the imaginative faith proposed by Schellenberg is essentially propositional, but in practice, it is likely to also include some mental images used as tools. Note that the random images described in the passage above are meant to be "non-sectarian." It has to be said, though, that, in Western culture, the letter omega is easily associated with the Book of Revelation, and the image of light refers right back to the beginning of Genesis.

I will now examine Schellenberg's proposal by offering another thought experiment similar to the one introduced above. I want to show that ultimistic faith can include mental images that are more than instrumental, that is, images that are proper and important components of faith. I will claim, moreover, that due to such images, this faith looks doxastic.

Suppose there are two persons, D and E, who have recently converted to ultimism. Earlier in their lives, D was a sincere, practising Muslim, and E was a sincere, practising Christian. It is no wonder, then, that some old "sectarian" religious images persist strongly in their minds, even if the images are now less clear. While practising simple ultimism, D and E have spontaneously formed some images of the ultimate reality that grounds the natural world. The propositional content of their faith regarding (the metaphysical component of) simple ultimism is the same, but the images associated with the doctrine are different. At some point, D notices that her images of the ultimate reality bear features reminiscent of the monotheistic God. She realizes that she pictures, albeit vaguely, the ultimate reality as an infinitely powerful living person and the creator of everything else. The relevant ultimistic images in E's mind are very similar, except that, as he suddenly realizes, he vaguely pictures the ultimate reality as involving a kind of divine trinity. As new, enthusiastic members of the ultimist community, D and E struggle to set aside those apparently "sectarian" images. They want to purify their faith, not from wrong beliefs but from wrong mental images. Their propositional faith is right, but the images

[37] Schellenberg, *The Will to Imagine*, 4.
[38] Ibid., 36.

associated with the propositions in question are wrong. As prescribed by their new faith, they abstractly *imagine that* there is an ultimate reality, but when they picture the reality, they slip into traditional religious images. Perhaps ultimism, being a *propositional* faith, can accommodate these deviant images, and D and E should not worry after all. For they have abandoned all specific religious *beliefs*, and they do not deviate from the *propositional* content of their ultimistic faith. At the same time, it would seem that their images of the ultimate reality are a part of their faith, and that is precisely where D's faith differs from E's faith.

Now suppose there is a third ultimist, F, whose mental images of the ultimate reality do not include any recognizably "sectarian" features. Her images represent the ultimate reality as a vast, all-embracing metaphysical space that has a particular colour and extends beyond the universe. She has not voluntarily constructed those images; rather, the images were spontaneously formed in her mind at one time and now reappear as she practices her religion. The images are fairly abstract and yet specific, as they go beyond the propositional content of simple ultimism.

Finally, suppose that in 10,000 years, humankind gains conclusive evidence that the ultimate reality exists but that it has no monotheistic, let alone trinitarian, features. It would seem, then, that the relevant images in the minds of D and E were incorrect, although D and E were correct in their propositional faith. Furthermore, in that far future, it turns out that the ultimate reality has the colour that F imagined it to have. So the ultimistic faith of F was correct not only propositionally but also imagistically.

According to Schellenberg, the imaginative faith regarding simple ultimism is propositional and yet beliefless. *Imagining that* something is the case is not *believing that* it is the case. However, this faith is not only propositional but also includes mental imagery as an important component. As shown above, the imagistic imagination of a faithful ultimist can go far beyond the abstract propositional content of simple ultimism. It seems that, by forming and repeatedly experiencing certain mental images of the ultimate reality, the ultimists D, E, and F ascribe specific features to that supposed reality. Their images represent the reality as being in a certain way. In a sense, they believe, correctly or incorrectly, the ultimate reality to have those features. It seems that their faith comes close to belief.

We learn from this and the previous imaginative scenario that faith can involve mental images that may turn out to be correct or incorrect representations of religiously significant reality. It seems that such images can be components of doxastic as well as non-doxastic faith and add important details to the propositional content of faith.

The persons A, B, C, D, E, F and their mental states, as described above, are hypothetical. My aim so far has been to show that the conceptual boundary between beliefs and mental images, in the domain of religious faith, is in some respects unclear and needs further, careful examination.

Belief and Imagination Intertwined

While the above discussions of the relationship between belief and imagination were confined to the field of religious faith, I now want to take a second look at the common definitions of belief and imagination in contemporary Anglophone philosophy. I will try to use the conclusions of the previous parts of the article to challenge the standard definitions. According to the reliable and widely used *Stanford Encyclopedia of Philosophy*:

> Contemporary Anglophone philosophers of mind generally use the term "belief" to refer to the attitude we have, roughly, whenever we take something to be the case or regard it as true.[39]

Belief is often contrasted with imagination precisely on the basis of the idea that the former aims at the truth while the latter does not.[40] Thus, to quote from the same source:

> *To imagine* is to represent without aiming at things as they actually, presently, and subjectively are. One can use imagination to represent possibilities other than the actual, to represent times other than the present, and to represent perspectives other than one's own. Unlike perceiving and believing, imagining something does not require one to consider that something to be the case.[41]

Now, in the scenarios presented above, the persons A, B, D, E, and F imagined certain transcendent realities—the bodily resurrection, eternal life, and the ultimate reality—to have certain specific features. They did not fantasize. Rather, I am tempted to say, they believed those specific things by way of imagistic imagination. On the standard understanding of belief, however, I should not say that, because, unlike mental images, beliefs are concerned with propositions:

---

[39] Eric Schwitzgebel, "Belief," in *Stanford Encyclopedia of Philosophy*, edited by Edward N. Zalta (2019), https://plato.stanford.edu/entries/belief/.

[40] See Nishi Shah and J. David Velleman, "Doxastic Deliberation," *Philosophical Review* 114, no. 4 (2005): 497–534. However, some philosophers have explicitly disputed this view. For example, Van Leeuwen argues that "imaginings share many of the characteristics of belief: many (maybe all) imaginings appear to have a weak truth aim (in the relevant sense) as well." Neil Van Leeuwen, "The Meanings of 'Imagine' Part II: Attitude and Action," *Philosophy Compass* 9, no. 11 (2014): 791–802, 794. There are also philosophers who speak of "belief-like" imaginings; see, e.g., Schellenberg, "Belief and Desire." For other comparative studies of the properties of belief and imagination, see, e.g., Sinhababu, "Imagination and Belief," and Anna Ichino, "Imagination and Belief in Action," *Philosophia* 47 (2019): 1517–1534.

[41] Liao and Gendler, "Imagination;" italics original.

> Most contemporary philosophers characterize belief as a "propositional attitude." Propositions are generally taken to be whatever it is that sentences express… […] A *propositional attitude*, then, is the mental state of having some attitude, stance, take, or opinion about a proposition or about the potential state of affairs in which that proposition is true…[42]

But why must we think that the only way to believe something is to believe a proposition? Perhaps there are other ways of believing as well, such as the one described above. Why couldn't we say that, in some cases or respects, the content of belief is imaginative and not (only) propositional? The two scenarios presented in the previous sections of the article were intended to show that imagistic imagination can add important details to propositional belief and propositional imagination, and also that mental images can be the vehicle of such properties as correctness and incorrectness. According to the first scenario, persons A and B both *believe that* there will be a bodily resurrection, but every time they *picture* the resurrection, A does so in a specific way that is different from the way B does. The propositional part of their belief is the same, but the imaginative part is different. In the second scenario, persons D, E, and F *imagine that* (but do not *believe that*) there is an ultimate reality. They all assent to the same proposition, but every time they *picture* the ultimate reality, each does so in a different, specific way. Their images represent the ultimate reality as having certain specific features that are not mentioned in the proposition they assent to. In a sense, they believe the ultimate reality has those features, but they do so, to a large extent, through imagistic imagining.

The same line of thought used here to describe religious beliefs and images can be applied to far more mundane matters. For example, in one of the original Gettier cases, there are two characters, Smith and Jones, both applying for a job.[43] A proper analysis of the Gettier cases is beyond the limits and scope of this article, but I want to point out the role that imagination can play in such cases and contexts. According to the scenario, Smith has strong evidence to believe that (1) "Jones is the man who will get the job, and Jones has ten coins in his pocket." Proposition (1) entails another proposition that Smith also believes to be true: (2) "The man who will get the job has ten coins in his pocket." As it turns out, however, Smith himself gets the job, and he also happens to have ten coins in his pocket.

Suppose that both Smith and Jones believe proposition (2). Unlike proposition (1), proposition (2) does not specify who exactly is "the man" that "will get the job." However, suppose that Smith imagines, imagistically, "the man" to be Jones, and Jones imagines, imagistically, "the man" to be Smith. The images in question seem to be a part of what they believe. Smith gets the job, and each of them happens to have ten coins in his pocket. It turns out that they

---

[42] Schwitzgebel, "Belief;" italics original.

[43] Edmund L. Gettier, "Is Justified True Belief Knowledge?" *Analysis* 23, no. 6 (1963): 121–123.

were both correct in believing (2). At the same time, Smith was wrong when he pictured Jones getting the job, whereas Jones was correct when he pictured Smith getting the job. It seems that mental images can be parts of beliefs, and thus, they can aim at truth. As in the cases of religious belief discussed above, here, too, imagination can add important details to what is believed in the standard sense of "believe."

Finally, the line of thought presented here can be applied to simple, everyday situations in which new beliefs emerge. I hear a certain noise through a living-room window. Based on similar experiences I have had before, I immediately form the belief that there is a cement-mixing machine outside, somewhere on the nearby construction site that I have passed by many times. My belief includes a spontaneously formed mental image of the machine. According to the image, the machine is entirely brown. I go out of the house and look around. What I see is indeed a cement-mixing machine. So I had formed a propositionally true belief. At the same time, I see, to my surprise, that the machine is completely blue. My image of the machine, which was a part of my belief, turned out to be incorrect. When I heard the noise through the window, I formed a mixture of belief and image, a compound "belief-image" that was correct in one respect and incorrect in another. When I formed the "belief-image," I had a compound doxastic-imaginative experience.[44]

In light of these and the above observations, it seems that the standard conceptions of belief and imagination need reconsideration. The standard description of belief as a "propositional attitude" appears to be too restrictive because mental images can also be parts of beliefs.

Problems and Replies

In this section, I will raise two problems concerning the main claims made in the article and try to answer them.

One of the claims was that mental images can be parts of religious beliefs and add important details to the propositional content of faith. I envisaged cases in which the beliefs of two individuals have the same propositional content but different, even conflicting, imaginative contents. This gives rise to the problem of how to deal with conflicting images in the domain of faith. By way of response, I would say that first, we need to find out what the actual specific images are like in the minds of believers. The images might be of interest not only to philosophers, psychologists, and theologians but also to the believers themselves. The answer to the question of what religious beliefs one has is not complete if it includes propositions but leaves out mental images. If it turns out that

[44] This is somewhat similar to Langland-Hassan's view that some imaginings have "hybrid contents" involving "both discursive and imagistic representations." Peter Langland-Hassan, "Imaginative Attitudes," *Philosophy and Phenomenological Research* 90, no. 3 (2015): 664–686.

individuals agree on religious propositions, but their relevant images are in conflict, it is a matter of private and public discussion on whether or how to solve those conflicts. I presume that the images can be modified while leaving the propositional content of the beliefs untouched. At the same time, I certainly do not wish to suggest that religious authorities should try to gain control over people's imaginations.

The article also claimed that, in principle, the imaginative contents of religious beliefs might turn out to be correct or incorrect representations of transcendent realities. As these supposed realities are beyond human ken and the representational capability of mental images is limited, one can question the epistemic significance of the relevant images. In response, I would say that, from the epistemological point of view, propositional beliefs about transcendent realities are also problematic, which is why analytic philosophers of religion have intensively and variously dealt with the justification of such beliefs. What I propose is to broaden the scope of epistemological inquiries by looking closely at the mental images involved in religious beliefs. The specific images discussed in the article were hypothetical, but there are actual images to be examined in the minds of believers. A compound analysis of the propositional and imaginative contents of those beliefs may give valuable insights into the nature of faith.

Conclusion

This article aimed to show that religious beliefs and religious mental images can be intertwined to the extent that a sharp and exclusive conceptual distinction between them oversimplifies matters and undermines the role that those images play in faith. It argued that mental images can be parts of beliefs, and thus, they can aim at truth, not only in the context of religious faith but also, more generally, in everyday life situations. Accordingly, it claimed that the familiar conception of beliefs as propositional attitudes is too restrictive and needs revision. The argumentation used Plantinga's model of the Christian faith as an example of classical religious epistemology, in which beliefs are seen as wholly distinct from imaginings. It also showed that Schellenberg's ultimistic faith, which is meant to be non-doxastic, can include religiously important mental images that make this faith look doxastic.[45]

[45] The author would like to thank Uku Tooming for his helpful comments on a draft of the paper and Chris Springer for copyediting the text.

Faith as Imagination and the Despair-Problem

Carl-Johan Palmqvist

Introduction

According to non-doxasticism, an important view in the contemporary analytical philosophy of religion, religious faith can be in a crucial sense belief-less.[1] However, as I have recently argued elsewhere,[2] such non-doxastic faith is vulnerable to the despair-problem commonly associated with the analysis of hope. In analytical philosophy, hope has traditionally been analysed as requiring esire and epistemic possibility. For hope to beat cancer, you must desire to survive and regard it as uncertain that you might. However, despair also requires desire and possibility – you can only despair over your prospects of beating cancer if you desire to survive, and it remains uncertain whether you will survive or not. Therefore, an analysis of hope that lacks the capability of properly distinguishing hope from despair seems unacceptable since, intuitively, the attitudes should be mutually exclusive. Since non-doxastic faith implies hope, the problem carries over to the analysis of such faith as well. Arguably, the problem is even more severe in relation to non-doxastic faith since the exclusion of despair must be considered a minimum requirement for any acceptable analysis of faith.

In what follows, I will suggest one possible solution to the despair-problem for non-doxastic faith. My contribution is, first of all, an attempt to advance our understanding of non-doxastic faith, and I will show how my solution to the problem gives us reason to prefer some non-doxastic theories over others. Obviously, the contemporary discussion concerning the feasibility of non-doxastic faith is but one of many important philosophical discussions on faith, and while I do hope that my results have some significance also outside this context, it falls outside the scope of this essay to explore any such implications in detail.

---

[1] For important contemporary accounts, see William Alston, "Belief, Acceptance and Religious Faith" in *Faith, Freedom, and Rationality*, eds Jeff Jordan & Daniel Howard-Snyder (London: Rowman and Littlefield Publishers Inc., 1996), 3-27; Lara Buchak, "Faith and Steadfastness in the Face of Counter-Evidence" *International Journal for Philosophy of Religion* 81 no. 1-2 (2017): 113-133; Daniel Howard-Snyder, "Propositional Faith: What It Is and What It Is Not" *American Philosophical Quarterly* 50 no. 4 (2013): 357-372; Daniel McKaughan, "Action-Centered Faith, Doubt and Rationality" *Journal of Philosophical Research* no. 41 Issue Supplement (2016): 71-90; J. L. Schellenberg, *Prolegomena to a Philosophy of Religion* (Ithaca: Cornell University Press, 2005).

[2] Carl-Johan Palmqvist, "Desiderata for Rational, Non-Doxastic Faith" *Sophia* (Forthcoming): 14-19.

I suggest that understanding faith in terms of imagination provides a conceivable way of overcoming the despair-problem. In particular, I think Schellenberg's analysis of faith in terms of voluntary assent to an imagined picture of a desired epistemic possibility has the resources needed to properly distinguish faith from despair.[3] Schellenberg himself does not address this issue, and my key contribution in this article is to demonstrate the incoherence between imaginative faith and despair.

My arguments rest on the account of imagination offered by Kind[4] and an account of despair indicated by Calhoun.[5] According to Kind, imagination has an irreducibly phenomenological character, and according to Calhoun, despair consists of having a negative phenomenological idea of the future. Together, these accounts suggest that both imagination and despair should be understood in terms of their phenomenological content. Given that assumption, it does not seem far-fetched to hold that one cannot give voluntary assent to an imagined phenomenological picture of reality where what one desires is true, and at the same time entertain in one's imaginative faculty an incompatible phenomenological picture where what one desires is not true. Or so I will argue.

Even though much attention will be given to the notion of a phenomenological *picture*, I want to make clear from the start that I am not aiming to capture the complete phenomenology of either faith or despair. I am concerned with conceptual definitions in terms of necessary and sufficient conditions, and such analyses are not intended to do full justice to the phenomenology involved. In the analytical treatment of notions like faith or despair, the focus is on cognition, propositional content, and intensional attitudes. Emotional aspects are standardly downplayed, as are considerations regarding how these states are experienced. I would not deny that a more phenomenological take on the matter might yield interesting results, but for the present purposes, I stick with the analytic approach.

In the upcoming sections, I will first introduce the non-doxastic approach to religion. It is followed by a presentation of the despair-problem, where its relevance for present accounts of non-doxasticism is explained. Then follows a section on Schellenberg's analysis of propositional faith in terms of imagination, and a section dedicated to showing how an imagination-based account of faith is able to handle the despair-problem. In the last part of the text, I clarify and develop my argument by considering some major objections before I end with some concluding remarks.

---

[3] I will concentrate on Schellenberg's most recent formulation of the view, in J. L Schellenberg, *Evolutionary Religion* (Oxford: Oxford University Press, 2013), 91-115. For the original account, see Schellenberg, *Prolegomena to a Philosophy of Religion*, 127-166.

[4] Amy Kind, "Putting the Image Back in Imagination" *Philosophy and Phenomenological Research* 62 no. 1 (2001): 85-109.

[5] Cheshire Calhoun, *Doing Valuable Time* (Oxford: Oxford University Press, 2018).

A Brief Presentation of Non-Doxasticism

The basic idea of non-doxasticism is that one can make a religious commitment while lacking outright religious belief. Faith is standardly viewed as a composite attitude which can be analysed by identifying its constituents. In this analysis, most accounts include some substitute for belief in terms of a weaker cognitive attitude, like hope, acceptance, or belief-less assumption. However, some more radical authors suggest that non-doxastic faith can be analysed without including any such cognitive belief-substitute.[6]

Non-doxasticism must not be conflated with religious fictionalism, which treats religious language as fiction and religious life as a game of make-believe.[7] On fictionalism, the truth-value of religious language is irrelevant, and religion is practised only for its moral and spiritual value, as a means of human flourishing not too different from other cultural activities. By contrast, non-doxasticism rests on a realist interpretation of religious language and the epistemic possibility that the relevant religious propositions might be true is all-important. Unlike the fictionalist, the non-doxasticist is generally conceived as taking part in the same project as the believer.

While the exact nature of non-doxastic faith varies with the account, there is also a common core to the approach, which can be summarized in terms of two necessary conditions. Here follows a formulation of these requirements from an earlier paper of mine:

For S to have a non-doxastic pro-attitude towards some state of affairs *p*, it is necessary that the following two conditions are met:

ND1: S desires that *p* or judges that *p* is an overall good thing.

ND2: S believes *p* to be epistemically possible.[8]

---

[6] For an important account in terms of hope, see Louis Pojman, "Faith Without Belief" *Faith and Philosophy* 3 no. 2 (1986): 157-176. For acceptance, see Alston "Belief, Acceptance and Religious Faith" and for belief-less assumption, see Daniel Howard-Snyder "The Sceptical Christian" in *Oxford Studies in the Philosophy of Religion Volume 8*, ed. Jonathan Kvanvig (Oxford: Oxford University Press, 2017), 142-167. For the most well-known philosopher who does not include any weaker cognitive attitude, see Buchak "Faith and Steadfastness in the Face of Counter-Evidence".

[7] For an accessible introduction, see Robin Le Poidevin, *Religious Fictionalism* (Cambridge: Cambridge University Press, 2019).

[8] Carl-Johan Palmqvist,"The Proper Object of Non-Doxastic Religion: Why Traditional Religion Should Be Preferred Over Schellenberg's Simple Ultimism" *Religious Studies* 55 no. 4 (2019): 560. I have later come to reject ND1 as a general requirement for non-doxasticism. The reason is that ND1 excludes non-doxastic fear, which should be viewed as a viable alternative to faith and hope (see Carl-Johan Palmqvist "A Non-Doxastic Fear of Hell: On the Impact of Negative Factors for an Agnostic Religious Commitment" *Religions* 11 no. 8 (Early View):1-12). However, ND1 still holds as a requirement for non-doxastic *faith*, which makes it suitable for present purposes.

The first condition is mainly about motivation. Since the subject lacks belief, a religious life becomes entirely voluntary, which is why some non-epistemic reason to commit is required. While such reasons are often ambitious and religious in character, like aligning with the divine in order to achieve salvation, a minimal requirement is that the subject must desire the truth of the religious proposition towards which her faith is directed or consider such truth an overall good thing. If you do not find God's existence a good or desirable thing, you cannot have non-doxastic faith that God exists.

The second condition concerns epistemic possibility, and it should be read as excluding the possibility that the subject considers *p* an epistemic possibility *and* believes or disbelieves *p*. Non-doxastic faith excludes the possibility of outright belief, but it also excludes the possibility of outright disbelief.[9]

The second condition is the key requirement of non-doxasticism. It requires uncertainty, that the subject is agnostic concerning the truth of *p*. The subject for which non-doxastic faith is a possibility believes that for all she knows, it could well be the case that *p* is true, but it could at least as easily be the case that *p* is false. In such circumstances, *p* is considered an undefeated epistemic possibility.

ND1 and ND2 coincide with the standard account of hope, which suggests that non-doxastic faith implies hope. In other words, if you have non-doxastic faith that *p*, you will also hope that *p*. This also means that philosophical problems concerning the standard analysis of hope can be relevant for non-doxastic faith. As I have previously suggested[10], this certainly seems to be the case when it comes to the despair-problem.

The Despair-Problem for Non-Doxastic Faith

The despair-problem originates from the literature on hope. It demonstrates that the conditions of the traditional, standard account of hope (in terms of desire and epistemic possibility, as captured by ND1 and ND2) are not sufficient since a subject might satisfy these conditions without hoping. Worse still, she might even satisfy them while despairing. The problem is that the conditions do not uniquely identify hope, and the focus is usually on despair to stress its seriousness. Clearly, there is something wrong with an account of hope which cannot rule out the possibility that the subject is in despair. The problem

[9] This formulation rests on the assumption that outright belief and disbelief in *p* is something qualitatively different from finding *p* somewhat probable or improbable. If one thinks belief could come in degrees, the account needs to be reformulated accordingly.

[10] Palmqvist, "Desiderata for Rational, Non-Doxastic Faith," 14-19.

has prompted much new work in the philosophy of hope, with the goal of finding a more adequate analysis.[11]

To get a feel for the despair-problem, it is helpful to consider a common illustration from the literature on hope.

> Two men, Andy and Red [from the movie *Shawshank Redemption*], have been serving life sentence for murder in a brutal prison. They are in many ways similar. They are equally resourceful, they understand equally well the workings of the prison and the ways of the prisoners and guards inhabiting it, and *they have an equal grasp of the very small chances* of escaping. At the same time, neither of them has lost the *desire* to be free again (though some more veteran prisoners have lost this desire). And yet, Andy lives in the hope of escaping, whereas Red despairs.[12]

For many accounts of non-doxastic faith, the despair-problem is as pressing as it is for the standard account of hope, and it is safe to say that an analysis of faith that is unable to distinguish faith from despair is even more problematic than an analysis of hope with the same exclusion problem. A correct account should be true to the intuition that it is both rationally impossible and psychologically unfeasible to have faith that *p* while at the same time despairing over the prospects that *p* (of course, one can be torn between faith and despair and alter between the attitudes, but one cannot hold both at the same time).

The despair-problem concerns non-doxastic faith because it is belief-less (outright belief that *p* prevents despair over *p* – if you believe that your wife survived the accident and is well, you do not despair over her safe return) and because it rests on ND1 and ND2, which are identical to the standard account of hope. However, since ND1 and ND2 are only part of the analysis of non-doxastic faith, the despair-problem does not affect non-doxastic faith in general. It could well be the case that some further condition is able to prevent the rise of the problem. I will argue that this is indeed the case with Schellenberg's imagination-based faith. First, however, I will demonstrate how some other leading accounts succumb to the problem.

The despair-problem is most pressing on accounts of non-doxastic faith, which does not substitute belief with some weaker cognitive attitude. These accounts simply say too little about what is going on in the subject's mind to be able to exclude despair or any other attitude which intuitively should conflict with having faith. Consider the account offered by Buchak. In addition to considerations very similar to ND1 and ND2, Buchak makes the following requirement for faith:

---

[11] See for example Adrienne Martin, *How We Hope: A Moral Psychology* (Princeton: Princeton University Press 2014); Ariel Meirav, "The Nature of Hope" *Ratio* 22 no. 2 (2009): 216-233; Carl-Johan Palmqvist "Analyzing Hope: The Live Possibility Account" *European Journal of Philosophy* (Early View): 1-14.

[12] Meirav, "The Nature of Hope," 222, italics added.

Act A is an act of faith that X, for S, if and only if:

(i) S performing A constitutes S taking a (subjective) risk on X

(ii) S chooses (to commit to A before he examines additional evidence) rather than (to postpone his decision about A until he examines additional evidence).[13]

On Buchak's account, faith consists in acting instead of collecting more evidence, taking a risk on some desired epistemic possibility. While these conditions capture an important intuition regarding what it is to act on faith, they are not sufficient for an analysis of faith, since one can perform such actions while holding a variety of other mental attitudes.

Consider the case of a starving man and his child, marooned on a small, desolate island. The man decides to go fishing on the assumption (X) that there is edible fish in the sea. He does so without gathering more evidence, and the risk is obvious – if the sea around the island contains no edible fish, he and his child will die. The starving man satisfies ND1 and ND2 since he desires to catch the fish and since the existence of edible fish constitutes an epistemic possibility. Does this mean that the man has faith rather than being in despair? Certainly not. The man might well despair over the prospect of catching edible fish, and the fact that he tries rather than just give up might be explained by some other desire. Perhaps he wants to keep his child from despairing too, or perhaps he wants to do his duty as a good parent until the very end.

While the problem with an account like Buchak's is that it is cognitively underdefined, simply adding any weak cognitive attitude is not enough to overcome the problem. Many of the attitudes suggested as belief-substitutes are too modest to be incoherent with despair. Consider, for example, the attitude of acceptance, which has been advocated as a basis for non-doxastic faith by Alston. To accept *p* means to voluntarily adopt a policy to use *p* as a basis for action and reasoning. On Alston's account, the voluntary attitude of acceptance differs from belief mainly by the fact that unlike the believing subject, the accepter does not feel it to be the case that what she accepts is true. In other aspects, acceptance is a lot like belief. Like the believer, the accepter tends to affirm the truth of *p*, and acceptance is sensitive to the evidence since Alston thinks that one can only accept the alternatives one finds most likely. Few non-doxasticists require such strong evidence, and in many ways, Alstonian acceptance is one of the most belief-like cognitive attitudes suggested as a replacement for belief proper. Consequently, if acceptance cannot exclude

---

[13] Buchak, "Faith and Steadfastness," 115.

despair, it is hard to see how the more modest non-doxastic attitudes suggested by other philosophers could do so.[14]

As it happens, adding acceptance to the picture does nothing to overcome the despair-problem. Consider the starving man again. He is obviously accepting the proposition that there is edible fish in the sea as a basis for his actions. We can also add that he might well accept it as a basis for rational reasoning, planning for the future for him and his child on that assumption, for example, by making plans on how to escape the island. As an Alstonian accepter, he must now consider the possibility that there is edible fish in the sea to be at least as likely as the possibility that there is no such fish, although he will still not feel it to be the case. Can the man still be in despair? Yes. He can act and plan for the parenting reasons already mentioned. Since he does not feel it to be the case that there is fish, despair seems possible, at least in the case where the man finds the proposition that there is edible fish as likely as its negation. In short, acceptance is not an attitude incoherent with despair.

It must be noted that Alston also thinks that a subject will be surprised if what is accepted turns out not to be true. Such a surprise might seem incoherent with despair since if you despair over *p*, you will standardly not be surprised if you learn that -*p*. However, such a surprise seems unreasonable in a case where you accept a proposition which you regard as on par with the alternatives. If *a* and *b* seem equally likely to you, you should not be surprised if *b* turns out to be true, even if you chose to accept *a*.

It is often suggested that faith implies some sort of trust.[15] Trust is obviously incompatible with despair – I cannot be said to trust you to rescue me from the burning building if at the same time, I despair over the prospects of being saved. However, as I have previously argued, if non-doxastic faith is to be considered a rational attitude, it cannot involve trust. Trusting implies expecting certain outcomes that one cannot rationally expect if one lacks belief. If I trust you to deliver a package to me, I must expect as an outcome that I am going to receive the package, but how can I expect that if I do not also *believe* that you will deliver it?[16] Therefore, the despair-problem cannot be handled by introducing trust. It can, however, be handled by an account of faith in terms of imagination.

---

[14] Alston "Belief, Acceptance and Religious Faith," 7-14. The distinction between belief and acceptance was first introduced by Jonathan Cohen to separate the kind of belief-like states which are the result of conscious and voluntary deliberation from beliefs proper, which are involuntary and the product of automatic cognitive processes (see Jonathan L. Cohen, *An Essay on Belief and Acceptance* (Oxford: Oxford University Press, 1992)). Also see Howard-Snyder's critical assessment of Alstonian acceptance, which helps clarify Alston's position (Howard-Snyder, "The Sceptical Christian").

[15] Alston, "Belief, Acceptance and Religious Faith," 12-14. Also see McKaughan, "Action-Centered Faith".

[16] Palmqvist, "Desiderata for rational, non-doxastic faith," 9-14.

Schellenberg's Faith in Terms of Imagination

According to Schellenberg, to have faith is to be guided in thought and action by an imagined picture of reality where some desired epistemic possibility is realised:

> Faith without belief is realized in circumstances where you don't believe the relevant proposition (call it p) but (1) you nonetheless think it would be *good* for p to be true... and (2) you take p to be epistemically possible, holding that it can't reasonably be *dis*believed either... although you're not being involuntary represented-*to* in the manner of belief, (3) you deliberately represent or picture the world *to yourself* through the power of imagination as including the truth of p. Moreover (4) you form the intention to be mentally guided by this picture on an ongoing basis when relevant things come up, that is, to think accordingly and as a matter of policy; and (5) you follow through on this policy.[17]

The first two conditions (together with the requirement that you do not believe *p*) are simply restatements of ND1 and ND2. The remaining conditions specify what is unique to Schellenberg's imagination-based account of faith.

Condition (3) is where imagination enters the picture. Here, imagination is presented in contrast with belief: while belief is involuntary and passive, imagination is an active and deliberate process in which the subject pictures the world to herself in a certain way. What one pictures to oneself in faith is the possibility that what one hopes for (according to ND1 and ND2) is true. In faith, one is "imagining the world to oneself as including the relevant state of affairs."[18] For example, if I hope that God exists, to have faith I must also use my imagination and picture the world as a world where the proposition "God exists" is true.

Only imagining that *p* is not enough for faith. A faith solely in terms of imagination would reduce to daydreaming, and that would surely be an unacceptable result.[19] Therefore, we also need something like (4) and (5), requiring the subject to be steadfast in her imagination and to let the imagined picture guide her thoughts and actions. Schellenberg calls this "a policy of voluntary assent".[20] Therefore, to have non-doxastic faith that God exists, it is not enough that I picture the world to myself as a world where it is true that God exists, I must also adopt a policy of voluntary assent where I resolve to act and think according to this imagined picture of the world.

To appreciate what kind of faith-attitude Schellenberg's account leads to, it is helpful to consider Schellenberg's recurring example with a runner slightly out of form, who prepares himself mentally for a big race:

[17] Schellenberg, *Evolutionary Religion*, 102-103.

[18] J. L. Schellenberg, *The Will to Imagine* (Ithaca: Cornell University Press, 2009), 3.

[19] Carl-Johan Palmqvist, "Faith and Hope in Situations of Epistemic Uncertainty" *Religious Studies* 55 no. 3 (2019): 329.

[20] Schellenberg, *Prolegomena to a Philosophy of Religion*, 134.

> Think of a runner who is considering whether he will do well in the important race that is about to begin. Loosening up and stretching behind the starting line, he broods about how on this day of all days his condition is not exactly favourable to success, because of various physical ailments. (2) Going over the relevant evidence, which at first he is inclined to treat very negatively, he notices that it does not *establish* that he must fail... But all in all the evidence on which he reflects still is insufficient to cause in him the belief that he will do well; it takes him from disbelief to doubt but no further. At this point he realizes that he will have to do something about his frame of mind if he is to have any chance of beating the odds. (1) Winning the race, or at least placing in the top three, would obviously be a good thing; so he tells himself to contemplate on that good thing for a bit. (3) As he focuses his attention on it, the unsettling feelings associated with his doubt recede to the background; there is no longer any room for them at the forefront of his consciousness. (4) Keeping that picture in place before his mind as he positions himself with the other runners, he mentally affirms over and over that it corresponds to the way things are: "Yes, I will do this, yes, I will do well".[21]

Already at an intuitive level, it seems reasonable to suggest that if one has the kind of imagination-based faith suggested by Schellenberg, one will not at the same time despair. Clearly, it is in order to avoid attitudes such as despair that the runner adopts faith. However, we need not restrict ourselves to an intuitive level. Given some reasonable assumptions concerning the nature of imagination and the nature of despair, it is possible to demonstrate this incoherence in a more thorough fashion.

Why Imagination-Based Faith is Incompatible with Despair

For the nature of imagination, we turn to the account offered by Kind. Kind's analysis is somewhat controversial since she defends the view that imagination always includes mental imagery, something which has been questioned when it comes to propositional imagination, i.e., imagination that *p*.[22] However, I do not think we must embrace the idea that *all* imagination includes mental imagery to find Kind's theory useful for understanding the kind of imagination suggested by Schellenberg. Even though Schellenberg is explicitly concerned with propositional imagination, it is clear that he intends such imagination to be understood in terms of images. One cannot very well picture the world to oneself in a way not including mental imagery. Therefore, Kind's image-centered account, at the very least, captures imagination in the sense used by Schellenberg, and that is sufficient for present purposes. Kind presents her view as follows:

> There are three characteristic features of imagination which must be accommodated within any satisfactory account of this phenomenon:

---

[21] Ibid, 129-130, italics in original, numbers added.

[22] For an instance of this criticism, see Neil Van Leeuwen "Imagination Is Where the Action Is" *Journal of Philosophy* 108 no. 2 (2011): 55-77.

(i) *Directedness*: In imagining X, I direct my imagining at something.

(ii) *Activity*: To imagine X is to do something.

(iii) *Phenomenology*: Imagining X has a qualitative character.[23]

The conditions are clearly in line with Schellenberg's account. What my imagination is directed at (i) is a desired possible state of the world, and it is clear that Schellenberg would agree that (ii) imagining is a voluntary activity. However, what really clarifies the picture is Kind's idea that (iii) imagination has a qualitative or phenomenological character. I assume Schellenberg would agree with (iii) given his examples and emphasis on picturing, even though he does not offer any more detailed treatment on the imagery of imagination. The following quote captures the gist of Kind's account:

> Suppose that I were to imagine my friend's orange dress. My imagining clearly has a phenomenology. Moreover, the qualitative feel involved in my imagining is essential to it. Most importantly, however, there is nothing special about this particular imagining that provided it with its phenomenology. No matter what I imagine, my imagining will involve an experiential aspect... The experiential aspect of imagining is very much like that involved in several other mental activities, including hallucinating, dreaming, and perceiving.[24]

If we understand imagination along the lines suggested by Kind, we can elaborate Schellenberg's account of non-doxastic faith and say that such faith consists in actively conjuring and holding in one's mind a phenomenological picture of a possible state of the world in which some desired possibility *p* is true.

According to the account of despair offered by Cheshire Calhoun,[25] despair is also characterized by its phenomenological content, which is viewed in the imagination. Calhoun claims that we have "a phenomenological idea of the future", which should not be conflated with our "planning idea of the future". While the latter builds on rational considerations, the former is "not a fully reasons-responsive state," building instead on a plurality of psychological sources like unconscious generalisations from previous experience. The phenomenological idea of the future is supposed to capture one's basic and unreflective sense of the future, the idea of the future one "inhabits," so to speak:

> Having a phenomenological idea of the future is a matter of inhabiting the future. We inhabit the future by being drawn to *previsage a particular future in our imagination*... we inhabit the future now by living now under an unreflective sense of what the future will be like.[26]

Calhoun explicitly considers the phenomenological idea of the future to be an object of the imagination, in the sense that the imagination is identified as the faculty in which we view this phenomenological picture. This strongly suggest

[23] Kind, "Putting the Image Back," 89-90.
[24] Ibid, 93-94.
[25] Calhoun, *Doing Valuable Time*, 68-89.
[26] Ibid, 72, italics added.

that the phenomenological picture is of the same kind as the imagery of imagination described by Kind.

On Calhoun's account, despair is to be understood in terms of having a special kind of phenomenological idea of the future. It is when we have a determinate picture of the future, including the failure of our present endeavour:

> Those who hope, despair and merely fret may differ not in their probability assignments of what the future will be but, rather, in how they fill in the content of the determinate future they previsage in reflective imagination and that operates as a background idea of the future... Those who despair use the undesired unsuccessful future.[27]

Calhoun is mainly concerned about despair's role when it comes to action, and that is why she speaks only about despair concerning some future outcome. I take it to be obvious that one can despair over other things than the future. In all situations where one can take on a non-doxastic attitude according to ND1 and ND2, that is, in situations where some state of affairs is desired but uncertain, one can always despair over the prospects of *p* being true (note that the easily overlooked desire-component is as vital as the epistemic possibility since you cannot despair over something you do not care about). For example, if you are a pro-religious agnostic who finds God's existence an overall good thing, you might well despair over the existence of God.

To accommodate for despair over unknown things other than the future, Calhoun's theory needs to be expanded. I suggest that we add a phenomenological picture *of the world*, analogous with the phenomenological picture of the future. Just as the phenomenological idea of the future is distinct from our planning idea, the phenomenological picture of the world must be distinct from our rational, belief-based view, building partly on non-rational and perhaps even unconscious sources. I do not find it implausible to suggest that we have such a basic and unreflective view of the world, especially if we consider cases of the alleged conflict between this picture and our rational and belief-based view. Consider, for example, how one might struggle with bias and prejudice even though one rationally believes all men and women to be equal, or how one might be afraid of the dark even though one does not rationally believe the dark to hold any dangers. Or consider how many people answer questions like "Does God exist?" based on gut-feeling rather than theoretical reasons. The idea of a phenomenological picture of the world offers a plausible explanation regarding the origin of such gut-feelings.

If we extend Calhoun's account to cover despair over the unknown, we can say that to despair over some unknown but desired state of affairs *p*, one's phenomenological picture of the world must include the actualization of *-p*

[27] Ibid, 85. As is implied here, Calhoun suggests that her account can address the despair-problem for hope. I think we have good reason to reject Calhoun's suggested solution, since it certainly seems possible to hope against one's phenomenological picture of the future (Palmqvist, "Analyzing Hope," 7).

rather than *p*. When the despairing subject unwittingly and unreflectively imagines the world, it will be a world where *-p* is true.

I want to stress that I do not suggest that we should develop an account of despair that mirrors all conditions of Schellenberg's analysis of faith. Despair differs from faith in several important aspects. Most importantly, it is an involuntary attitude, while faith is voluntary. It is beyond the scope of this article to spell out a detailed account of despair in terms of necessary and sufficient conditions. Fortunately, the basic idea that a negative phenomenological picture of the world and/or the future is the defining feature of despair is enough to demonstrate the incompatibility between faith and despair.

Now, we have reached the point where it is possible to see that imagination-based faith and Calhounian despair are mutually exclusive. If faith that *p* consists in imagining a phenomenological picture of the world where *p* is actualized, and if despairing over *p* consists in imagining a phenomenological picture of the world where *-p* is actualized, one cannot have faith and despair at the same time.

Elaborating the Argument

My solution to the despair-problem is based on the idea that one cannot, at the same time, entertain two mutually exclusive phenomenological pictures of the world. Stated a bit more formally, the argument goes as follows:

P1: Faith that *p* consists of imagining a phenomenological picture of the world where *p* is actualized.

P2: Despairing over *p* consists of imagining a phenomenological picture of the world where *-p* is actualized.

P3: One cannot imagine two mutually exclusive phenomenological pictures of the world at the same time.

Conclusion: One cannot despair over *p* while having faith that *p*.

P1 and P2 follow from the accounts of faith, imagination, and despair offered by Schellenberg, Kind, and Calhoun. It is outside the scope of this essay to defend these accounts in detail, so I will simply take their characterization of faith, imagination, and despair for granted. P3 is essential to my argument. Only if one cannot imagine two inconsistent phenomenological pictures of the world at the same time does imaginative faith exclude despair. But is this premise as obvious as I suggest? In exactly what way are the two pictures supposed to be incompatible?

Clearly, the imagination can sustain two contrasting images at the same time. For example, if I am a scientist pondering two mutually exclusive theories regarding some phenomenon X, it seems plausible to suggest that I could simultaneously imagine the world as it would be on both these theories in order to evaluate which is the best and most probable explanation of X.

However, Schellenberg's account of faith and Calhoun's account of despair do more than simply suggest that these attitudes should be understood in terms of imagination. According to Calhoun, the subject of despair "inhabits" the picture of the future she imagines, and the subject of Schellenbergian faith gives voluntary assent to her imagined picture. What is suggested here, are attitudes much more potent than ordinary, every-day imagining. Also, in both Calhoun's and Schellenberg's views, the imagined picture is taken to be a picture of the actual world; it is no mere fantasy or consideration of hypothetical possibilities. It seems highly unlikely to suggest that one could imagine two inconsistent pictures of the world in this strong and reality-centred way. Therefore, faith and despair should be viewed as psychologically incompatible attitudes.

It follows from my argument that one can take on faith to get rid of one's despair. This is because faith is a voluntary attitude, while despair is involuntary. If the attitudes are incompatible but only one of them voluntary, it will standardly be the case that one can take on the voluntary attitude to replace the involuntary attitude. This result is in line with Schellenberg's account of faith. In the example with the runner, it seems that the main purpose of conducting the kind of imaginative, mental exercises the runner is occupied with is to block out any conflicting idea or phenomenological picture. It also seems intuitively right to regard faith as a way of combatting or preventing despair.

Obviously, this does not mean that one can always replace despair with faith. There might be many reasons why a specific subject does not find it within her power to do so (heavy grief, exhaustion, a negative disposition, etc.). My point is only that in standard cases, faith will be an option even if in despair.

Perhaps an objector would suggest that I overstate my case. Why stick my neck out and make claims about empirical matters such as psychological incompatibility? Is it not enough that the phenomenological pictures in question are logically inconsistent since the actual world cannot contain both *p* and *-p*? Should I not rest content with demonstrating this logical inconsistency?

However, the objector is wrong to suggest that logical inconsistency is enough to solve the despair-problem in a satisfying way. If holding both attitudes at the same time is psychologically feasible, and if faith and despair are only logically inconsistent, despair will standardly prevent faith. Since non-doxastic faith is a rational and voluntary attitude, a subject cannot take on faith in a situation where this will result in rational inconsistency. If one is in despair, which is an involuntary state, one will realize that adopting faith in addition to despair will lead to rational inconsistency and therefore refrain from doing so. This picture contrasts sharply with the intuition that faith can be a way out of despair, an intuition we should certainly strive to preserve. To that purpose, we need psychological incompatibility so that faith replaces despair on adoption.

Before rounding off the discussion, I wish to consider two further possible objections. The first is an objection that could be directed at P1, concerning the possibility of adequately imagining an important religious state of affairs. In the literature on imagination, there is an objection against the idea that propositional faith has phenomenological content, based on the claim that one can imagine what one cannot visualize. This point has been colourfully put by Van Leeuwen: "When I imagine, on reading *Lord of the Rings*, that elves can live forever, I'm fictionally imagining a proposition I couldn't imagine using mental imagery. It would take too long!"[28]

Now, if we cannot imagine things like immortal elves, it seems that there are many religious propositions that suffer a similar fate, like "God exists" (since God supposedly has truly mind-blowing attributes like omnipotence and omniscience). This objection seems to suggest that we must either abandon the accounts of imagination and/or faith offered by Schellenberg and Kind or conclude that one's faith cannot be directed at things like God. Both options would be highly unsatisfying, given the present approach.

However, as explained by Kind, the phenomenological content of imagination does not have to be unique and does not have to perfectly capture what is imagined. She gives the example that one might imagine Bill Clinton doing budget calculations in his head just by imagining Bill Clinton looking very thoughtful.[29] Likewise, one might imagine the immortality of elves by, for example, picturing an elf in a ruined city, lost in memories from the foundation of the city millennia ago. Or whatever comes to mind.

Concerning the kind of imagination employed in Schellenbergian faith, I think it is important to note that what one imagines is the world as it would be if some state of affairs was actualized. You do not have to imagine God in ungraspable glory to imagine that God exists, you only have to imagine the world as it would be if God exists. Since you already hold God's existence an epistemic possibility, that is, since you already hold that the actual world might be this possible world, this act of imagination might, in fact, require less of an effort than one might originally suppose.

The second objection I wish to consider is that the introduction of imagination might seem redundant on my account. Is it not the idea of a phenomenological picture rather than an account of imagination that does the heavy philosophical lifting? Could not the argument be restated without reference to the imagination? After all, this would make the argument less controversial since there are philosophers who deny that we possess a distinct imaginative faculty.[30]

---

[28] Neil Van Leeuwen "The Meanings of 'Imagine' Part I: Constructive Imagination" *Philosophy Compass* 8 no. 3 (2013): 222.

[29] Kind, "Putting the Image Back", 103-104.

[30] See for example Peter Langland Hassan "Pretense, Imagination and Belief: The Single Attitude Theory" *Philosophical Studies* 159 no. 2 (2012).

However, it seems unclear to me what kind of images these phenomenological pictures would be, if not images of the imagination. Other image-producing faculties, like memory or perception, produce pictures clearly distinct from the phenomenological pictures under consideration. In short, it is hard to conceive of a faculty other than the imagination with the capability of producing phenomenological pictures with the characteristics described by Kind and Calhoun, and we cannot have phenomenological pictures without them being produced by some kind of cognitive faculty. Of course, the objector could always postulate some special "phenomenological picturing faculty," but that seems an unmotivated departure from folk psychology. Also, it seems that such a "phenomenological picturing faculty" would function very much like the faculty I call "the imagination," reducing the matter to a verbal issue.

Concluding Remarks

Non-doxastic accounts of faith must deal with the despair-problem commonly associated with hope. An account of faith must be able to exclude despair, but how can that be done if faith neither implies belief nor trust? I have suggested that the problem can be overcome by framing both faith and despair in terms of having a phenomenological picture of the world in one's imagination. Understood this way, the attitudes become incompatible due to the impossibility of entertaining two explicitly inconsistent pictures of the world.

Since I am aware of no other solution to the despair-problem for non-doxastic faith, my argument speaks strongly in favour of an imagination-based account. If one is unwilling to accept this conclusion, two options remain: reject the entire notion of non-doxastic faith or provide an alternative solution to the despair-problem. In the absence of an alternate solution, we should treat imagination-based faith as the only viable kind of non-doxastic faith.

Finally, I want to point out that my claims concerning the incompatibility between imagination-based faith and despair are in no way restricted to non-doxasticism. If voluntary assent to an imagined picture of reality is truly incompatible with despair, this remains the case even if we hold that faith must be based on belief. Of course, we would have to find another label than "faith" to name this strong, imaginative stance, but that is merely a verbal issue. What remains important is that we have identified a voluntary mental state where despair can be overcome by the use of the imagination.

Instructive and Transcendent Uses of Imagination in Medieval Philosophical Psychology

Ritva Palmén

Introduction

Our ability to imagine all kinds of things, be they real or unreal, is considered as one of the basic capacities of the human mind. Imagination is usually conceived as something positive and innovative, allowing us to envision the world and ourselves from various perspectives. While the imagination has its numerous uses in everyday speech, it is also one of the central concepts in various theoretical fields of thought. Much of the contemporary discussion of imagination has been concerned with the particular roles that imagination is supposed to play in various domains of human understanding and activity. Researchers have been eager to identify the role of imagination in the process of understanding, in acquiring knowledge about possibilities, engaging with the arts, thinking creatively, and interpreting figurative language. Arguably, imagination has its own role to play in moral theorizing and religion as well.[1]

As this anthology demonstrates, the philosophers of religion have also been interested in disclosing and investigating recent advances in the study of imagination, evaluating its potential roles and uses as well as its limits in theology and philosophy from a fresh angle. I am entirely convinced that in order to progress in understanding such an elusive and hard-to-define concept as imagination we need to be aware of the achievements of our predecessors as well. I do not think that we should treat their works as authoritative sources of truth but, by engaging with them, we may be confident that real insights into

---

[1] The literature on imagination is extensive. For recent developments in philosophy, see, e.g., *The Routledge Handbook of Philosophy of Imagination*, ed., Amy Kind (New York: Routledge, 2016); *Knowledge Through Imagination*, eds., Amy Kind and Peter Kung (Oxford: Oxford University Press 2016); *Perceptual Imagination and Perceptual Memory,* eds. Fiona Macpherson and Fabian Dorsch (Oxford: Oxford University Press, 2018). For a contemporary phenomenological tradition and the philosophy of religion exploiting imagination, see, e.g., the collection of essays *Imagination Now: A Richard Kearney Reader*, ed. M. E. Littlejohn (Lanham: Roman & Littlefield, 2020), for an investigation of imagination in current research and the problems of interdisciplinarity, see Julia Jansen, "Phenomenology, Imagination and Interdisciplinary Research" in *Handbook of Phenomenology and Cognitive Science*, eds., Julia Jansen, Shaun Gallagher, Daniel Schmicking (Dordrecht: Springer, 2010), 141–158. For the entry in the Stanford online encyclopaedia of philosophy, see https://plato.stanford.edu/entries/imagination/ .

imagination and other similar concepts can be found. Where the differences between historical accounts of imagination and contemporary understanding of it seem to be deep and genuine, we should try to discover and articulate the sources of those differences.

It is not surprising that the history of philosophy witnesses several insightful attempts to understand and analyse imagination, trying to explain its place in human life and thought. Researchers interested in the historical accounts of imagination have mostly referred to Immanuel Kant's *Critique of Judgement*, known for its profound interpretation of the imagination, presenting it as an essential ability in aesthetics as well as knowledge acquisition. Several scholars have remarked on Samuel Coleridge's differentiation between imagination and phantasy and a discussion of the imagination as a source of creativity[2] or analysed the writings of iconic figures of continental philosophy such as Edmund Husserl and Jean-Paul Sartre, who understood imagination as a vital element in phenomenology and essential for explaining human consciousness.[3]

For a philosopher of religion who is keen to explore the role of the imagination, medieval philosophical theology and psychology offer stimulating leads as well. Deeply embedded in Christian faith and institutions, the medieval intellectuals attempted to formulate and explicate a number of classical philosophical questions, such as the role of the imagination in human life. I will substantiate my theses by investigating the account of the imagination offered by Richard of St. Victor (d. 1173) as it is presented within his two books, *Benjamin Minor* and *Benjamin Major*.[4] Researchers have acknowledged the monastery of St. Victor for its unusual combination of daily spiritual life and advanced intellectual study, as well as its considerable interest in teaching.[5] Richard was one of its most prominent teachers, known for his interest in spiritual

---

[2] For a historical account of imagination, see, e.g., Eva T.H Brann, *The World of the Imagination: Sum and Substance*, (Lanham: Rowman & Littlefield, 1991).

[3] Julia Jansen, "Husserl", in *The Routledge Handbook of Philosophy of Imagination*, ed., Amy Kind (New York: Routledge, 2016), 69–81.

[4] *De duodecim patriarchis sive Beniamin minor* (Les douze patriarches ou Beniamin minor), eds. Jean Châtillon, Monique Duchet-Suchaux, Jean Longère, (Paris, 1997) [= PL 196, coll. 1–64, *Bm*]; *De contemplatione (Beniamin maior)*, ed. Jean Grosfillier, (Turnhout, 2013) [Sous la règle de saint Augustin, 13. L'œuvre de Richard de Saint-Victor, [= PL 196, coll. 63–202, *BM*].

[5] William Champeaux founded this community of canons regular in 1108. The historical, political and ideological aspects of the foundation and growth of the monastery of St. Victor have been discussed by Margot Fassler, *Gothic Song. Second edition. Victorine Sequences and Augustinian Reform in Twelfth-Century Paris* (Notre Dame: University of Notre Dame Press, 2011), esp. 187–240.

questions.[6] Although his monastic literature is not philosophical as such, it contains substantial elements of philosophical deliberation. As part of his theological anthropology and guide to spiritual life, Richard argues strongly in favour of the use of the imagination. His ideas on the imagination have remained relatively unknown, and research has only recently acknowledged his impact on later developments in the conception of imagination.[7] In this article, I will analyse Richard's theoretical discussion of the imagination, explain why it is a constitutive element in religious life, and introduce examples of the recommended activities of the imagination.

In their recent anthology, Amy Kind and Peter Kung have suggested that imagination seems to have two different and apparently incompatible uses in human life. The first is the *transcendent use of imagination*, meaning that we use our ability to imagine in order to escape or move from the everyday reality to look beyond the world as it is. The second is the *instructive use of imagination*, which is the idea that imagination enables us to learn something about the world and its phenomena, predict the future, and help as we make decisions. Kind and Kung ask how one mental activity can help us to detach from the world and fly freely, while teaching us something about it, calling this question the *puzzle of the uses of imagination*.[8] This puzzle appears in philosophers' tendency to analyse both its transcendent use and its instructive use in isolation from one another. Richard's inclusive theory of imagination stands as an exception to this rule. In Richard's account, imagination turns out to be a necessary precondition for human reasoning in general (*instructive use*), but it also reveals the religious metaphors and sets the contemplative process in motion, functioning as a link between the lower levels and the higher spiritual levels of contemplation (*transcendent use*).

Richard's comprehensive theory of the imagination builds on his commitment to Christian Neo-Platonic metaphysics, which both allows an extensive range for the imagination, while setting clear limits to its use. The Neo-

[6] Our knowledge of Richard's life is sparse. He was probably born in Scotland in the early part of the twelfth century. He arrived in Paris, the leading scholarly and administrative centre of that time, by 1140. Richard succeeded in his studies and soon after his entrance he was teaching at the external school of St. Victor. In 1159, he became sub-prior of the monastery, and he was elected prior in 1162. Richard died in March 1173. For the details and literature, see Dale Coulter 2006, 246. *Per visibilia ad invisibilia. Theological Method in Richard of St. Victor (d.1173)*. Bibliotheca Victorina XIX (Turnhout: Brepols, 2006), 246.

[7] Some Dante scholars, Mira Mocan among others, have suggested that Dante Alighieri knew Richard's theory of imagination well and utilized it as a literary method within his own masterpiece *The Divine Comedy*. Peter Cheyne, in turn, has noted Richard's impact in Samuel Coleridge's ideas of the imagination and contemplation; see his *Coleridge's Contemplative Philosophy* (Oxford: Oxford University Press, 2020), esp. 130–1.

[8] Amy Kind and Peter Kung, "Introduction", in *Knowledge Through Imagination*, eds. Amy Kind and Peter Kung (Oxford: Oxford University Press, 2016), 1–2.

Platonist dualism divides the hierarchy of being into two major levels, material and spiritual. These two levels are hierarchically structured to form an organized ascending pattern from the lowest to the highest levels of being. This hierarchy is revealed in various respects in the division between visible and invisible reality and in the individual himself and his soul. This conception of reality has important effects on Richard's psychology, spirituality, theory of language and signification, as well as his theological method in general. In a typically Neo-Platonist way, Richard attempts to find the appropriate way to bridge the gap between the visible and invisible spheres, or divine and created objects. Imagination plays a fundamental role in this endeavour since it turns out to be a crucial mediating principle between visible and invisible realities.[9]

The philosophical analysis of Richard's works is challenging since he does not present imagination in a scholarly fashion with clear definitions and classifications, preferring to describe its operation and the objects of its attention. For the purposes of this article, I have picked three main themes related to the imagination, highlighting Richard's wide-ranging treatment of it. My analysis is by no means complete, but aims to illuminate some of the ways that Richard deliberates on the nature and uses of imagination in religious life.[10]

1. Imagination as a handmaid of reason
2. Imagination and religious metaphors
3. Imagination as an image of the creative power of God

These three themes form the outline of the article, which starts with the discussion of the most elementary function of imagination in knowledge acquisition and then proceeds to consider the role of imagination in the formation of religious metaphors and moral theology. The article ends by analysing the possible analogy between divine creativity and the imagination.

Imagination as a handmaid of reason

Both historical and contemporary accounts of imagination agree that imagination plays a role in the acquisition of knowledge, and many philosophical arguments typically invoke imagination when they appeal to metaphysical modal

---

[9] This principle, manifest in several twelfth-century anthropological treatises, is inspired by Neo-Platonist worldview. One of the most influential of these treatises was a booklet about the union of the spirit and body (*De unione corporis et spiritus*) written by Richard's teacher, Hugh of St. Victor. In his account, Hugh exploits the philosophical as well as medical sources of his time, suggesting imagination as a mediating principle between reason and the sensible world. *De unione corporis et spiritus*, ed., A. M. Piazzoni. *Studi Medievali* 21, (1980): 883–888.

[10] For a fuller account of Richard's theory of imagination, see my *Richard of St.Victor's Theory* of *Imagination* (Leiden: Bill, 2014).

knowledge. However, the link between rational thinking and imagination has remained unspecific, and the philosophical discussion about the differences between belief and imagination has remained lively. The main question concerns the truth criterion. While the norm of truth is constitutive of the attitude of belief, it is not constitutive of the attitude of imagination. From the point of view of the philosophy of religion, this seemingly unbridged difference between belief and imagination causes an undeniable challenge. As Shah and Velleman formulate it, the very concept of belief includes a standard of correctness to the effect that a belief is correct if and only if it is true.[11] Indeed, we may imagine something that we know is false, whereas belief aims at the truth. If the activities and productions of the imagination may lead us astray from truth, what is their value in knowledge acquisition? Is there any role for imagination in religious life, which is allegedly concerned with the truth? As the following analysis shows, Richard recognizes these problems but still recommends that religious people should understand the basic functions of imagination, identify the problems it may cause, learn to moderate its activities, and exploit it optimally in spiritual rehearsals. The key is to study the different uses of imagination.

In their discussion of the instructive and transcendent uses of imagination, Kind and Kung similarly distinguish the apparently different ranges of knowledge and imagination by asking how we use imagination and what the actual relation between imagination and reason is. They remark that in contemporary philosophical thought, the transcendent use of imagination has prevailed, and the link with the instructive use has remained vague or non-existent. In order to find compatibility between these apparently contradictory roles of the imagination, they suggest that its expansive powers should be reined in. Imagination can be exploited in these seemingly disparate uses because they do not differ in kind but in degree, based on the degree of constraint on imaginings. The use of transcendental imagination instructively requires that imagination be anchored to the real world.[12] King and Kung write: "When there are constraints for imagination, either architectural constraints or constraints that we are willing to impose and when these constraints ground the imagination in the world in the right way, imagination can help us to discover truths about the real world."[13]

Many authors in the history of philosophy refer to imagination and its different uses within their system of thought, as does Richard, who examines both the instructive and transcendent roles of imagination within a person's spiritual life. The core issue in Richard's spiritual writings concerns the art of

---

[11] Shah, Nishi and J. David Velleman, "Doxastic Deliberation," *The Philosophical Review* 114, no: 4 (2005): 497–534. doi:10.1215/00318108-114-4-497.

[12] Ibid, 16.

[13] Kind and Kung, "Introduction," 2.

contemplation, the clear sight of the mind that directs it first to sensible objects of reality, then through an ordered process ascends to reflect on one's own soul and its structures, and eventually proceeds to understand even the invisible and divine objects. The starting-point of the contemplation is in the real, visible world, which is explored by means of the senses and the imagination. Even though imagination plays a constitutive part in the process of contemplation, Richard also addresses the complications that overly free functioning of the imagination may involve. Hence, by mentioning how the individual should set the limits on the free play of one's imagination, he agrees with Kind and Kung.

Next, I will proceed to examine Richard's account of imagination more closely, exploring how he attempts to address the gap between imagination and reason as well as other uses of the imagination. I will begin by analysing *Benjamin Minor*, one of Richard's best-known works. This treatise's basic objective is to produce an idea of the soul and its operation, which would be as useful as possible for the contemplative life, guiding the students of St. Victor's school in their spiritual exercise and self-reflection. Richard is keen to use the imaginative means within his teaching, and his pedagogical methods serve as an example of the possible instructive and transcendent uses of the imagination.

Benjamin Minor concerns the basics of monastic life and religious matters, extending to analysis of technical questions of the soul and its parts as well. Richard explains his idea of the soul's basic functions to his novices by offering a novel interpretation of the Biblical story of Jacob and his two wives and their handmaids found in Genesis. He suggests that the students should consider their souls as like a growing family, where each member of Jacob's family represents a particular affect or faculty of the soul, or even a combination of the soul's faculties. In Genesis, Jacob begets 12 sons and a daughter altogether with his wives and their handmaids.[14] These children are born in the Bible successively, in a particular order which, as Richard explains, describes how the parts of the soul develop and learn to co-operate with each other. This original literary technique is called personification allegory.

Leah and Rachel, the main wives, are personifications of affectivity and rationality, the two most prominent powers of the soul.[15] Richard describes how Rachel (*ratio*), the wife whom Jacob loves more, is like a beautiful mistress. She represents reason, right doctrine, and teaching, and she meditates, contemplates, and makes distinctions.[16] For reason to operate like this, it needs sense perceptions. The soul is able to approach the invisible, immaterial objects rationally only by studying the various aspects of the world of sensible objects. However, this divide between senses and reason establishes a problem for the

---

[14] Gen. 29–30, 34–35, 49.

[15] *Bm* III, p. 96.3–5.

[16] *Bm* IV, p. 100.24–30.

soul. Richard explains that "The young, beautiful, and sensitive daughter can neither roam the streets nor is the servant allowed to rush into her mistress's private bedroom. Reason (*ratio*) cannot step out; senses (*sensus*) cannot come in."[17] The divide between the visible and invisible world is bridged by imagination (*imaginatio*), because it is the only faculty that can operate between the senses and reason, providing a link between them. Richard writes straightforwardly that "without imagination reason is unable to know anything (*sine imaginatione ratio nichil sciret*)."[18]

Imagination, this link between the senses and reason, is represented by the handmaid called Bilhah. Richard describes imagination as an active and quick ability of the soul that acquires material from outside through the fleshly senses (*extrinsecus haurit per sensus carnis*). It immediately represents this material inwardly (*intus repraesentare*) for the service of reason. Its activity is ceaseless. Even if the operation of the senses fails, the imagination does not stop providing material for reason. For example, when a human being is placed in the dark and is able to see nothing, he can still imagine anything.[19]

While imagination is indispensable for reason, it is not a harmless companion, having its distinctive vices. Thus imagination is sometimes dangerously overactive, producing plenty of unnecessary material for reason to use. Too much pictorial sense-data disturbs reason. Richard warns how Bilhah-imagination is a chatterbox that continually repeats everything that a person has seen or heard, said and done, without the soul actually needing all this material. She maintains the discussion even though nobody listens, which is why she sometimes acts as an aged gossip or senile man.[20] Hence, the soul should be aware of an over-active imagination, making an effort to restrict its activity. Richard's account of imagination is innovative, but the underlying idea is still traditional and much discussed in classical and medieval sources. Imagination is a useful, even crucial ability of the soul, but its activities should be strictly guarded – at least at the beginning of spiritual rehearsal.

A few years after completing this work, Richard wrote a parallel book, which is nowadays known as *Benjamin Major*. In this considerably more wide-ranging speculative treatise, Richard continues to develop his theory of imagination further. While *Benjamin Minor* was aimed at preparing the soul for the contemplation, the highest mental activity, the soul proceeds to contemplation itself in *Benjamin Major*. Addressing the experts in spirituality, Richard explains that six different kinds of contemplation can be distinguished on the basis of the cognitive faculties or their combination that are used (imagination, reason, and understanding). Imagination is actively involved in the first three

---

[17] *Bm* V, p. 102.23–27.
[18] *Bm* V, p. 102.4–7,12–18.
[19] *Bm* V, p. 102.6,12–15,27–30; Bm V, p. 104.31–33.
[20] *Bm* VI, p. 106.11–22, 25–27.

kinds of contemplation.[21] Having accomplished the spiritual rehearsal of *Benjamin Minor*, the moderated and disciplined soul may fully employ the potential of imagination in contemplation – this time without the constant worry of its unwanted or overly active functions.

The importance of imagination for contemplation is evident since the first stages of contemplation are entirely dependent on its functioning. The very first stage of contemplation is said to happen in the imagination and according to the imagination only. The soul examines only sensible things, the impressions of which it has received through the bodily senses. These are forms and images of visible things. Arguments and reasoning do not inform this purely imaginative activity. A new aesthetic function appears alongside imagination as the soul wonders and venerates all the objects examined by the imagination. Richard writes: "Thus, our contemplation is employed in imagination and is formed according to imagination only when we seek nothing by means of argumentation and investigate nothing by means of reasoning, but rather our mind runs freely here and there, wherever wonder moves it in this kind of manifestation."[22]

While the free movement of the imagination is pleasurable and rewarding, the soul should continue to strive upwards within its journey. Richard's psychological innovation is to claim that imagination and reason may together form different modes of collaboration, which employ the full potential of both. In order to proceed to the second kind of imagination, the soul should learn to use imagination and reason simultaneously and in co-operation. The role of imagination as a handmaid of reason becomes more evident. The connection is close: Richard describes how reason leads imagination around and directs it. The second kind of imagination takes place in imagination, but reason informs its operation. While the objects of contemplation are sensible, the soul attends to the rational principles of these objects. The aim of the joint effort is to examine the reason, order, cause, utility, mode, disposition, and effect of any given imaginable object; i.e., to acquire knowledge of the sensible world.[23]

Richard's examination of the second kind of contemplation reveals his interest in natural philosophical speculations. He calls the entire visible reality the machine of the world (*mundana machina*), suggesting that the second kind of contemplation concerns the rational analysis of the reasons for the various phenomena, the disposition of the world, and the powers of the elements. The co-operation between imagination and reason provides access to an understanding of the world and enables natural philosophical investigation.[24] Hence, we rely on the imagination to achieve a scientific understanding of the world.

---

[21] *BM* I, VI, p. 102–108.
[22] *BM* I, VI, p.102.5–21.
[23] *BM* I, VI, p. 104.22–28.
[24] *BM* II, VII, p. 168.10–16.

These descriptions of imagination in *Benjamin Minor* and *Major* exemplify the instructive use of imagination where it allows the individual to know and understand something about the world and its phenomena, aiding rational thinking. Next, we move to examine the possibility of the transcendental use of imagination, describe its basic function, and ask whether it is compatible with the instructive uses of imagination.

Imagination in moral conduct and creation of metaphors

As we have learned from the previous section, reason employs imagination in order to know and has a clear, instructive use. However, Richard sees more potential in imagination, suggesting that people are able to voluntarily direct the imagination and thence produce a special kind of rational imagination. He acknowledges the intentional nature of the imagination, exploring its potential in religious life. Richard's idea of rational imagination allows him to address two major discussions related to imagination, i.e., the role of imagination in moral theology and the use of imagination in creating and understanding religious metaphors, both of which exemplify the transcendent use of the imagination.

In *Benjamin Minor*, Richard explores the story of Jacob and Rachel further by asking why Rachel-reason is infertile and what this means for a religious person. Rachel, reason, passionately desires offspring; i.e., suffers, cries, and experiences pain when attempting to attain wisdom. The desolate Rachel-reason offers her handmaid Bilhah (imagination) to Jacob (the personification of the intellectual soul), so that she can at least have children through her. Bilhah begets two children, who are then adopted by Rachel. This is how the two sons of Bilhah, Dan, and Naphtali, are born. These sons are by the handmaid through birth but by the mistress through adoption. They are born from Bilhah but governed by Rachel. In Richard's psychological schematization, they are typified as two forms of rational imagination.[25]

With the help of this personification allegory, Richard teaches how some acts of the imagination are voluntary, and the individual may guide them at will. Rational imagination operates voluntarily and forms some new images based on bodily sensations. These new images are created by joining, separating, reducing, and enlarging sensible pictures in the mind. Richard writes that one can fabricate something else from what the human being acquires through the bodily senses by imagining. Interestingly, the output may presumably also be something fictional, non-existent, or false. The human being can, for example, form images of gold and a house and connect them as an image of a golden

[25] *Bm* XIII, p. 124.5–7; *Bm* XVI, p. 132.9–10.

house. An animal is not able to do so, but a rational being such as a human can.[26]

As it appears, two forms of rational imagination differ from each other. The first-born son, Dan, is imagination directed by reason. Controlled by reason, it produces new images on the basis of seeing visible objects. The individual uses this kind of rational imagination when, according to the known image of the visible thing, the mind creates some other visible image. Richard straightforwardly adapts rational imagination in the realm of ethics. With the help of imagination, the individual may create morally educational images. Richard writes that good and evil in the world are always mixed, never absolute. However, one can gather from experiences acquired through the external senses what kind of good or evil might be the highest.[27] Hence, the rational imagination enables the individual to create thought experiments about her/himself either in heaven or hell.

Dan-imagination, a kind of lower-order rational imagination, may envisage absolute evil, that is, the future torments of hell. This is an important and useful technique in religious life. By constructing images of hell, the mind guards itself against drifting into shameful thoughts. The individual may punish himself with a series of images of destruction before the impermissible thoughts find time to grow and become indecent desires and sinful acts. The individual does not know where hell is located and exactly what horrors there will be, everyone producing different images according to his own will. [28] People often make decisions via thinking about counterfactuals, or what would happen if things had been different from how they, in fact, are. Imagining the flames of hell does not represent counterfactuals *per se,* since the possible scenario resides in the future. However, the imaging of possible future evil and punishment subjectively, for oneself, is an efficient tool for fighting against sinful thoughts and building one's moral personhood.

While Dan-imagination tries to imagine something absolutely evil, the Naphtali-imagination, second-born son of Bilhah, attempts to imagine a good which can be realized only in the future, i.e., in the life to come in heaven. Again, imagination assists in the reasoning process and thus helps one to proceed from individual images to generalizations through induction; in other words, one is able to construct the image of a perfectly good object on the basis of many fairly good objects.[29] The imagination of future torments, as well as

---

[26] *Bm* XVI, p. 132.9–14.

[27] *Bm* XVI, p. 132.14–29.

[28] *Bm* XVIII, p. 136.18–24; *Bm* XIX, p. 140.13–23.

[29] *Bm* XVIII, p. 138; 148. This technique is similar to Aristotle's idea in *De anima* that the human being is able to make use of concrete images or fantasies in his moral consideration. When the soul chooses between various operations, one can estimate different options and calculate the best possible alternative. See *De anima* 434a5–10.

pleasures based on real-world experiences, is a prime example of the combination of the instructive and transcendent uses of imagination: imagination is anchored to the real world through reason but is free enough to employ its creative capacities.

Rational imagination is essential in religious life since it enables us to instigate the right kinds of emotion, which are necessary in order to guide our moral conduct. However, this idea evokes two questions. First, imagination and belief have a functional difference concerning their characteristic connection with emotions. If someone truly believes that she is in danger, she is afraid, but not if she merely imagines this. While belief evokes genuine emotions toward real entities, imagination does not. The second question concerns the correctness of imaginary scenarios. One may ask how accurately potential rewards and punishments can be described using the imagination since the imaginary expressions do not have a truth-value and are voluntary.

Richard is not worried whether the fictional imaginations of the future are accurate or not. The co-operation between reason and imagination obviously guarantees proper operation, so that both Dan and Naphtali can protect the soul faultlessly. The images they create have enough congruence with reality to function as effective thought experiments on one's future state. Moreover, the descriptions of heaven and hell derive from the authoritative Biblical texts. Dan can show a sufficient number of images of hell and guide the mind to focus on the right thoughts. Naphtali neither resorts to soothing the soul in vain nor allowing wicked people to enjoy false pleasures, attempting to create internal peace between the various thoughts. When Dan threatens, Naphtali will conciliate, rightly calming the soul with the hope of eternal happiness.[30]

Richard is by no means the only theologian who has utilized fearsome images in moral deliberation.[31] The Church Father Augustine of Hippo teaches that the first step to wisdom is to awake the feeling of fear. This is achieved by scaring and wounding oneself in the imagination.[32] Their ideas contrast with Aristotle's account, which differentiates between fantasy (*phantasia*) and belief (*doxa*). Belief is accompanied by a conviction about its truthfulness, and only the conviction stirs feelings such as fear. However, fantasy does not demand truthfulness or necessarily stir up a feeling more than a painting that

---

[30] *Bm* XXXIII, p. 180.5–13.

[31] For references, see Mary Carruthers, *The Craft of Thought: Meditation, Rhetoric, and the Making of Images, 400–1200*. Cambridge Studies in Medieval Literature 34 (Cambridge: Cambridge University Press, 1998), 104, 308.

[32] *De doctrina christiana* 2.7.9. Practising fear was a natural part of both the novices' life as well as the daily spirituality of the more advanced members of the community. Carruthers, *The Craft*, 266.

describes some frightening or encouraging thing.[33] Remarkably, contemporary philosophers are more likely to support the view that imagined content could play a direct role in actual attitudes and behaviour. In affective transmission, an emotional response generated by an imagined situation may limit or guide subsequent behaviour.[34] Moreover, Noël Carroll has suggested that literary thought experiments, characterizations of virtues and vices, in particular, invite us to self-reflection and cultivate our capacity for moral deliberation. Even though these thought experiments are literary productions they can afford knowledge of concepts of virtue, simulate real life, and have argumentative structure.[35]

Richard's allegory has the clear educative aim of cultivating the capacities of the soul through reading. In addition to moral conduct, two forms of rational imagination are essential in analysing religious language. In his examination of Naftali-imagination and images of heaven, Richard proceeds to analyse the function of religious metaphors, how they can be created, and how they should be interpreted. The biblical descriptions of hell can be interpreted literally, but the descriptions of heaven are mostly metaphorical. The activity of rational imagination is a necessary means for a foundational transition from the literal interpretation and the material images of the Bible to the spiritual interpretation of the text.

Richard separates two different techniques that the rational imagination, or Naphtali-imagination, may employ. These are comparison (*comparatio*) of images and translation (*translatio*) of images.[36] Richard's attempt to integrate classical rhetoric as part of his theory of imagination and religious language can be seen by the fact that comparison and translation are both standard rhetorical terms, used already by Quintilian.[37]

Translation is the more demanding act. For Richard, translation is a technique by which the individual can move through the combinations of visible

---

[33] *De anima* 427b15–25. For Aristotle's attempt to define fantasy in relation to sensing, conceptual thinking, and belief, see Victor Caston "Why Aristotle Needs Imagination," *Phronesis* 41, no: 1 (1996): 20–55.

[34] For instance, Gendler has developed a notion of *alief*, an affect-laden and action-generating mental state that differs from belief in a sense that its contents are fictional and they do not carry truth-value. "Alief and Belief," *The Journal of Philosophy* 105, no.10 (2008): 634–663. doi:10.5840/jphil20081051025. Jonathan Gilmore, "Aptness of Emotions for Fictions and Imaginings," *Pacific Philosophical Quarterly* 92, no: 4 (2011): 468–489. doi:10.1111/j.1468-0114.2011.01407.x.

[35] Noël Carroll, "The Wheel of Virtue: Art, Literature, and Moral Knowledge," *The Journal of Aesthetics and Art Criticism* 60, no.1 (2002): 3–26. I wish to thank Ingrid Malm Lindberg for pointing me towards Carroll's interesting suggestions about thought experiments.

[36] *Bm* XXII, p. 148.

[37] See Quintilian's *Institutio oratoria* 8.6.4–9.

images to the signification of an invisible object.[38] As he suggests, rational imagination is actually able to convert almost everything written into spiritual understanding.[39] Richard utilizes the image of light as an example of translation. In Scripture, it has been written that God 'is living in the light which cannot be approached' (I Tim. 6:16). Now the human being can imagine what kind of entity this immaterial light might be. Here one may formulate an analogy: just as the exterior light illuminates the external eyes of the body, so the spiritual light illuminates the eyes of the heart. The exterior light and its relation to outer eyes are a metaphor for the invisible light that enlightens our souls and, in this case, the light signifying God's wisdom.[40]

In *Benjamin Major*'s description of the third kind of contemplation, Richard gives a fuller account of the co-operation between reason and imagination as a means for the spiritual interpretation of the world and the Bible. Unlike the two earlier kinds of contemplation, the third is formed in reason according to imagination. Richard writes that reason draws imagination with it to study higher things. This co-operation between imagination and reason is described as a shared journey during which the imagination rises above itself. Richard even writes that the imagination is the beginning of all argumentation (*omnis ratiocinatio et argumentatio ab imaginatione fundamentum sumit, et firmamentum capit*), calling the imagination a kind of leader of reason, because it represents the external forms of things to reason and leads it to examine the invisible properties of objects.[41]

The third kind of contemplation involves the use of similitudes (*similitudines*). In Richard's scheme, similitude means a specific kind of relation between the sensible object and the invisible object. This relation is asymmetrical, the corporeal similitudes offering a necessary point of departure for knowledge. Richard's asymmetrical epistemology is justified by the Neo-Platonist ontological hierarchy, which considers that the invisible things of creation are seen in the visible world. The corporeal similitudes may be found in the images of visible objects, similitudes which are needed to grasp the qualities of invisible objects. Similitudes can be found everywhere in creation, but they reside above all in Biblical texts.[42] Thus, the third kind of contemplation offers a theoretical framework and justification for the allegorical method of Biblical interpretation since the association between reason and imagination produces a combination of the mind's abilities through which the allegory becomes a meaningful

[38] *Bm* XXII, p. 148.26–28: "Utitur nichilominus, ut dictum est, translatione, quando rerum uisibilium quamlibet descriptionem transfert ad rerum inuisibilium significationem."

[39] *Bm* XXII, p. 150.35–36, 39–43.

[40] *Bm* XXII, pp. 148, 150.28–35. Cf. *Bm* V, p. 102.20–23.

[41] *BM* I, VI, p. 104.43–50.

[42] See the discussion and the references in Palmén, *Imagination*, 177–194.

form of expression. Hence, imagination helps reason to transcend the mere literary level of the text.

Imagination as an image of God's creative act

These examples teach us how simple imagination may link the senses and reason; and how we can combine the abilities of imagination and reason and learn to use rational imagination. It has become evident that imagination is indispensable for our knowledge of the outer world, important for reading and understanding the religious texts and useful for directing our morality through images of heaven and hell. However, can we describe these activities of imagination as creative, or is the imagination just a mimetic capacity, which repeats and remodels the images?

The central role of imagination in creative processes is generally recognized in both everyday speech and theoretical deliberation. Historically, the idea of imagination as a source of aesthetic creation is often traced back to Immanuel Kant, who refers to artistic geniuses as paradigmatic examples of creativity. The possibility of aesthetic judgement requires a special interaction between the powers of imagination and understanding; an interaction that Kant calls free play.[43] As Dustin Stokes puts it, the foundational component in creation is a cognitive manipulation performed by imagination.[44]

In general, Richard is clearly interested in proposing the idea of creative imagination, discussing the issue in several passages of *Benjamin Major*. He calls imagination a creator (*creatrix*).[45] Elsewhere he explains how the rational soul uses the powers of the imagination in order to create fictional places. These worlds of phantasms are voluntary productions; i.e., first, the individual chooses the images appearing and then remodels them according to his will. "When it wishes, does the rational soul not create daily by means of the imagination new heaven and a new earth, and in that phantastical world, as if it were another creator, according to its will, it every hour causes actions and forms creatures of that sort and however great you like?"[46]

---

[43] See Donald W. Crawford's essay "Kant and Creative Imagination" in *Kant's Critique of the Power of Judgment: Critical Essays*, ed., Paul Guyer (Lanham: Rowman & Littlefield, 2003), 143–170.

[44] For a more detailed discussion of the criteria of the role of imagination, see Dustin Stokes, "The Creative Imagination" in *The Philosophy of Creativity: New Essays*, eds., Paul, Elliot Samuel and Scott Barry Kaufman (New York: Oxford University Press, 2014), 157–184.

[45] *BM* III, I, p. 268.20: "Quid hic facit fantasmatum corporalium creatrix, moderatrix, reparatrix imaginatio?"

[46] *BM* III, XXI, p. 334.28–31: "Nonne per imaginationem animus cotidie nouum celum, novam terram cum uoluerit, creat et in illo fantastico mundo quasi alius quidam creator quantaslibet eiusmodi generis creaturas omni hora actitat et pro arbitrio format?" Here

In the last pages of *Benjamin Major*, Richard examines how we, human beings, carry the image and similitude of God within ourselves. This is a standard and much-discussed idea in Christian theological anthropology. Augustine memorably wrote that memory, will, and reason reflect the divine trinity within the human soul. Richard, in turn, writes that humans can draw similitudes (*similitudines rationis*) within themselves from their very own souls, and understand something about the divine nature through analysing these similitudes. He enumerates three properties of the rational soul from which a rationale for similitude (*rationes similitudinis*) can be found. This reason for similitude means similarity between two things and justification of why they are alike. Indeed, the soul may achieve the first reason for similitude by considering its own ability to imagine. Richard asks us to draw an analogy:

> If you marvel how God, the Maker of everything, brought into actuality from nothing at the very beginning of the world so much and so many various species of things just as He willed, think now how easy it is for the human soul to fashion by means of imagination images of things of whatsoever at any hour and to form some unique creatures (*quasi sui generis*), as it were, as often as it wishes, without pre-existing material (*sine preiacenti materia*) and from nothing as it were (*uelud ex nichilo formare*) … In the foregoing you will discover a very remarkable thing: that [God], who is the supreme truth, reserved the truth of things for Himself; but he granted to His image the power of forming images of things at whatever time.[47]

In this connection, Richard outlines a clear parallel between the operation of the human imagination and the creative activity of God. First, he compares various species created by God to individual pictures imagined by the human being. Second, he notes that God creates whatever He wants and whenever He wants to. Similarly, the human being can imagine whatever he wants, whenever he wishes. Third, Richard writes that God creates beings from nothingness (*ex nihilo*) into actuality, whereas the human being creates without the preceding matter (*sine praeiacenti materia*) as it were from nothingness (*velut ex nihilo*).

There is no doubt that Richard utilizes the terminology clearly related to the idea of creation here: the soul creates (*creare*) by means of imagination; in this way, the soul is a kind of a creator (*quasi creator*). The imagination also functions as one of the reasons for similitude to God's creative act. Drawing on this

---

Richard describes the idea of an inner scene of action that imagination produces. In this fantastic world, imagination models various kinds of creatures according to the will of the rational soul, putting them into action to perform.

[47] *BM* IV, XX, p. 452.23–30: "Si miraris quomodo ille omnium opifex Deus tot et tam uarias rerum species prout uoluit in ipso mundi exordio ex nichilo in actum produxit, cogita quam sit humane anime facile omni hora quaslibet rerum figuras per imaginationem fingere, et quasdam quasi sui generis creaturas quoties uoluerit sine preiacenti materia et uelud ex nichilo formare, et incipiet minus esse mirabile quod prius forte uidebatur incredibile. In quo et illud inuenies ualde notabile, quod rerum ueritatem, qui summa ueritas est, reseruauit sibi, rerum uero imagines qualibet hora formandas sue concessit imagini."

last idea, Richard indeed seems to argue that imagination is the very symbol of the divine creativity in the human being. By examining its function, it is possible to understand something about the ways that God creates. This idea is original and thought-provoking, resembling some later accounts of imagination in the Romantic era, such as Samuel Taylor Coleridge's well-known ideas of imagination in his *Biographia Literaria* (1817).[48] The analogy between imagination and God's creative work emphasises the transcendent use of imagination. Moreover, it demonstrates how the imagination not only aids in unravelling the symbols and metaphors but is a symbol in itself.

Conclusion

In the first part of this article, we learned how Richard suggests that imagination is capable of acting as the main link between visible and invisible realities, uniting the body and soul and helping to proceed from the visible things to investigate the invisible things. The ultimate purpose of imagination, however, is to aid the human being to encounter transcendental reality and God.

The second part of the article focused on discussing so-called rational imagination. Initially, Richard was convinced that imagination was able to cooperate with the upper abilities of the soul like reason and understanding, and thence, the soul could produce a more flexible and creative disposition towards the objects of its attention. The combination of imagination and reason allows one to understand and use metaphorical language or invent rhetorical devices within one's speeches. Richard's own literary style and the imaginative use of Biblical texts suggest how Richard understood the ways in which one is able to use biblical and religious language. The means for both creating and explaining symbols is the joint use of imagination and reason.

The third and last section of this article questioned what we can know about imagination through introspection. Like many twelfth-century authors, Richard supports the idea that the individual should know and understand the very structures of one's soul in order to understand something about her creator. Hence, Richard encourages us to reflect on the abilities of our soul, such as imagination. He urges us to ask what the nature of this ability is, how we can use imagination and what the limits of imagination are. This discussion also addressed a significant question about the possible creative acts of imagination, asking whether it can create something completely new without any preceding matter. For Richard, imagination is active in the lowest stages of contemplation, but in the highest levels of spiritual rehearsal, we should study its characteristics and, through understanding its functioning, learn some particular information about the Creator himself.

---

[48] See Coleridge's *Biographia Literaria*, vol I, 13, ed. Adam Roberts (Edinburgh: Edinburgh University Press), 205–206.

These three examination areas have shown that imagination can have multiple functions in medieval philosophical psychology and religious thought. Richard's strong reliance on a Neoplatonist dualist worldview and his presumptions in theological anthropology enable him to give the imagination a prominent role within his thought system, demonstrating how the metaphysical commitments have a clear effect on the accounts of imagination. It also seems that Richard has a personal interest in lively literary expressions and the use of creative interpretations of Biblical stories within his teaching, both of which enforce and motivate him to develop an original and multifaceted theory of imagination further. In sum, Richard's extensive and analytical theory of imagination manifests how imagination can have both instructive and transcendent uses in human life and how these uses may converge in Christian spirituality and the theory of contemplation.

Imagination in a Living Universe: on Bruno's Renaissance Magic

Jonna Bornemark

Introduction

The question of the place of imagination is an important and too often neglected question in Western philosophy. It affects what we think is real, how we understand human thinking in relation to reality, how humans are involved in creating reality, how humans are part of a universe that goes beyond them, and so on. The question about imagination thus relates to many central philosophical questions.

One period of time in western philosophy, where imagination plays a central role, is the renaissance, not least due to its syncretistic and experimental thinking, where for example, magic, Christianity and philosophy were intertwined. We find this among renaisannce thinkers such as Marsilio Ficino, Picco della Mirandola, and Tommaso Campanella. Another central person in this line of thinking is Giordano Bruno (1548-1600). In Bruno, imagination is the prime human faculty and deeply entrenched in the relation between the human being and her world. Hence, I will explore a Bruneian framework of imagination, which includes a metaphysical understanding both of his magical world and of magic as a way to act in the world.

Bruno's thought is elaborated at the intersection between Christian mysticism (but against its passivity), Neo-Platonism (but with an appreciation of the body), early science (but in an enchanted universe), and hermetic magic as he is inspired by Nicholas of Cusa, Plotinus, Copernicus, and Hermes equally. Early on, he was a Dominican monk, and Thomistic Aristotelianism permeates his work and is something he reacted against. In Bruno, there are no distinctions between physics, metaphysics, and religion. His discussions touch upon the physical world as well as upon ideal entities and religious goals. Bruno also lived in an enchanted universe, breathing of vitalism and animism, and life is such a central idea in his work that he tends to see matter itself as being alive.

However, in order to understand Bruno's understanding of imagination, I would claim there is one thinker who is more important than the others, namely Nicholas of Cusa (1401-1464). To some extent, Bruno enters Cusa's epistemology and develops his theory of imagination from there. The relation between Cusa and Bruno also illustrates some central differences between negative theology and magic. Nicholas of Cusa was deeply influenced by the tradition of apophatic mysticism and of Neoplatonic philosophy, but also by Aristotelian scholasticism.

Nicholas of Cusa

Nicholas of Cusa, as well, gives imagination a certain place within human knowledge processes In "*De coniecturis*" Cusa initially places human knowledge between intellectual unity and sensuous otherness, and between these two edge points, tying them together, we find rationality and imagination. These different capabilities are not in conflict with each other, but seems to slide into each other as knowledge is developed. The movement between these capabilities is the movement of the divine as a differentiating and creative power through which knowledge is produced. Cusa calls this differentiating power *non-aliud*, and it keeps together what it at the same time differentiates between.

To be more specific, in one description, knowledge starts in sense perception, but sense perception is not knowledge in itself, and it is limited when it comes to mass, time, gestalt, and space, and therefore imagination is needed. Imagination perceives more than the senses, since it relates to what is not there. Sense perception is thus continued in imagination, which continues the perception of images, but it is also different insofar as it goes beyond the presence of sense perception. Its forms come from within rather than from without.[1] In sense-perception, there are no borders between things; we, therefore, create borders employing imagination, which is connected to meaning/sense (sensui) rather than to sense perception (sensus). An image of that which does not necessarily is there is thus created.[2]

Imagination, in turn, is continued in rationality, which both continues the movement of creativity as its forms come from within rather than from without, but it differs from imagination as it moves toward the field of oppositions, abstractions, and calculations, as the categories of ratio separates themselves from sense perception. The ratio opens up for knowledge as it can understand for example, gravity as such, which neither sense perception nor imagination can do.

The intellect continues the movement of ratio and relates to calculation but focuses on its measures rather than on calculation itself. The intellect thus picks up on the categories, values, and direction of ratio. Where ratio sees "hot" and "cold," and can measure these, the intellect apprehends "temperature." The

---

[1] Nicholas of Cusa, "De coniecturis" [1441] in *Philosophische und theologische Schriften,* edited by Eberhard Döring, translation Anton Scharpff (Wiesbaden: Marix Verlag, 2005), 200-203. English translation; Jasper Hopkins, *On Surmises* (Minneapolis: The Arthur J. Banning Press, 2000).

[2] Nicholas of Cusa, "Idiota de mente" [1450]. English translation Jasper Hopkins, *The Layman on Mind* (Minneapolis: The Arthur J. Banning Press, 1996), 73.

intellect always looks for the categories that bind together what is separated and contrasted against each other in the ratio. This also means that there is a coincidence of opposites (*coincidentia oppositorum*). Finally, the intellect moves to not-knowing. They both share the free movement of not-knowing but are separated as the intellect participates in the creation of new categories and values, while not-knowing does not have such a creative side.

This movement goes in both directions. Something of sense perception moves into imagination, something of imagination into ratio, something of ratio into the intellect, something of the intellect into not-knowing. But also the other way around. The mobility of not-knowing moves into the intellect, abstraction moves from the intellect to ratio, the power to create images moves from ratio to imagination, and the space of images moves from imagination to sense perception.[3]

However, this is not the end of the story. The relation between these different parts of cognition does not only go both ways, but the endpoints also meet each other. The reason is that Cusa's philosophy is firmly based in relation to not-knowing, and not-knowing does not only exist at the end of abstraction, after a motion toward larger and larger categories, finally going beyond categories. Not-knowing also exists in the *minima*, in the smallest, such as specific situations and individuals which goes beyond the generalizations of *ratio*. Thus, it also exists a not-knowing in sense-perception as the senses relate to the specific. But not-knowing always stands in relation to the intellect. Standing in this relation means that the intellect is aware of overflowing horizons, but at this limit, it perceives qualities in the *minima* (we will come back to this).[4]

This is also the reason why the sense perception as a *minima* can never fully be verbalized. Words are always formed through former experiences. But as the minima always have a uniqueness, and thus newness, to it, it can never be fully known through concepts since the latter formulate something that is repeated in our experience. Two situations are never the same in time and position, and therefore, one of them cannot be the measure of the other. Therefore, nothing can be used as a complete measure for something else. Cusa claims that the closer we come to this not-knowing, the closer we come to truth. No

---

[3] Cusa, "De coniecturis", 199-206.

[4] Ibid., 177, Mariano Álvarez-Gómez,"Die lehre vom menschlichen Geist (intellectus/Vernunft) in den Sermones des Nikolaus von Kues," in *Mitteilungen und Forschungsbeiträge der Cusanus-Gesellschaft 31: Die Sermones des Nikolaus von Kues II. Inhaltliche Schwerpunkte. Akten des Symposions in Trier vom 20. bis 22. Oktober 2005*, eds. Klaus Kremer and Klaus Reinhardt (Trier: Paulinus 2006. XXIX, 333), 211-243, 219-220.

knowledge is so precise that an infinitely greater precision would not be possible.[5]

Thus, in the movement between different capacities in "De coniecturis" Cusa puts imagination between sense perception and ratio. Cusa does not discuss this, but I think Bruno picked up on this point and saw a similarity in imagination and the intellect, namely the capacity to have a direction and pick up "whatnesses," what he calls *quidditas*, in relation to horizons of not-knowing.

The capacity to pick up on *quidditas*, i.e., on whatness, qualities, or essences, is namely central to the intellect in Cusa's theory. The stream of experiences is infinite as there is an infinite stream of whatnesses – but whatnesses not yet made into calculable concepts with strict definitions. These *quidditas* are what the ratio has as a starting point when it creates its categories and definitions. But since it is impossible for the human being to experience all *quidditas* at once, that which is different from one point of view becomes similar from another. When we, for example, count trees, we ignore the difference between pine trees and leafy trees, and we draw a line between bush wood and trees and ignore their similarities. Sense perception is multifaceted, but just as when many people speak to you at once, you only understand the one toward which your attention is directed. This directionality is the light of *ratio*, which thereby separates and ties together.[6]

Ratio should thus not be understood as a neutral mirror that reflects an outer world. *Ratio* needs to fixate its categories, definitions, and dichotomies: in order to start calculating one needs to fixate that which is counted. This need for fixation ignores the movement through which the ratio itself is formed. *Ratio* itself cannot perceive new or transformed *quidditas* either. That is one of the tasks of the intellect.

Thereby, the intellect, through its own relation to that which cannot be known, provides the ratio with its founding direction and values. Through the reflection upon the categories and an experience of the limits of knowledge and ratio, *what* is important appears – a human capacity that is lacking or decreased in for example depression. In Cusa, however, this is not connected to imagination.

Cusa also discusses the role of images. This discussion takes place in an apophatic tradition where God cannot be known, and our most true relation to God is not-knowing. God provides the formation of everything but has no

---

[5] Nicholas Cusanus, „De docta ignorantia" [1440] in *Philosophische und theologische Schriften,* 52-63, 85-86, 130. English translation; Jasper Hopkins, *On Learned Ignorance* (Minneapolis: The Arthur J. Banning Press, 1981).

[6] Nicholas of Cusa, "De quaerendo Deum" [1445], in *Philosophische und theologische Schriften*, 214. English translation; Jasper Hopkins, *On Seeking God* (Minneapolis: The Arthur J. Banning Press, 1994).

specific form in Godself. But this does not stop humans from trying to relate to the divine by the means available to them. Humans continue to provide God with names and make images of "God," even if none is fully correct.[7] This situation results in a complicated relationship to images. They seem both to be needed in human knowledge and to be something that the intellect and *ratio* can go beyond.[8] He is also attacked from opposite directions on this question. Johannes Wenck, a scholastic theologian, accused him of collapsing every distinction and believing in the possibility of moving beyond images. On the other hand, Dominican monks accused him of putting too much emphasis on sensible images instead of focusing on affections beyond images.[9]

This position also places Cusa in a quite unique position regarding the problem of universals and the medieval battle between nominalists and realists. In this combat, the basic question is if universals, i.e., those words that apply to many objects such as "blue" and "free," exist on their own or only in singular objects. The main positions were on one side the realist or Platonist position which claimed that the universals existed beyond words and on their own and that human knowledge picks up these universals. On the other side were the nominalists who claimed that the universals only are fabrications without any actual existence.

Cusa's position in this combat was neither of the above. He claimed that the only thing that has true reality is the concrete universe and its individuals, things, etc. The universals do not exist beyond these, but they do exist within them. The universe only exists concretely, in its actualization, just as a line and a surface does not exist without a body. The line exists on its own only through abstraction from the body, and this abstraction is the work of the ratio. Our abstractions are intellectual images with their starting point in similarities found in many things. This means that the abstractions are there in the concrete things, or the basis for the abstraction is there, but the universals are formed through the abstractions. They do not exist beyond them.[10] Cusa thus argues that words never are precise; they are not the essences of the concrete things. They arise through intellectual reflection.[11]

In Cusa, the intellect picks up *quidditas*, for example, universals, that exist within the concrete world, and in order to make them into categories of the ratio, categories that can be counted, there needs to be clear definitions and differences – and these are also produced by abstractions. A more thorough

---

[7] Cusa, "De docta ignorantia", 74-76, 91.

[8] Ibid., 149.

[9] K. Meredith Ziebart, *Nicolaus Cusanus on Faith and the Intellect:* A *Case Study in 15th-Century Fides-Ratio Controversy* (Boston: Brill, 2013), 64-72, 138, 164.

[10] Cusa, "De docta ignorantia", 100-102.

[11] Nicholas of Cusa, De venatione sapientiae, [1463] in *Philosophische und theologische Schriften*, 383.

discussion on the role of imagination might be helpful at this point. Cusa connects imagination to images as variations of sense perception but does not really connect it to the power of formation. At the end of the day, the most important knowledge is to be found in abstractions and in not-knowing. He continues an apophatic tradition where images tend to be part of decay. Bruno provides us with an alternative to this evaluation of images and offers a different understanding of the role that imagination plays in both knowledge processes and life processes.

Giordano Bruno

Self-forming matter

Bruno makes an important distinction between principle and cause. A cause affects something from without. The cause and that which is affected are two different things. In contrast to a cause, a principle moves something already existing from within or contributes to the creation of a thing and remains within it.[12] God can be understood from both these aspects, both as external to the beings, a demiurge or creating God, and as the internal principle in pantheistic or panentheistic conceptions of God. We could even understand the concept of an outer cause as connected to a theological idea of a demiurge God, and to science where natural laws are understood as something beyond matter as a similar idea: thinking through and by means of causes.

Even if Bruno acknowledges the need for both thinking by means of causes and of principles in metaphysical questions, he leans toward a thinking through principles. Hence, he is against ideas about God as something outside of the creation, or as conceived by mechanistic science. He is instead interested in matter as something self-forming, governed by its inner principles. Matter is, in his conception, simply the *taking form* of being and life. Matter is never without form and is in itself the *capacity to exist*. Matter is also potency in its constant change of forms. It is the receiver of forms, but the forms do not exist somewhere else beyond matter, rather "all the forms together must be taken merely as various dispositions of matter, which come and go and cease and renew themselves."[13] At this point, it is easy to see the influence of Cusa. The forms are both universals as they can come and go, but also always unique *minimas* as they are played out in matter. As in Cusa, however, the universals do not exist beyond matter.

In this way, matter tends to include all the other concepts: intellect, form, idea, etc. This tendency is explicitly stated in the dialogue:

---

[12] Giordano Bruno, *De la causa, principio et uno* [1583]. English translation; Sidney Greenberg, "Cause, Principle and Unity," in *The Infinite in Giordano Bruno: With a Translation of his Dialogue Concerning the Cause, Principle, and One* (New York: King's Crown Press, 1950), 110-111, 20.

[13] Ibid., 134.

- Why do you wish that it includes all, rather than that it excludes all?

- Because it does not come to receive the dimensions from without, but sends them out from and casts them out as from her womb"[14]

Matter is a female principle in the western tradition, in contrast to form that is understood as male, and it is this gendered tradition that Bruno plays with here. The femininity of matter becomes more and more explicit as it also becomes more and more active, and no longer a pure potency, as it sends forth the forms from herself.[15] It is also explicit from the start of the dialogue that the discussion on matter is a discussion on the female (maybe not as women and sex, but rather as a principle, and thus as gender).[16]

There is here a feminine matter with the power to take on forms, and the discussion on universals suddenly becomes a discussion on the role of men: Are they lovers that come and go, or are they superfluous as the forms rather are born from within matter in a non-sexual reproduction?

As this self-forming matter tends to include all other concepts, it is also a name on God. The idea of self-forming matter includes an intimate connection between all beings. This connection is rooted in the relation between finite beings, the infinite numbers of finite beings, and the infinite as a constant flow of finite beings. God here is infinity, as a perpetually giving birth and infinite form-taking.

Creativity is the life-nerve of this form-taking as its essence is the birth of forms; forms that are related but do not connect as model and image.

To summarize:

- Nature is an infinite series of finite beings.
- Matter is constant concretisation.
- God is the constant movement of matter. A pure giving, which never can be an object to knowledge as it does not have a specific form itself.

Ideation and universals

So, how should we understand thinking and ideas concerning such a self-forming matter? Thinking is clearly not another sphere outside of matter. It takes place within matter and influences it, just like other kinds of movements in matter influence thinking. Ideas are a different kind of concretisation. But ideas are also always connected to forms of matter. Today we might call such a thought contextualization or perspectiveness. But this does not help us understand what thinking and ideas are in a universe where everything is form-taking matter.

---

[14] Ibid., 153.

[15] Ibid., 153.

[16] Ibid., 103-108.

Maybe one important clue here is that matter in Bruno's conception is movement. The basic substance here is not passive *res extensa*, but movement. This movement that constantly takes form can also, in a second step, turn back to itself. It can relate to itself, creating a layer of perception, consciousness, thinking, and ideas. These are thus part of the same movement as the extension, continuing the same movement. Matter thus holds the possibility of consciousness within itself, as consciousness always is connected to matter, too. The human body is thus both extended matter with a specific form, always continuing to take form, and a soul, i.e., a form with self-consciousness, in the capacity of matter to turn back to itself. One movement, taking two shapes.

Thinking is an individual consciousness that arises and perishes, just like a form in matter arises and sooner or later willperish. But this individual thinking is only one of the avatars of consciousness. Other forms are ideas and universals etc., which live their lives across consciousnesses; i.e., ideas are not independent of individual consciousnesses, but can be independent of specific individual consciousnesses. They cannot be reduced to individual consciousness, pretty much as an individual consciousness is not independent of an extended body but cannot be reduced to one either. The well-known Bruno scholar Frances Yates points out that, in *De umbris idearum*, ideas are magical or astral images.[17] The world is only a world to live in through ideas organizing it. The idea of "life" is, for example, a concept through which we experience the world. We live in a world of meaning. It is the living capacity of the intellect to infuse words with power and thus with meaning. These ideas exceed the individual. In short, individuals live within ideas rather than ideas exist within individuals. Ideas are also a gathering of earlier experiences and are in that way a kind of memory. We live in this memory, and it makes our perception comprehensible, but it is also larger than any perception – just as the perceptions, as *minimas* are larger than any idea and even larger than a "full memory." These ideas thus exceed humans, but humans connect to them using images.[18]

Individuals are here also bound together in the self-forming matter, whose movement Bruno understands as the soul of the world. Just as one's living in the human body causes vision in the eyes, hearing in the ears, or taste in the mouth, Bruno claims that the soul of the world produces different subjects and

---

[17] Frances Yates, *Giordano Bruno and the Hermetic Tradition* [1964] (London: Routledge, 1978), 290.

[18] For a discussion on a Brunian art of memory and a Deleuzian understanding of memory see Jonna Bornemark, "Giordano Bruno's Mnemonics: A Deleuzian reading," in *Monument and Memory*, eds. Jonna Bornemark, Mattias Martinson and Jayne Svenungsson, (Zürich: LIT Verlag, 2015).

different actions. Vision can only immediately and without motion grasp what is distant since it belongs to an outspread soul.[19]

This is also possible only as everything is connected to everything else in the form-taking matter. There is always an opening toward the other. The universe as an extension is thus not a container of individual beings, but an interval and space as everything moves within and through the moving efficient cause and principle.[20] The position of everything can only be defined in relation to another object. On this point, Bruno also connects to Cusa as the idea of coincidence of opposites becomes important here. The coinciding of opposites means here that each thing is within every other; they only exist in relation to each other, in similarity and dissimilarity, pretty much as in the logic of non-aliud. This is also why we can understand the world since the world is in us and we are in the world as a nesting micro- and macrocosmic structure. Therefore, to understand is to distinguish without separating. Ideation and universals pick up on the similarities in the moving forms, they exist, but nothing exists independently.

Human beings

The human being is in this way a part of a concretisation and a continuation of the "world soul" or God. Every species is thus an arrest of movement. But this concretisation is not a fall or even subordinated to the divine. There is no reaching toward a hidden beyond in not-knowing, as in Cusa. There is room for an epistemological transcendence, the movement as such, what can be called "God" or "world soul," which is always larger than the intellect and thus incomprehensible. But this infinity of the divine has two surprising consequences. One result is that this not-knowing is not an end to knowledge but a possibility to move. The other is that human understanding can always be greater than it is, whereas God cannot be greater than God already is.[21] Furthermore, the human intellect, in its infinite creativity, takes on the infinite act, whereas the absolute act, God, is immovable and thus betrays its constant creativity. God, as the constant movement of the self-forming matter, is *continually* moving, i.e., stands as always the same. On the other hand, humans are born and thus finite, but they are born as always giving birth to understanding and new forms. As giving birth, it can mirror the continual changing and thus the pure act, but it cannot give birth to this standing. However, this is not a loss but rather a mad overcoming of the position of God. This standing of God is not what should or ever could be comprehended; exactly on this point, the

---

[19] Giordano Bruno. "De magia" [1588]. English translation; Robert de Lucca and Richard J. Blackwell, "On Magic," in *Cause, Principle and Unity* (Cambridge: Cambridge University Press, 1998), 111-112.

[20] Bruno, "Cause, Principle and Unity," 164.

[21] Ibid., 141.

human intellect should embrace its own creativity and become a *magus*, i.e., someone who continues the creating movement of which we all are made. The human being is thus finite creativity.[22]

All beings are here part of the same movement. Life and reality are movements of self-forming matter. Life is taking shape as me right now, right here. This might sound too vitalistic and too romantic to many contemporary readers, yet it is not far from many contemporary experiences. Let me take but one example. In giving birth, many women testify to how the power of labour is not theirs to own and control but comes from somewhere beyond them. In labour, the woman needs to follow the waves of labour pains and work with these. She needs to follow them and direct them, breathe through them when it goes too fast, and push with them when the time is right. The labour pains go through her and most often results in a new life. A life separated from hers and yet intimately connected. In labour, the birth-giver might also feel connected to generations of women giving birth in a chain of lifeforms.

This movement is a specific kind of movement and action. It is not the action of an autonomous individual with free will, and thus a cogito separated from *res extensa*. This freedom is freedom from within. As such, it breaks the borders between passivity and activity thought of as an either/or. In labour, the women receive the labour pain as waves from beyond her agency. She is, in a way, passive in relation to these. But she cannot stay passive; the labour pain demands activity. To go against the labour pain, to try to escape them or panic, will make the birth harder. But this activity receives all its powers from beyond itself. In breathing through the labour pain or pushing with them, the person giving birth is neither passive nor active; she is *pactive*.[23] She continues the wave that comes from beyond and gives it a direction.

Giordano Bruno's understanding of matter is aligned with such a pactive movement. Matter as the capacity to be formed and form is traditionally an activity. "Form-taking matter" thus combine activity and passivity. But in his emphasis on movement, passivity and activity are connected in a more intimate way, which also becomes explicit when it comes to living beings. To begin with, no living being has formed itself. We are born in a certain shape, at a specific place, in a specific time – we are passive in regard to these presuppositions, but to be alive means to continue a chain of lives, to "take on" the possibility to act and think and in this way making the wave of life, or the form-taking matter, into a "me." This means that the creativity of the form-taking

---

[22] Ibid., 139-141, 17.

[23] Pactivity is a concept I have invented, see for example Jonna Bornemark, "Life beyond Individuality: A-subjective Experience in Pregnancy," in *Phenomenology of Pregnancy*, eds. Jonna Bornemark and Nicholas Smith (Huddinge: Södertörn University, *Södertörn Philosophical Studies 18*, 2016), 268-270.

matter is continued in the actions of the human being. And it means that pactivity is the structure of life.

Magic

Taking part in this movement, pactively continuing it as human beings means to act. It means that the divine direction does not aim toward a not-knowing as striving beyond the world. Not-knowing instead continually opens up a space for action. The central not-knowing thus lies in the minima rather than in the maxima. This is the move from negative theology to magic. The magician is also, in Bruno's definition, "a wise man who has the power to act."[24] The magician is part of the living universe and forms it according to its desires and values, and thus through the *quidditas* that are picked up from this position. As a living being with a certain form, the magician wants to maintain its form and continue its desired direction. The magician, therefore, manipulates parts of the living universe by, for example, evoking its desires to move in a certain direction. And since every being contains an opening to everything else, the magus can entice the desired form into existence. The matter is the womb of any form and continually changes form. This changing of form is what the magus wishes to be active in. Magic includes understanding the intertwinement of beings and the different expressions of one and the same, as well as being an active and acting part of the intertwinement and its expressions. Magic is the insight into the natural connections of things.[25]

Magic is also a sensitivity to the minima, which can never fully be exhausted. Bruno writes: "But if the same figure comes exactly, It does not run in the same numbers or in one colour; Let a place's structure, the situation of its junction vary its shape, Assisting the change according to its multiple conditions."[26] At this point, there is a possibility to be sensitive to the minima of "the same thing." If we look close enough, it never comes back in exactly the same figure. Magic, therefore, needs a sensitivity to the minima: "not all things are influenced by everything else, and not all effects happen to everything in the same way."[27] Just as different harmonies bind different persons, different magicians bind different spirits.[28]

The practice of magic is a practice of bonding and of binding together in order to influence. Binding is in a way a practice of ideation, but an ideation that takes place within, rather than outside the concrete world. It uses connections and similarities in order to form new shapes. And it is a pactive movement

[24] Bruno, "On Magic," 107.

[25] Ibid., 90.

[26] Bruno, *On the Composition of Images Signs and Ideas*, 47.

[27] Bruno "On Magic," 134.

[28] Ibid., 135.

as it gets its power from beyond itself, takes these over, and continues its own forms and desires.

The pactivity of binding is only possible through the means of imagination. In binding, the magician forms *what does not already exist* but not from a vacuum. Instead, it binds things together in new ways. It lets matter and ideas take new forms. Imagination is thus not to make things up from nowhere. It is taking part in the movement of self-forming matter. Imagination is the capacity to throw new patterns before oneself, from which a binding pattern then can follow. Binding things is possible because everything contains everything else, i.e., to transform the horse into a unicorn is only possible because the horse already has a part in the idea of a narwhal; they both come from the same self-forming matter. In this way, binding creates a gestalt that did not exist before, with a starting point in existing patterns and individuals.[29]

Let me be a bit more specific, though. What does this practice look like? To begin with, binding demands attentiveness to what lets itself be bound and how. The magician needs to listen to the *minima*, the unique situation and constellation that make up a certain individual. This also includes a double bind between the binder and bound. The binder (the magician) first needs to be bound him/herself in order to want to bind. It also means that we are different in this binding. Some things are easier to pull forth than others, and one binder binds some things easier than another binder. Yet, as everything is connected to everything, anything can be bound – it is just more or less difficult.[30]

Binding is not easy, and to create new constellations also always excludes others and those that existed before. Within the movement of matter is also a conservative tendency to remain the same. Thus, there is a force that stands against the continual movement, and that is the power to preserve the form that is present in each individual. This is present in the stone's hardness but also finds a more intense form in living beings as the whole movement of an individual life is to continue and uphold its form.

This is also the starting point of bad magic. The desire to keep the present forms is also part of the binder's own motivation. The magician also wants to keep its own form and its beloved form. It can lead to evil magic, which at its kernel is motivated by a desire to freeze the world, hindering flux. Good magic, on the other hand, would then include one's willingness to be transformed.[31]

Bruno points to different binding practices. Binding can, for example, take place through arguments. Arguments become stronger if the binder him/herself

---

[29] Giordano Bruno. "A general Account of Bonding," in *Cause, Principle and Unity* (Cambridge: Cambridge University Press, 1998), 145-176.

[30] Ibid., 151-152.

[31] Bruno, "On Magic," 107-115. See also my interpretation of this in "Matter, Magic, and Madness" in *Madness, Religion, and the Limits of Reason* (Huddinge: Södertörn University, Södertörn Philosophical Studies 16, 2015), 114.

is bound by the argument. It also binds stronger if the binder picks up on what the person to be bound already accepts. In this way, the binder makes the other person see a slightly new constellation in repetition with a difference.

Binding also takes place through affects. For example, in love, the binder is already bound by the one (s)he loves and wants to bind the loved one to him/herself. The task is here to make the other person see a new constellation of "us." In a similar way, binding takes place through habits. There already exist habits that we are bound by, and the binder draws them in a different direction. Habits are part of the counterforce to the constant movement and create stability in the world. In relation to ideas or God that move through individual consciousnesses, they bind us (or even play with us), just as we can bind and use them.[32]

For binding to take place, there is one active ingredient that is the source of all bounds, and that is love or desire. Love both make everything endure (for a while) and lets the new come. Love makes the living detour from themselves. It ties the world together and opens up certain connections. It is paradoxical as it makes us want to be where we are and have what we have, but at the same time, be everywhere and have what we miss.

It is the affirmation of love and desire that directs the imagination. And the other way around, only through imagination, the possibility for the world to be different, can there be love. Imaginations are not bound by the present constellation and are the foundation for the freedom to move and shape a possible future. Imagination opens up love, and love provides imagination with direction. Rationalization, however, comes after both love and imagination.

Images

Through binding new patterns and new constellations are created, and images play an important part in this. Images are in Bruno kinds of shadows of ideas, but as noted above, these ideas do not exist somewhere else, but they move around in the concrete as avatars of consciousness. In *On the Composition of Images, Signs and Ideas,* images stand at the centre, and Bruno states that our intellect only sees through images, shapes, likeness, and signs. Perception and understanding thus come forth through images.[33]

We have a pactive relation to images as they move around; we inherit images, live in and with them, perceive through them, and shape and re-create them. Images are therefore described as vestiges that functions as a starting-

---

[32] Ibid. 173-174.

[33] Giordano Bruno, *De imaginum, signorum et idearum compositione* [1591]. English translation; Charles Doria, ed. Dick Higgins *On the Composition of Images Signs and Ideas* (New York: Willis, Locker & Owens, 1991).

and end-point in perception.[34] The images of perception should here not be understood according to a theory of correspondence, as a copy of an object; rather, it is "the world made picture," as a contemporary scholar has put it.[35] This means that the world flows in its form-taking, is picked up by the experiencing person and pactively received as images. The images are not only there for us to adopt or contemplate; they demand the soul to be active in perception and thinking, and this activity is what Bruno calls imagination.

Imagination here turns out to be central to perception, understanding, and action as it is intimately connected to sense-making. It inherits some central tenets of Cusa's understanding of the intellect as a picking up on the *quidditas* that are of greatest importance in a specific situation. As we have seen, this picking up means to connect to something that goes beyond the individual and overflows every knowledge, but at the same time, this picking up has a creative feature, a making of images in perception and understanding. A making that does not stay at a theoretical level but also makes action possible as it guides our actions through which we continue the transformation of the world.

Imagination is, therefore, by Bruno understood as the most general sense organ and prime body of the soul, and he even calls it the sense of senses. Other senses such as hearing, sight, etc., are sense administrating, and as such, always relating to imagination as the common sense.

> All the while, this inner sense [imagination] remains intact in all its parts; for it hears with the whole spirit and sees with the whole, whence it shares some things with some, and others with the rest of the senses, and, as it were, radiates and casts innumerable lines from a single center out to the fullness of its circumference, lines which go out from there as if from a common root, and go back into it as if participating in the eternal, where for the most part we live; an indivisible unit, it creates and receives all the senses that there are.[36]

Imagination is both receiving and creating, and thus pactive. As such, imagination is the central human capacity, it puts us in contact with ideas carrying earlier experiences, i.e., with memory. Affections are also an important part of this capacity, since affections such as anger, greed, love, hate, fear, hope, joy, sorrow, and astonishment open up the memories present in ideas and give us access to them.[37]

Thus, human knowledge and action are not rooted in a capacity to correctly represent the world beyond, but to a certain kind of creativity and activity in relation to it. Human knowledge and action continue the movement of the universe.

---

[34] Giordano Bruno, *De umbris idearum* [1582]. English translation; Scott Gosnell, *On the Shadows of Ideas* (Port: Huginn, Muninn & co, 2013), 28.
[35] Alia Al-Saji, "The Memory of Another Past: Bergson, Deleuze, and a New Theory of Time," Continental Philosophy Review, 37:2 (2004), 203-239, 220.
[36] Bruno, *On the Shadows of Ideas*, 50.
[37] Ibid., 85.

Conclusion

If the relation between man and his universe, between understanding and matter, is often understood as a relation of rationality, correspondence, and representation, Giordano Bruno provides us with an alternative where imagination stands at the centre.

Bruno inherited from Nicholas of Cusa an understanding of an overflowing world, an appraisal of the concrete without underestimating the power of abstractions and images. Cusa defends a position in the medieval problem of universals, where he rejects both a realist position and a nominalist position, and instead shows how abstractions and images are formed (or in a more Bruneian languish, come alive) with starting-point in similarities in the concrete. These similarities do exist, but they are picked up and isolated through conceptualization. Cusa does not understand this as the work of imagination and gives imagination a limited role. Bruno agrees with Cusa on these points, but in a *non-aliud* movement, he also develops it into a magical materialism where imagination plays a crucial part.

Bruno describes matter as a movement guided by its own inner principles. Matter is self-forming and continually takes on new forms. As this movement of matter also can turn back upon itself, consciousness, perceptions, abstractions, images, and ideas are born. Such earlier ideations move around in the world which human individuals are born into. Imagination is the way the human being as a conscious creature is part of the self-forming matter. She is basically a *magus* who pactively continues a stream of formtaking. She forms the world, although not as an external cause, but as a part of it. She picks up on earlier forms, as she is also formed by them, and creatively gives them new shapes. She picks up *quidditas* and gives them distinctiveness and direction. The creativity of the universe that continually finds new forms thus continues in the imagination of human beings.

Imagination and the Origins of Religion in Thomas Hobbes's *Leviathan*

Or why the Sovereign must be Visible

Esben Korsgaard Rasmussen

Introduction

Just from looking at the frontispiece of Thomas Hobbes's *Leviathan,* we are cautioned that the doctrine contained within does not exclusively pertain to reason. The famous image of the sovereign state's imposing figure points to the fact that political power essentially involves an *aesthetic* dimension. It is the theoretical underpinnings of this aesthetic dimension of Hobbes's political doctrine that I shall explore in the present article.[1]

In particular, I shall attempt to show that the need for political power to appear in a specific way is primarily determined by Hobbes's conception of the origins of religion. According to Hobbes, religion is a natural phenomenon with roots in human finitude. Consequent to this finitude, human life is marked by an anxious desire to stay alive that translates into a specific structure of thought and action. This structure is, in turn, determined by a system of *imaginary representations*. The fact that these representations are "imaginary" does not, however, imply that they are somehow not real. Rather, it implies that they have their root in the faculty of imagination understood as a fundamental human capacity of relating to and understanding one's environment. Yet, because these representations intimately structure human life, they have an inherent potential for conflict. Insofar as they act as a response to the desire to stay alive, they concern the very existence of man. Divergence will thus tend to produce deadly strife – a fact well established by the religious wars following the reformation. Hence, I ultimately argue that Hobbes's sovereign state and its grand figure can be seen as an effort to aesthetically reform divergent systems of *religious imaginary representations.*

In the first part of this article, I sketch out Hobbes's concept of the imagination. In particular, I shall explore the way imagination relates to sensation, passion, and what Hobbes calls "mental discourse." The latter is the pre-linguistic structure of human thought and is essentially generated by the way our bodies

---

[1] I will not deal explicitly with the frontispiece. See, however, Horst Bredekamp, *Thomas Hobbes – Der Leviathan: Das Urbild des modernen Staates und seine Gegenbilder. 1651-2011* (Berlin, Boston: De Gruyter 2020).

interact with those outside us. This interaction is, in turn, determined by our fundamental desire to stay alive.

In the second part, I proceed to a closer examination of how this desire leads to a never-ending search for power, which acts as the root of a complex system of social stratification rendered manifest by a set of shared imaginary representations.

In the next section, I will attempt to show that religion, according to Hobbes, must be considered as a specific, but historically dominant, case of such social stratification. It is ultimately the natural desire to stay alive that prompts humans to create imaginary representations of divine powers that are thought to aid them in their endeavours. But as these powers are imagined to be invisible, visible mediation by way of a common set of practices, rituals, and signs becomes an urgent need in order to appease the fundamental human uncertainty. This is where religious institutions come into the picture.

Finally, I shall briefly elucidate the role that the visible figure of the sovereign plays in relation to the imaginary representations embodied by religious institutions. In the guise of a conclusion, I will thus attempt to answer the question stated as the subtitle of this article: why must the sovereign be visible?

Hobbes on the Imagination

In the second chapter of *Leviathan,* Hobbes defines imagination as "nothing but *decaying sense.*"[2] On the face of it, this definition is in complete accordance with Aristotle's definition in his *Rhetorics.*[3] It does, however, involve at least one major difference. For Aristotle and a large strand of the Scholastics, sensation is a question of receiving so-called *species* from things outside the soul.[4] As these species are formally identical both within and outside the soul, they assure that what we sense is indeed the existing world and not just a figment of the mind. For Hobbes, on the other hand, sensation is a purely mechanical process. Ultimately, it is nothing but matter in motion:

---

[2] Hobbes, *Leviathan,* 26. Though with some variation, Hobbes's definition of imagination is comparable across his different works. See Thomas Hobbes, *The Elements of Law,* ed. Ferdinand Tönnies (London: Frank Cass and Company, 1969), 8; Thomas Hobbes, *De Corpore. Elementorum philosophiae sectio prima,* ed. Karl Schuhmann (Paris: Librairie philosophique J. Vrin, 1999), 272; Thomas Hobbes, *Critique du* De mundo *de Thomas White,* ed. Jean Jacquot and Harold Whitmore Jones (Paris: Librairie philosophique J. Vrin, 1973), 350-351.

[3] Aristotle, *Ars rhetorica,* ed. W.D. Ross (Oxford: Clarendon Press, 1959), 1370a28.

[4] For the *locus classicus* concerning the need of *species*, see Aristotle, *De anima,* ed. W.D. Ross (Oxford: Clarendon Press, 1963), 431b29. As it is not the stone itself that is in the mind when we perceive it, it must be something else originating from that stone. That something is the *species* or εἶδος. For Thomas Aquinas's account of *species,* see Thomas Aquinas, *Summa Theologica,* ed. Leonina (Bologna: Edizioni Studio Domenicano, 2014), I, q. 78, a. 3. Here, Aquinas explicitly denies that sensation can be caused by mechanical causation.

> The cause of Sense, is the Externall Body, or Object, which presseth the organ proper to each sense (...) which pressure, by the mediation of Nerves, and other strings, and membranes of the body, continued inwards to the Brain, and Heart, causeth there a resistance, or counter-pressure, or endeavour of the heart, to deliver it self: which endeavour because *Outward,* seemeth to be some matter without. And this *seeming,* or *fancy,* is that which men call *Sense.*[5]

Sensation is a mere "seeming" exactly because it is only the appearance or representation of something that exists outside the mind and not the reception of a *species,* formally identical in both the perceiver and the perceived object.

Although the representation of the cause that exerts pressure on the sensorial organs needs not resemble that cause itself, sensation, however, still needs the presence of an external body. It is in this regard that it differs from imagination. In sensation, the object that moves our organs is present, in imagination, it is absent.[6] Again, the reason why we retain a representation of an object even when it is no longer present is not because a *species* remains in our mind. Rather, we retain such a representation due to the nature of local motion, or, to be more precise, due to the principle of *inertia.*[7] This principle states that "what is moved is understood to be always moved unless there is something else exterior to it because of which it comes to [be at] rest."[8] Applied to the imagination, this means that motion originally caused by the object of sense remains in the perceiving body unless something else stops it. This is why sensation only decays when new sensations cause motions that hinder the original motion:

> [A]ny object being removed from our eyes, though the impression it made in us remain; yet other objects more present succeeding, and working on us, the Imagination of the past is obscured, and made weak.[9]

Imagination is thus appearance remaining of an original sensation but made weak by subsequent sensation constituted by new motions in the body of the perceiver.

This continuity of motion, or, more accurately, the "coherence of matter" where such motion is produced, has further implications for Hobbes. For not only does the original motion never cease unless stopped by something else, it also ties together different motions first produced in sense. If I have repeatedly experienced one ball hitting another causing it to move, these two events will

---

[5] Hobbes, *Leviathan,* 22.

[6] Ibid., 26.

[7] For the implications of Hobbes's adaptation of the principle of inertia, see Thomas Sprangens, *The Politics of Motion. The World of Thomas Hobbes* (London: Croom Helm, 1973), 63-75.

[8] Hobbes, *De corpore,* 91: "quod movetur, semper moveri intelligitur, nisi aliud sit extra ipsum, propter quod quiescit." See as well Hobbes, *Leviathan,* 26.

[9] Hobbes, *Leviathan,* 28.

remain connected in my mind. Although presently I only see one of the events, my mind will proceed to the thought of the other because the motions caused by the previously experienced connection are continuous. Every sensation has consequently tied to it a series of past sensations retained by the imagination. These series constitute what Hobbes calls "the Consequence or TRAYNE of Imaginations."[10] Now, because these series or "trains" multiply as our experience increases, the connection among their different elements is never completely stable: "...because in sense, to one and the same thing perceived, sometimes one thing, sometimes another succeedeth, it comes to passe in time, that in the Imagining of any thing, there is no certainty what we shall Imagine next."[11]

While the determination of the specific series of imaginations seems to be random,[12] they are, however, always regulated. The structuring principle of any given "mental discourse" might not be perceptible to the imagining subject, but that does not exclude the fact that such a principle does indeed exist. As Hobbes explains: "When a man thinketh on any thing whatsoever, His next Thought after is not altogether so casuall as it seems to be."[13] Though Hobbes subsequently distinguishes between a "regulated" and an "unregulated" train of thoughts, the latter is not simply derived of coherence. Rather, the principle behind that coherence remains imperceptible to the imagining subject. To understand what might be the structuring principle behind this coherence, we need to take a closer look at Hobbes's understanding of sensation and its relation to the passions.

As we have already seen, sensation is produced by an exterior motion against our sensorial organ(s). Yet, for there to be sensation, a certain counter-motion must be produced. In *Leviathan,* that counter-motion stems from the heart.[14] This is of crucial importance. For not only is the heart the "origin of all

---

[10] Ibid., 38. In fact, in *De corpore* Hobbes denies that a single sensation is ever to be found *in rerum natura.* See Hobbes, *De Corpore,* 271.

[11] Ibid., 38.

[12] At one time Hobbes thought they might be, see Hobbes, *Elements,* 13: "The succession of conceptions in the mind (...) may be casual and incoherent (...) and it may be orderly." In the same direction, see Arnaud Milanese, "Le désir de pouvoirs chez Hobbes: De l'ontologie à l'anthropologie," *Klesis – Revue Philosophique* 12 (2009), 8-11. Although I generally agree with his line of interpretation, Douglass fails to consider the difference between the treatment of the imagination and its relation to "mental discourse" in the *Elements of Law* and *Leviathan.* See Robin Douglass, "The Body Politic "is a fictitious body." Hobbes on Imagination and Fiction," *Hobbes Studies* 27 (2014): 128-133.

[13] Hobbes, *Leviathan,* 38.

[14] Ibid., 22. This is the case in all works posterior to *The Elements of Law* where the counter-pressure is exerted by the brain. See Hobbes, *Elements,* 6; Hobbes, *De corpore,* 270; Hobbes, *Critique*, 349-350. It is worth noting that Hobbes in his treatise on optics from 1643, seems

sensation" it is also the source of our *passions*.[15] According to Hobbes, passions are the "beginnings of Voluntary Motions" and receive a mechanical explanation as well.[16] When the motion of an exterior object moves our sensorial organs that motion proceeds to the heart, where it either aids or hinders our so-called "Vitall motion." If it aids, it causes a counter-motion towards the object, if it hinders, it causes a motion away from the same. The former is called "appetite", the latter "aversion." When it is considered as an *appearance,* "appetite" is defined as "delight" while aversion appears to us as "displeasure."[17] While these appearances cannot immediately be identified *as* cognitive content, they are always intimately coupled with a mental representation of the object that causes the counter-motion in the heart. Sensation and passion are thus intimately associated. On this point, Hobbes is absolutely clear:

> [T]hough the nature of what we conceive, be the same; yet the diversity of our reception of it, in respect of different constitutions of body, and prejudices of opinion gives every thing a tincture of our different passions.[18]

But this is not all. For seeing that imagination is nothing but "decayed sense," it is clear that even the representations retained by the imagination must be intimately intertwined with our passions as well.

This fundamental entanglement of emotive and cognitive appearance stems from the fact that the counter-motion of the heart that produces both is a function of the same motion, that is, vital motion. Insofar as both sense, passion, and the derived imaginations are effects of the way motions of external bodies interact with the motion of our heart, they stand in a necessary connection to a more profound motion that seeks to perpetuate itself. This latter motion constitutes what Hobbes in *De corpore* calls the "primary endeavor" (*conatus primus*). This fundamental "desire" must indeed be considered foundational in relation to the differentiated desire and aversion insofar as both derive from

---

to derive the idea of the heart being the origin of both sensation and passion from the fact that we *experience* these two as intertwined. See Thomas Hobbes, "Tractatus Opticus (Harley Mss. 6796, ff. 193-266)," ed. Franco Alessio, *Revista critica di Storia di Filosofia* 18, 2 (1963), 199.

[15] Hobbes, *De corpore,* 270; Hobbes, *Tractatus Opticus,* 209.

[16] Ibid., 78.

[17] Ibid., 82.

[18] Ibid., 62. See as well Hobbes, *Elements,* 29. As concerns *Leviathan* it is impossible to accept Fiaschi's dualistic account of Hobbes's anthropology. See Giovanni Fiaschi, *Il desiderio del Leviatano. Immaginazione e potere in Thomas Hobbes* (Catanzaro: Rubbettino Editore, 2014), 76-83. That does not mean, however, that passion and sensation could simply be identified as Springborg seems to suggest. See Patricia Springborg, "Liberty Exposed: Quentin Skinner's *Hobbes and Republican Liberty,*" *British Journal for the History of Philosophy* 17, 5 (2009), 1050. As passion indicates a body separate from the object of sensation, that is, of our *own body,* it needs to be distinguished from sensation. See Hobbes, *De corpore,* 278.

it.[19] Desire, aversion *and* their annexed cognitive and emotive representations are differentiated precisely as a function of their respective relation to vital motion.[20]

If this is so, we seem to have found an explanation for the coherence of the trains of thought that are not guided by a conscious scope. Although particular series of thought must ultimately derive from the material of past sensation, the sheer multiplicity of sensation precludes that the constitution of a particular series can stem *only* from that material. Yet, insofar as the original sensations from which subsequent chains of thought are derived were necessarily "colored" by the passionate make-up of the observer, only an ensuing desire – whether explicitly available to the subject or not – can act as a sufficient cause for the production of a particular chain of thought.[21] A determinate relation between singular thoughts cannot be provided by the fact of sense itself, exactly because the multiplicity of merely contiguous appearances precludes *any* determination of the specific imagination to follow upon another. Thus, the coherence of thought, even when un-directed by a determinate scope, is ultimately due to the fundamental desire that generates the complex nexus between sensation, passion, and imagination. Human thought is not a matter of a self-sufficient subject contemplating whatever it pleases. Rather, it is a process deeply informed by the most practical of all endeavours: staying alive.

---

[19] Hobbes, *De corpore,* 279.

[20] In the same direction, see Yves Charles Zarka, *La décision métaphysique de Hobbes* (Paris: Librairie philosophique J. Vrin, 1999), 261-262. Though the topic is too broad to be treated here, let it be noted that Hobbes does not consider the mere preservation of one's physical existence as parallel to the ancient's *summum bonum.* Staying alive is a condition *sine qua non* for an existence in which we can continue to desire. In this direction, see Dominique Weber, "L'anthropologie Hobbesienne du désir," *Klesis – Revue Philosophique* 12 (2009), 33-37. See as well Thomas Hobbes, *De homine. Elementorum philosophiae sectio secunda,* ed. Josep Monserrat Molas (Paris: Librairie philosophique J. Vrin, 2018), 128: "Bonorum autem primum est sua cuique conservatio. Natura enim comparatum est ut cupiant omnes sibi bene esse. Cujus ut capaces esse possint, necesse est cupiant vitam, sanitatem, & utriusque quantum fieri potest securitatem futuri temporis."

[21] See as well Hobbes, *Leviathan,* 104. The difference in the quickness of thought depends upon the difference of passions "and therefore some mens thoughts run one way, some another." It is common to notice but not to interrogate the coherence of unguided mental discourse. See Samantha Frost, *Lessons from a Materialist Thinker* (Stanford: Stanford University Press, 2008), 48-59; Anne Herla, *Hobbes ou le déclin du royaume des ténèbres* (Paris: Éditions Kimé, 2006), 126. Paganini rejects Barnouw's use of the term "unconscious" in connection with Hobbes. Of course, Hobbes does not use that vocabulary but the doctrine of *Leviathan* does indeed point in that direction. See Gianni Paganini, "Hobbes Philosophical Method and the Passion of Curiosity" in *Interpreting Hobbes's Political Philosophy,* ed. S.A. Lloyd (Cambridge: Cambridge University Press, 2019) 66; Jeffrey Barnouw, "Hobbes's Psychology of Thought," *History of European Ideas* 10, no. 5 (1989): 522-523.

Yet, to see how this fundamental desire generates a specifically religious structure of thought, we first have to a look at what Hobbes calls "the restlesse desire of Power after power."[22]

The Desire for Power

As we have seen, pleasure and displeasure are the appearances of what either helps or hinders vital motion. We *desire* the former and have an *aversion* for the latter. Conceived in this way, desire is in itself pleasurable and not merely the expectation of something that will eventually procure us pleasure: "[A]ll Appetite, Desire and Love, is accompanied with some Delight."[23] Hence, the object of desire is not something foreign to desire but somehow desire itself. Or, in other words: we desire to desire.

In this regard, it is crucial that desire involves a specific temporality. Obviously, desire by definition implies the absence of its object and a consequent orientation towards the future, that is, towards the point in time at which the desired object will be present. When desire has itself as an object, however, the implied temporal horizon expands beyond the finite limit of a simple relation between desire and its object.[24] If I desire an apple, the future I foresee merely stops at the getting of that apple. It does not stretch beyond that limit. This is not the case when the object of desire is desire itself. Here, the temporality implied is expanded *ad infinitum* as the procurement of the object of desire necessitates continued anticipation of the time to come.[25] This is why Hobbes asserts "[t]hat the object of mans desire, is not to enjoy once onely, and for one instant of time; but to assure for ever, the way of his future desire."[26] Humans

---

[22] Hobbes, *Leviathan,* 150.

[23] Ibid., 82.

[24] On the face of it, this structure of desire would seem to derive directly from its definition. However, animals, though they have desires, do not perceive an indefinite future. Hobbes even suggests that animal desire can be satisfied despite his initial conflation of pleasure and desire. See Hobbes, *De homine,* 131. The topic cannot be treated here, but the specificity of human desire seems to stem from a fundamental orientation towards the future rather than from the structure of desire itself. In this direction, see Pierre-François Moreau, *Hobbes. Philosophie, science, religion* (Pars: PUF, 1989), 57-60. In fact, Hobbes's argument suggests that it is temporality as such that makes human desire indefinite and not the indefinite structure of desire that makes human beings temporal. From a formal point of view, the latter argument would equivocate on the meaning of desire insofar as animals are not involved in a search after power. It would thus be the specifically human desire that conditions the search after power and the attempt to employ the power of others. Social interactions are, seen in this light, derived from the more fundamental temporal character of human desire.

[25] For Hobbes's most radical expression of this thought, see Hobbes, *De homine*, 132: "Ipsa cupiti Fruitio tunc cum fruimur appetitus est, nimirum motus animi Fruentis per partes rei qua fruitur."

[26] Hobbes, *Leviathan,* 150.

are riddled by a desire to make sure that the continuation of their desire will be possible throughout an indefinite future. The only way to safeguard that continuation is by procuring *power.*

In *Leviathan,* Hobbes defines power thus: "The POWER *of a Man,* (...) is his present means to obtain some future apparent Good." Following this general definition, Hobbes distinguishes two sorts of power of which one is called "natural," the other "instrumental." The former consists in the "eminence of the Faculties of Body, or Mind: as extraordinary Strenght, Forme, Prudence, Arts, Eloquence, Liberality, Nobility," while the latter "are those Powers, which acquired by these, or by fortune, are means and Instruments to acquire more."[27]

At first sight, this distinction seems somewhat awkward. Seeing that natural powers are said to be one possible source for obtaining instrumental powers, it is not clear how the fact that the latter are "means and Instruments to acquire more" should separate them from the former. The distinction used to separate them would seem to hold for both. However, as Hobbes proceeds to exemplify the instrumental powers, we get a better hold of the distinction itself. According to Hobbes, instrumental powers are "Riches, Reputation, Friends, and the secret working of God, which men call Good Luck."[28] It now seems as if instrumental powers are "instrumental" in that they are not restricted to the employment of the power of a single person. Rather, they involve the employment of more than one. Whereas natural powers are not natural in the sense of being innate qualities – both arts and eloquence are clearly not –, but because they have a natural limit due to the finitude of each person endowed with these powers, instrumental powers lack any upper limit.[29] If these powers are not limited by the natural finitude of each person, it is because they consist in the utilization of the power of others.

However, to utilize the power of others is not a simple procedure as it is impossible to transfer actual power from one person to another.[30] If I am to use the powers of another, it must be that he or she will place them at my disposal, yet, they will only do so if they gain something by doing so. If a person is to place his powers at the disposal of another, it is thus a necessary condition that the former perceives the latter to possess a power sufficient to help him. In this way, *perception* is crucial for the constitution of instrumental power. As Hobbes says: "Reputation of power, is Power; because it draweth with it the adhaerence of those that need protection."[31] If others perceive me as powerful,

---

[27] Ibid., 132.

[28] Ibid.

[29] In the same direction, see Milanese, "Le désir," 17-19 and Frost, *Lessons,* 144-146.

[30] Thomas Hobbes, *De cive,* ed. Howard Warrender (Oxford: Clarendon Press, 1983), 134.

[31] Hobbes, *Leviathan,* 132. In the same direction, see Sandra Field, "Hobbes and the Question of Power," *Journal of the History of Philosophy* 52, 1 (2014), 70-75.

they will tend to submit their will to mine as they can, thereby win my favour. Yet, as the mere reputation of power is itself power, it is clear that the recognition of another's power is by itself the creation of the power that such recognition purports to merely *find*. If I perceive another to be powerful, that perception will, insofar as it translates into specific actions, constitute a *sign to others* of the power that I recognize.[32] My recognition will entail the recognition of others because by signalling to others that I perceive another to be powerful, I effectively create or increase the power of the person in question. If I perceive someone to be powerful, I will tend to obey that person and thus constitute the power I perceived to be already existent. In this way, "the nature of Power, is in this point, like to Fame, increasing as it proceeds."[33]

Still, the specificity of instrumental power is not so much to be found in the fact that it is conditioned by a perception of power. "Eloquence" and "liberality" are listed under "natural powers," but both clearly depend upon a certain perception. Rather, instrumental power designates a specifically *social perception* as it is characterized by a perception of the way *others* recognize power. Or, to put it another way: the structure of instrumental power is *triadic* rather than *dyadic*.[34] That a person has friends, a reputation, or is favoured by God all constitute signs of the fact that others consider that person powerful. These signs will thus constitute an argument as to why I should do the same.[35]

The structure of these power relations finds expression in what Hobbes terms "honour." To honour another is an expression of the value we put on that person: "To Value a man at a high rate, is to *Honour* him; at a low rate, is to *Dishonour* him."[36] That value is again defined as the price we are willing to pay for his or her power.[37] If we "give way" or "speak to another with consideration," these are all signs that we think that that person has power.[38] Yet, insofar as these signs of honour create the very power they purport to find, they seem to involve a certain paradox, even contradiction. For only on the

---

[32] See as well Hobbes, *Leviathan,* 564: "[W]here a man seeth another worshipped, he supposeth him powerfull, and is the readier to obey him; which makes his Power greater."

[33] Ibid., 132.

[34] Despite appearances, "riches" do not constitute a counter-example to this reading. Hobbes stresses that "Riches joyned with liberality, is Power." When not, "riches" are the cause of envy. As such "riches" are not simply material wealth but the *general recognition* of the fact that this wealth is obtainable to others through the mechanisms of honour. People will only honour a rich person in so far as there is a perceived hope of getting a share in that person's wealth.

[35] See as well Thomas Hobbes, *Behemoth, or the Long Parliament,* ed. Paul Seaward (Oxford: Clarendon Press, 2010), 128: "For the Power of the mighty has no foundation but in the opinion and beleefe of the people."

[36] Hobbes, *Leviathan,* 136.

[37] Ibid.,134: "The *Value,* or WORTH of a man, is as of all other things, his Price; that is to say, so much as would be given for the use of his Power."

[38] Ibid.,136. See as well Hobbes, *De cive,* 225.

condition that we shall obtain some good do we undertake any voluntary action.[39] This means that we would only honour another on condition that we receive some good by that act. And this is indeed what Hobbes claims. We honour others because we either fear what they can do to us if we do not comply or because we hope to receive benefit from them. By honouring, we seek to render those honoured favourable to us, "not by Force, but by Compleasance." Honouring is "a winning of favour by good offices; as by praises, by acknowledging their Power, and by whatsoever is pleasing to them from whom we look for any benefit."[40] Notwithstanding how contradictory it may seem, honour is a social mechanism that seeks to increase one's own power by recognizing and, by that very fact, *creating* the power of others.

It is, in fact, this mechanism that creates what Hobbes calls the "restlesse desire of Power after power, that ceaseth onely in Death."[41] Given that the recognition of another's power is only comprehensible as long as it increases the power of the recognizer, no stable power could ever be constituted solely by way of instrumental power. I can only annex the power of another as long as that person acts according to the same general desire as my self, that is, the desire to stay alive. But on principle, that desire can never be extinct in those that recognize the power of others as such a desire is the condition *sine qua non* for the exchange of signs of honour. Hence, human desire will, as a direct consequence of the internal logic of instrumental power, eventually evolve into a desire for total domination of the social sphere. As long as recognition of my own power is contingent upon the desire for power of others, it can never be definitively safeguarded. As Hobbes memorably puts it: a person "cannot assure the power and means to live well, which he hath present, without the acquisition of more."[42]

The social stratification deployed by the mechanism of honour creates an inherently unstable situation. That situation is ultimately founded upon the universality of the search for power, which is, in turn, conditioned by a desire to stay alive. With this stratification follows a complex network of *publicly perceptible signs* directed at our fellow-men. Insofar as this network is the constitutive framework for the way we understand the action of others and ourselves, it would seem that what I have called the "imaginary representations" that structure human perception and thought are deeply informed by the way the desire to stay alive manifests itself through social interactions. Indeed, it is within this general framework that Hobbes considers the advent of religion to which I shall now turn.

[39] Hobbes, *De cive,* 101.

[40] Hobbes, *Leviathan,* 562. See as well Hobbes, *De homine,* 148.

[41] Hobbes, *Leviathan,* 150.

[42] Ibid.

The Origins of Religion

According to Hobbes, it is only in humans that we find the "seed of *Religion.*"[43] Consequently, there must be some feature of human nature to account for this fact. There are three such features. The first is to be "inquisitive into the Causes of the Events they see." This feature is not equally distributed since some find pleasure in the pure contemplation of causal chains while others are only concerned with observing causes insofar as they influence their own wellbeing. This latter preoccupation is, however, ubiquitous: *all* men are "curious in the search of the causes of their own good and evill fortune."[44] The second feature is connected to the first but seems to concern the very structure of human consciousness. Whenever we experience something with a beginning, we inquire into the cause "which determined the same to begin, then when it did, rather than sooner or later."[45] The third feature consists in a specific human relation to time as it is only humans that can remember and compare a sufficient amount of causal connection for them to have a "foresight of the time to come."

Concerning this last point, Hobbes had previously remarked that "things *to come* have no being at all; the *Future* being but a fiction of the mind."[46] It is the ability to retain and order a sufficient amount of past sensations that creates an "imaginary future," which is essentially an extrapolation from what has happened to what *will* happen. Past experience is, however, never sufficient to know what will actually take place. The future is but a "fiction of the mind," it is on principle uncertain as it has no existence outside the fallible imagination of man. This is indeed why "it is impossible for a man, who continually endeavoureth to secure himself against the evill he feares, and procure the good he desireth, not to be in a perpetuall solicitude of the time to come."[47]

Such anxiety is thus consequent to the very structure of human thought. Given that *everyone* is concerned with their future well-being, anxiety is inescapable to the extent that the future is a fallible projection created by simple experiential knowledge. To remedy this universal anxiety, humans tend to invent causes that function as a response to the ignorance of the real causes of events. Seeing that these fictive causes correspond to the lack of knowledge, they are correspondingly understood to be *invisible*. We can discern no particular cause for the events that we observe, yet, ensuing from the second feature enumerated by Hobbes, we cannot help but pretend that some cause was really there. This ignorance, that is, this *lack of knowledge,* is thus transposed to the *form* our fictions take: "when there is nothing to be seen, there is nothing to accuse, either of their good or evill fortune, but some *Power,* or Agent

[43] Ibid., 164.
[44] Ibid. See as well Hobbes, *De homine,* 151.
[45] Hobbes, *Leviathan,* 164.
[46] Ibid., 42-44. See as well Hobbes, *Elements,* 15; Hobbes, *De cive,* 120.
[47] Ibid.,164.

Invisible."[48] To these "invisible agents" is subsequently annexed a whole string of imaginations according to which they have been understood as "Ghosts" or "Spirits" that "appear, and vanish when they please."[49]

The imaginary representations that are consequently tied to a specific conception of the "invisible powers" are in turn differentiated according to the particularity of each person. Hobbes asserts that the natural seeds of religion "by reason of the different Fancies, Judgements, and Passions of severall men, hath grown up into ceremonies so different, that those which are used by one man, are for the most part ridiculous to another."[50]

When individuals are considered in isolation from all social contexts, it is possible to envisage a situation where each would worship a particular set of imaginary representations in his or her purely subjective manner. However, as might be expected from the consideration of Hobbes's concept of honour, this is only rarely, if indeed ever, the case.[51] In fact, Hobbes claims that "all formed Religion, is founded at first, upon the faith which a multitude hath in some one person, whom they believe not only to be a wise man, and to labour to procure their happiness, but also to be a holy man, to whom God himselfe vouchsafeth to declare his will supernaturally."[52]

The point needs to be pressed that the person in whom the multitude has faith is said to "labour to procure their happiness" and to do this through direct communication with God. Given that the "secret workings of God" were already enumerated among the instrumental powers,[53] the inference seems

---

[48] Ibid.,166.

[49]Ibid.,166-168. The fact that the powers imagined to control the fate of man are invisible does not preclude that they are also imagined to appear in the visual domain. Indeed, for the most part, they are derived from a lack of knowledge of the causes of dreams: "From this ignorance of how to Distinguish Dreams, and other strong Fancies, from Vision and Sense, did arise the greatest part of the Religion of the Gentiles." See Hobbes, *Leviathan,* 34. According to this primary form of religion, the divine is present in the mundane sphere of visibility though it takes the shape of "spirits" or "ghosts." Such spirits and ghosts have been imagined to take their seat in pictures and statues. See Hobbes, *Leviathan,* 174. This is not specific to the heathens. The idea of God taking seat in something visible and finite is also present in the Christian idea of transubstantiation, an idea that involves idolatry if taken literally. See Hobbes, *Leviathan,* 968, 1034-1036. See as well Karl Schuhmann, "Phantasms and Idols: True Philosophy and Wrong Religion in Hobbes," *Rivista di storia della filosofia* 1 (2004), 23-25.

[50] Hobbes, *Leviathan,* 170.

[51] Occasionally, Hobbes does conceive of such a possibility. See Hobbes, *Leviathan,* 1026: "if the people had been permitted to worship, and pray to Images, (which are Representations of their own Fancies,) they had had no farther dependence on the true God (...) but every man had governed himself according to his own appetite, to the utter eversion of the Common-wealth." See as well Hobbes, *Leviathan,* 446, 466.

[52] Ibid., 180.

[53] Ibid., 132.

warranted that the submission to a specific person, perceived to stand on a particularly good foot with God, is a consequence of the universal desire to stay alive.[54] We submit to the power of another because he or she is perceived to be recognized by God as deserving of special abilities. That submission is again justified by the help we hope to gain from God through the mediation of the person whose power we recognize. At the same time, the fact that we recognize this latter person's power will only serve as an argument for others to do the same, thus enhancing and to some extent rendering this power stable.

In this regard, the imaginary representations of God and the cult that he is thought to necessitate receive some uniformity from the unicity of the founder(s) of institutionalized religion. These founders have consciously used the anxiety essentially annexed to the representations of the divine as a means to obtain civil peace. Whether these founders were Christians or "Gentiles", they have utilized it "with a purpose to make those men that relyed on them, the more apt to Obedience, Lawes, Peace, Charity, and civill Society."[55] Such a method of more or less cynical manipulation has proceeded through the institution of uniform rites and practices, such that "the common people in their misfortunes, laying the fault on neglect, or errour in their Ceremonies, or on their disobedience to the lawes, were the lesse apt to mutiny against their Governors."[56]

Involved in institutionalized religion is, therefore, the uniformity of visible rituals, imagery, and behaviour towards those that seem to mediate the relation to the invisible God. In this sense, religion is never a matter of simply *believing* that something divine exists. Rather, it involves an affectively shaped structure of imaginary representations that concerns the very existence of each person. Seeing that the social stratification involved in religious practice is a consequence of the basic human desire, it is clear that institutionalized religion cannot be a matter of simple information. Or, in other words: religion is never a purely cognitive phenomenon. It always embodies an entire world of emotions, action, and thought.

This has at least one very important consequence. Religion, whether it be Christian or that of the Gentiles, is never a matter of either pure superstition or

[54] This reading is confirmed by what Hobbes has previously said: to believe what a person says without regard to the propositional content of *what* is said, is an "Honour done in Believing." See ibid., 102. See as well ibid., 162: "And this seed of Religion, having been observed by many; some of those that have observed it, have been enclined thereby to nourish, dresse, and forme it into Lawes; and to added to it of their own invention, any opinion of the causes of future events, by which they thought they should best be able to govern others, and make unto themselves the greatest use of their Powers."

[55] Ibid., 170.

[56] Ibid., 178.

an equally pure, but presumably correct rational relation to the one true God.[57] The fundamental anxiety annexed to religion and the latter's adherent structure of imaginary representations is always so ingrained in the way humans relate to and understand the world that its possible reform can never be a question of a self-assured rational enlightenment.

Reform is, however, necessary. If for no other reasons, then because recent history had all too clearly shown the bloody chaos that ensues when the uniformity of institutionalized religion starts to crumble.[58] Indeed, given that the entire structure of religious representation ultimately originates in a fundamental human desire and thus concerns human existence itself, it is no wonder that radical divergences in this regard can cause deadly strife. But if this is so, a possible reform, or even unification, of the structure of religious representations can never be a question of merely convincing people of rational truth. Rather, it must rely on a rhetorical strategy that situates itself *within* the boundaries of the structure of the fundamental religious representations.[59]

If this is a correct interpretation of what could be called the "pragmatic conditions" of Hobbes's *Leviathan,* it is to be grounded in his understanding of human imagination and the way it is structured in accordance with human desire. In fact, on this interpretation, it would be possible to explain why Hobbes's felt the need to dedicate such a large bulk of the *Leviathan* to what has rightly been termed a "hermeneutic of the religious imaginary."[60]

Conclusion

So, in the guise of a conclusion, I will briefly attempt to answer the question posed as the subtitle of this article: why, as Hobbes claims in the *Leviathan,*

---

[57] In the same direction, see Jean Terrel, "L'antropologie de la religion dans le *Léviathan,*" *Klesis – Revue Philosophique* 12 (2009), 51-55. For a more affirmative view of the possibility of rational enlightenment in Hobbes, see Herla, *Le déclin,* 312; Devin Stauffer, *Hobbes and the Kingdom of Light* (Chicago and London: The University of Chicago Press, 2018), 272.

[58] Among the reasons for the English Civil War that Hobbes enumerates in the *Behemoth,* three out of seven concern religious opinions. See Hobbes, *Behemoth,* 109-110. See as well Hobbes, *Leviathan,* 502-504 and Hobbes, *De cive,* 94: "nulla acrius gerantur bella quam inter eiusdem religionis sectas, & eiusdem reipublicae factiones, ubi certamen est vel de doctrinis, vel de prudentia politica."

[59] Such an approach would, however, differ from the otherwise important work of Quentin Skinner and David Johnston. While both stress the rhetorical aspects of Hobbes's works, they fail to take notice of the fact that such a rhetoric is ultimately conditioned by Hobbes's ontology. See Quentin Skinner, *Reason and Rhetoric in the Philosophy of Hobbes* (Cambridge: Cambridge University Press, 1996); David Johnston, *The Rhetoric of* Leviathan. *Thomas Hobbes and the Politics of Cultural Transformation* (Princeton: Princeton University Press, 1986).

[60] Milanese, "Le désir," 11.

must the sovereign be *visible*?[61] In short, the sovereign must be visible to avoid strife. As the religious sentiment of a personal God, or gods, that control the fate of humankind is a natural consequence of human desire, there can be no question of eradicating it. Humans will always tend to imagine invisible powers that control their fate. However, as these powers are thought to be invisible, honour, power, and trust are given to a very visible person, who, through rites and ceremonies, is meant to appease the possible anger of the gods. Such a visible mediation of what is thought to be invisible gives shape to the structure of imaginary representations insofar as it consists of a series of visible practices, signs, and modes of action. These are ultimately founded in human desire and given body through the mechanisms of honour.

It is in this regard that a common, *visible* sovereign is needed. For as long as the imaginary representation implied by the diverse conceptions of the divine are contingent upon trust in particular priests or institutions, that is, contingent upon the unstable bonds that honour tends to constitute, such representations can provide no staying guide for action. As soon as priests or institutions fall out of favour, people are no longer sure how to control their own fate. When the unstable bonds of honour finally crumble, more often than not, the result will be the deadly institution of novel religious structures. As Hobbes succinctly puts it: "I may attribute all the changes of Religion in the world, to one and the same cause; and that is, unpleasing Priests."[62] To institute a common horizon of imaginary representations that will avoid chaotic change, the sovereign must be a *visible* source of ill or good fate. This visibility is thus meant to replace and reform the imaginary structures that are tied to the mediation between the visible and the invisible supposedly enacted by religious institutions. Similarly, the visible figure of the sovereign must instil fear in its subjects insofar as a violation of its laws have fatal consequences and hope insofar as the observance of the same laws will allow for a contented life.[63]

But the sovereign is *not* God. The laws of the sovereign state are not a matter of obscure signs, prophecy, or the working of miracles. The manifestation of the sovereign is not the paradoxical and ultimately incomprehensible presence of the infinite in the finite. Rather, it is an attempt to create a common imaginary structure that will render human life peaceful and independent of the individual charisma of priests and religious institutions. This entails the commonality of sovereign visibility and the public promulgation of the laws that are to be observed.

---

[61] Hobbes, *Leviathan,* 254-255, 510-511. See as well Hobbes, *De cive,* 78. Hobbes is speaking of a "golden age," where sovereign power was not disputed but merely exercised. However, that exercise seems to be conditioned by the veneration of a *visible*, quasi-divine ruler.

[62] Ibid., 186. See as well Hobbes, *De homine,* 152.

[63] Ibid., 512: "so also in the Body Politique, when the spirituall power, moveth the Members of a Common-wealth, by the terrour of punishments, and hope of rewards."

Reality Imagined: Aesthetic Participation in Indian Ritual Visualisation

Alan Herbert

Introduction

The idea of imagination operating within religious praxis rarely sits comfortably with traditions searching for legitimacy in a currency of truth or reality. It can seem fanciful, at best an engaging with possibilities, implying uncertainty. Hence, it is often treated with caution, suspicion, or scepticism. When there is no denying its function in a religious practice that has the goal of revelation or liberation, descriptions connected with it can seem opaque or obfuscated. This chapter explores one such problematic description in an early modern Indian religious treatise. Its author assimilates and, it appears unwittingly, recasts a pan-traditional set of meditation rituals involving imagination into a paradox. The rituals are traditionally part of the worship of a deity through its representative image. The author's own descriptions of the internal rituals seem to conflate their imaginals with reality, considering mental-images non-imaginative. After recognising the problematic issues in the author's account, I offer a potential resolution to this paradox based on his treatise's explanation of mature devotion in which he analogically employs theories of dramaturgy and poetics. It is observed that aspects of an aesthetic reality present in this culminating explication are also prefigured in his descriptions of the meditation rituals.

The paradoxical description appears in *Bhakti-sandarbha*, the fifth volume of *Sat-sandarbha*, a seminal treatise attributed to the sixteenth century Gaudiya Vaishnava thinker Jiva Gosvami.[1] The treatise is written in Sanskrit and promotes theistic devotion, or *bhakti*. It can be thought of as the tradition's devotional commentary on its principal testimonial and doctrinal textual authority,

---

[1] Jīva Gosvāmī was born around 1517 and his death was recorded in 1608. His early life was spent in Bengal. Around the age of twenty-four, he moved to Vṛndāvana, Uttar Pradesh, to live as an ascetic. His treatise, *Ṣaṭ-sandarbha*, is generally thought to have been completed between 1555 and 1561. His Gauḍīya Vaiṣṇava tradition is presently located under the broad banner of Hinduism. A comprehensive overview of Jīva's tradition and treatise can be found in: Sushil Kumar De, *Early History of the Vaisnava Faith and Movement in Bengal, from Sanskrit and Bengali Sources*, 2d ed. (Calcutta: Firma K.L. Mukhopadhyay, 1961), 254-412 (*Ṣaṭ-sandarbha*). Apart from technical terms, I have purposely omitted most of the Sanskrit diacritics in this chapter, instead using Anglicized transliterations to make it easier for readers unfamiliar with the language. I maintain diacritics in the footnotes as references.

Bhagavata-purana, a text still highly regarded throughout India.[2] Jiva's treatise is further supplemented by references to various other canonical texts, among which are a number of Pancharatras that to an extent act as ritual manuals.

Jiva's problematic assessment of imagination is partially the result of his attempts to assimilate and re-present as consistent with his tradition's ontology an important set of meditation rituals enjoined in several earlier Pancharatra texts.[3] The main source for his ritual explanation is a Pancharatra entitled *Trailokya-sammohana-tantra*.[4] The rituals are standard practice among Indian traditions worshipping representative images. Nevertheless, they typically include a particular visualization that is challenging for Jiva's tradition. Practitioners are expected to imagine themselves uniting with the worshipped deity and then to subsequently reflexively worship this union under the rubric that to approach the divine, one has to become divine.[5] The problem is that this kind of unity is antithetical to Jiva's view of devotion, which insists on the perpetual duality of worshipped and worshipper. Although acknowledging the validity of the rituals by including them in his treatise, he also expresses his tradition's abhorrence of literal identity with the deity. One way he articulates this is by reinterpreting this imaginative unification in terms of an identity of relational proximity and intimacy; that is, he sees the practitioner as an ideal god-like companion or assistant of the deity rather than merged with it. Still, his reframing of the rituals to accommodate his tradition's version of reality begets a paradox. In avoiding the undesirable notions of uniting with the deity and of imaginatively generating a deity, despite the deity being visualized and attended to in rituals performed in the imagination, Jiva paradoxically claims that the deity is in fact real and independent of the practitioner.

Offering no explicit philosophical explanation or justification for this declaration of a real deity in imagination, Jiva potentially leaves himself open to criticism and his readers susceptible to confusion. His descriptions of the rituals offer no clear and direct means to reconcile this paradox. They do, however, tacitly anticipate an alternate uncontroversial role for imagination that can

---

[2] *Bhāgavata-Purāṇa* gives the time of its own compilation at around five thousand years ago. Many Indologists desist from dating any of the Purāṇas due to difficulties in pinpointing the dates of the oral traditions that they have emerged from. Those who do attempt to date *Bhāgavata-Purāṇa* place it between the eighth and ninth century. For an overview of the Purāṇas, see: Ludo Rocher, *The Purāṇas* (Wiesbaden: Harrassowitz, 1986).

[3] The meditation rituals performed in the imagination are: *bhūta-śuddhi*, a deconstruction and reconstruction of the practitioner's body element by element; *nyāsa*, a divinising of this new body via *mantras*; and *mānasa-pūjā*, a mental pre-enactment or independent enactment of the entire physical worship.

[4] *Trailokya-sammohana-tantra* is also known as *Sanat-kurmara-saṁhitā*.

[5] This idea is also supported by *Bṛhadāraṇyaka-upaniṣad*, which repeats several times: "...he becomes a god and joins the company of gods." Patrick Olivelle, *The Early Upaniṣads: Annotated Text and Translation*, South Asia Research (New York, N.Y.) (New York ; Oxford: Oxford University Press, 1998), 102-9.

resolve it, one that is couched in secular ancient Indian aesthetic theory. Jiva employs an aesthetic framework to explain mature devotion in his treatise's final volume. By prefiguring elements of this aesthetic theory in his earlier descriptions of ritual visualization, he gradually introduces his readers to an imagination praxis that doesn't violate the ontological underpinnings of his tradition. He can then assert that the object of the ritual is non-imaginative, for aesthetic participation and appreciation implies a phenomenological reality.

Before addressing Jiva's aesthetic theory and how it is prefigured in his descriptions of imagination in the meditation rituals, I will first outline the paradox as it appears in his treatise. Next, two possible reconciliations for his paradoxical statements are explored. Although valid, they are shown to be philosophically unsatisfying. Finally, the means for understanding imagination in the rituals is explained by way of Jiva's description in his final volume of the experience of mature devotion via aesthetic theory, this kind of experience being anticipated in his articulation of the non-imaginative imaginal.

Refining the Problem in Jiva's Descriptions of Imagination

Jīva's Gaudiya Vaishnavism defines devotion as service, specifically as participation with the divine.[6] The deity, a personal expression of the divine, is the most common object of this participation. The principal deity for Jīva's School is Krishna, the speaker of *Bhagavad-gītā*, subject of the tenth book of *Bhagavata-purana*, and, for them, the Supreme God. Since Krishna is ordinarily invisible, ordinary practitioners require perceivable images, symbols, or other kinds of sensible representations as mediums for participating with him. The representative image, known as "*murti*," is the typical medium in temples and homes.[7] The *murti* is made in the anthropomorphic (or in some cases zoomorphic) form of the deity. Jiva writes that it is non-different with the deity:

> I. The representative image is thought to have the nature of Krishna's form since: (1) their forms are identical; and (2) it is said that after meditation it is wrong to think: "Oh, have I considered the image of Krishna to be stone?" ... Moreover, on the topic of installing the *murti*, the following invocation is offered in *Hayashirsa-pancharatra*: "O Vishnu,[8] be present in this image." After a special *mantra* that causes this deity to appear in the image, the following *mantra* is then

[6] *Bhakti-sandarbha* 216.

[7] The representative image of a deity, or a god, is known as "*mūrti*; *pratimā*; [or] *arcā*." Image worship involves offering articles such as a lamp, incense, flowers, and prepared food to the image. This image possesses similar theological relevance to an Orthodox Christian icon. For explanations of this form of worship, see: Diana L. Eck, *Darśan: Seeing the Divine Image in India* (Chambersburg, Pa: Anima Books, 1985); Julius Lipner, *Hindu Images and Their Worship with Special Reference to Vaisnavism: A Philosophical-Theological Inquiry*, Routledge Hindu Studies Series (London: Routledge, 2017).

[8] Vishnu (Viṣṇu) is a distinct personal expression of the same divine that is Krishna.

> recited: "Your highest principle, including your body that consists of knowledge, let it all as one be merged in the *murti*. May this *murti* now awaken."[9]

The *murti* can be physically made of stone, wood, metal, earth, paint, sand, or jewels, or it can be mentally formed.[10] As a means to directly participate with the divine, the *murti* needs to be a transparent medium. In other words, it should possess no mediating qualities or properties that could obscure the deity. Transparency is esoterically conferred on the *murti* by tradition through following certain guidelines for its formation, installation, and engagement. In effect, the deity is asked to ontologically populate the image and, in this way, devotion to the image is devotion to the deity, the two becoming non-different.

Jiva accepts the authority of testimony without question, which is a main reason why he offers no extra philosophical analysis or apologetic on this relationship of non-difference in his treatise. With regard to worshipping the *murti*, he thus writes:

> II. The highest worshippers see the *murti* precisely as the Supreme. Since any manifested difference between the two would disrupt devotion, they are indeed expressed as identical.... Precisely because of this, in the *Vishnu-dharma* it is said: "After absorbing your mind in the *murti*, give up other refuges. Only that image helps you when it is worshipped and meditated on with devotion. While moving, standing, sleeping, and eating, think only of it, of the Supreme Self, stationed in front of you, behind you, above and below you, and to your side."[11]

Jiva then emphasises that the mind-*murti* is equally non-different with the deity:

> III. This mental worship is sometimes performed independently of physical worship because: (1) the mental *murti* is already one of the eight non-different forms of the divine; and (2) it is stated in *Bhagavata-purana* 11.3.50 that "one can perform worship either in the form of the physical image or in the heart."[12]

Jiva's declaration that the object of worship in the heart is the mind-*murti* (in Indian thought, heart and mind are frequently equated) is consistent with his next claim that such an object, being non-different with the deity (which includes everyone and everything connected with it), is not imaginative:

---

[9] *Bhakti-sandarbha* 286. The numbering of the excerpts (I)–(V) is mine. They appear in a different order in the treatise. Translations are mine. Full literal translations and the Sanskrit quotes are available in my doctoral thesis. Sanskrit for *Bhakti-sandarbha* taken from: Jīva Gosvāmī and Haridāsaśāstrī, *Śrī-Bhakti-Sandarbhaḥ*, Dvitīyasaṃskaraṇam ed. (Vṛndāvana, Jilā Mathurā, Uttara Pradeśa: Śrīgadādharagaurahari Presa, 1986).

[10] Jīva's source for the eight kinds of *mūrti* is *Bhāgavata-purāṇa* 11.27.12. Kṛṣṇa Dvaipayana Vyāsa and J. L. Shastri, *Bhāgavata-Purāṇa of Kṛṣṇa Dvaipayana Vyāsa, with Sanskrit Commentary Bhāvārtha-Bodhinī of Śrīdhara Svāmī* (Delhi: Motilal Banarsidass, 1999).

[11] *Bhakti-sandarbha* 286.

[12] Ibid., 286.

IV. Moreover, in the mental worship, those things related to Krishna's activities and his companions that are from the past are not made of imagination. Rather, they are certainly, as their objects, real.[13]

Jīva supports this claim regarding the mental landscape's reality by way of an initially confusing conceptual strategy that differentiates historical objects from perennial ones:

V. This is [a reality]because those activities and retinues of Krishna's, which were revealed in the past during his time on earth, perennially exist in his non-manifest abode in innumerable ways. However, in the mental worship wherein Krishna's past acts are visualized, the demons with which he fights should not be considered sentient beings but figurative representations (because they cannot enter the pure perennial realm). The historical events depicting these demons can instead be meditated on through Krishna's and his companions' play-acting these events in the perennial realm, which takes the form of "hide and seek, constructing a bridge, monkey-jumping, and so on."[14]

On face value, excerpts I to V are problematic in that they contain a paradox. Nevertheless, within them there seems to be a certain leeway that would allow us to find justification for Jiva's statements as a means to dissolve the contradiction. With this in mind, the following offers two possible explanations of his claim to a non-imaginative imaginal that, although viable, in fact demonstrates that such resolutions are philosophically unsatisfying.

Two Philosophically Unsatisfying Resolutions

(1) There is a sense that Jiva intends by his statements regarding the non-difference between *murti* and deity that there is a non-difference between objects. Krishna is the object of Jiva's meditation or worship, and in the context of the excerpts the deity is attended to through a mental-image. Amy Kind defines the difference between a "mental-image" and an "object of imagination" in terms of the former "capturing" the latter, in a similar way to which paint on the painted image of a tree captures the perception of an actual living tree, its object.[15] In Kind's example, the object-tree exists by virtue of its being the *conception* of a real tree. Isolated from conceptualizing, any visualizing of the physical world is, as Kant would say, merely an apprehending of the

[13] Ibid. 286.

[14] Ibid. 286. Jīva's descriptions of Krishna's play is connected with scenes from the *Rāmāyaṇa*. In this Epic, Rama searches for and eventually slays his wife Sita's kidnapper, Ravana, in Lanka. Having had his monkey friend Hanuman jump from the Decan to the island on a reconnaissance mission, Rama then, with the help of his monkey and bear army, builds a bridge of floating stones in order to emancipate her.

[15] Amy Kind, "Putting the Image Back in Imagination," *Philosophy and Phenomenological Research* 62, no. 1 (2001): 108. The living tree could be a particular tree known to the imaginer or a universal conceptualization of a known existing species of tree.

unconnected and un-unified manifold of impressions given to the senses. Objects, such as trees, emerge only when particulars or universals are conceptualised from this manifold. So, although Krishna may be invisible to the senses, once he is conceived as real – which for ordinary practitioners is achieved through hearing or reading testimony – he can then become the real object of the mind, imagination, or worship. The mental-image simply captures the real object, Krishna, through an internally visible copy.

On Kind's view, an object of the imagination inasmuch as the object is captured by a mental-image is a conception of something real. Distinguishing image and object in this way and then claiming that in the excerpts Jiva is only addressing the reality of objects renders his statements on a non-imaginative mental-image non-contentious. The image can be claimed to be non-imaginative if *per se* it merely functions as a reference to a real object. However, Jiva's additional claim (in excerpt III) that worship in the imagination is worship to the deity directly via its non-different mind-*murti* is problematic. The *murti* does not capture the deity, it is the deity. The paradox is therefore philosophically sustained on account of Jiva's not distinguishing ontologically between the mind-*murti*, or representative image, as it appears to the imagination (since direct vision is not implied through the rituals) and the real object of imagination.

(2) Jiva justifies the reality of the *murti*, or image, by way of citing its identical form with the deity (excerpt I.). This is an ontological claim of identity since he considers the divine form to be an intrinsic quality of the divine.[16] For ordinary practitioners who are yet to attain what Jiva describes as a direct perception of the deity and who are relevant to this ritual section of his treatise, such identity can only be understood theoretically. They can only be informed of it through testimony. It would be absurd to claim that metaphysical reality or identity is perceivable of the *murti* or that it can be imaginatively generated as such simply by theoretically understanding its relationship with the invisible deity. Since Jiva makes no distinction between the *murti* in the mind and what he speaks of in terms of the imaginal, it could thus be argued that at least in the ritual section of his treatise, imagination functions to generate images that strongly resemble the deity, the unseen object. In other words, resolution (2) is a claim that imagination creates images to resemble theoretical descriptions of reality.

Nelson Goodman notes that before human cognition can determine or recognise a resemblance between an image (physical or mental) and an object, including one known through description, the mind has to re-present the image

---

[16] Jīva discusses the non-difference between the divine and its intrinsic potencies, which includes divine form and name, in his second volume, *Bhagavat-sandarbha* 11-17.

along with its relevant resembling features to itself.[17] Goodman's claim is founded on his recognising that resemblance indicates a symmetrical relationship whereas representation implies a non-symmetrical one.[18] A representation may appear as a resemblance, but to effectively be established as such, its relevant resembling aspects, which can be many, need to be recognised, i.e., re-presented to the mind. For instance, an image or painting of Jiva Gosvami could resemble the actual person Jiva Gosvami, his brother, an ascetic, a human being, an Earth-dwelling carbon-based organism, another image or painting by the same artist, or all of the above and more. The natural entailment of Goodman's view is that images can only represent resemblances; and for a resemblance to be represented, an interpretation or convention is required. Jerry Alan Fodor comments that to make sense of or to gain some determinate information regarding an image's intended resemblance, there needs to be some discursive content attached to it, an associated description.[19] Similarly, in Jiva's case an image can only resemble a deity if its resembling qualities are re-presented by some accompanying information, such as testimony, which fixes the resemblance.

For ordinary practitioners who do not have direct visual access to the deity, an imaginal that resembles the deity is therefore literally a representative image – the image is a re-presentation of resemblance that, in this case, is informed by testimony. However, the problem of arguing that reality can be represented by way of the image's resemblance with the deity is that it again skirts around the original problem, namely Jiva's claim of non-difference between the image as mind-*murti* and the deity as a real object. Such an argument, though reasonable in ordinary circumstances, would be philosophically too weak to satisfy Jiva's strong assertion of non-difference.

In light of the unsatisfying philosophical implications of the above two attempted resolutions of the paradox. I suggest instead that the reality of the mental image should not be determined through its ontology but by the practitioner's engagement with it. Jīva's explication of mature devotion by way of ancient dramaturgic and poetic theory offers us a way to understand his pedagogy, specifically his preference for addressing the experiences of devotion, including its imaginative elements, over presenting a purely rational assessment of it. In a sense, his descriptions of the rituals anticipate his later explicit aesthetic and phenomenological approach to pedagogy.

---

[17] Nelson Goodman, *Languages of Art: An Approach to a Theory of Symbols* (Indianapolis: Bobbs-Merrill, 1968), 27-31.

[18] Ibid., 4.

[19] Jerry A. Fodor, *The Language of Thought*, The Language & Thought Series (Crowell: New York, 1975), 128.

The Anticipating of *Rasa* as a Means to Dissolve the Paradox

An imaginal is not only generated but is also experienced. Jiva's principal concern with mature devotional participation, imagined or real, is the practitioner's experience. In *Priti-sandarbha*, the final volume of his treatise, Jiva follows his uncle and preceptor, Rupa Gosvami, who in *Bhakti-rasamrita-sindhu* describes mature devotion by mapping out its experience with the help of secular aesthetic theory.[20] Drawing on ancient aesthetic theories, Rupa and Jiva outline the elements that make drama into a living experience. The theories address the means by which an author, character, actor, and audience are able to enjoy a play that can also portray ordinarily unenjoyable events.[21] Much of Jiva's approach and descriptiveness while transposing Rupa's and his own version of these theories onto mature religious experience is anticipated in his earlier volumes, including in his fifth volume explaining the meditation ritual.

The aesthetic theory Rupa and Jiva reference is often referred to as "*Rasa* Theory," which originates in ancient secular analyses in dramaturgy and poetics.[22] The word "*rasa*" ("sap; juice; taste")[23] in the dramaturgic context denotes the enhanced relish experienced in a drama by its author, characters, actors, and audience. It is also regularly applied to Krishna and his devotees in *Bhagavata-purana*; namely, they possess, bestow, and participate in it, though in the religious setting it connotes devotional relish or something in the spirit of

[20] Rūpa's *Bhakti-rasāmṛta-sindhu,* completed in 1541-2, is a precursor to Jīva's *Ṣaṭ-sandarbha* and it contributes greatly to it, especially regarding the higher levels of *bhakti*. Moreover, Jīva was *Bhakti-rasāmṛta-sindhu*'s main editor and also wrote a commentary on it entitled *Durgama-saṇgamana*. My Sanskrit source for Rūpa's work and Jīva's commentary is: Rūpa Gosvāmī and Haridāsa Dāsa, *Bhakti-Rasāmṛta-Sindhu, with Commentaries of Jīva Gosvāmin, Mukundadāsa and Viśvanātha Cakravartī* (Navadvīpa: Haribol Kuṭira, 1961).

[21] A similar analysis takes place in Aristotle's *Poetics*. However, "catharsis" is not a theory embraced in India.

[22] The Western term "aesthetics" cannot neatly be applied to any pre-modern Indian thought system. See: Sheldon I. Pollock, *A Rasa Reader: Classical Indian Aesthetics*, Historical Sourcebooks in Classical Indian Thought (New York: Columbia University Press, 2016), 2. Whether Rūpa and Jīva consider their descriptions of religious experiences to be explainable through secular aesthetics or whether such experiences are in themselves an extraordinary kind of aesthetics as defined by aestheticians is debatable. Pollock sees them as extraordinary aesthetics. Ibid., 306-10. Haberman and Wulff seem to see them as analogous with aesthetics. David L Haberman, *Acting as a Way of Salvation: A Study of Rāgānugā Bhakti Sādhana* (Motilal Banarsidass Publ., 2001), 31; Donna Marie Wulff, *Drama as a Mode of Religious Realization: The Vidagdhamādhava of Rūpa Gosvāmi*, American Academy of Religion Academy Series (Chico, Calif: Scholars Press, 1984), 25-27.

[23] The translation "taste" is not in the sense of good or bad taste but is instead like the adding to a preparation of different spices and condiments to create a particular flavour.

rapture.[24] Rupa sees the term's appearance in the Purana as central for understanding its concept of devotion to Krishna. He subsequently and conveniently finds the analogical model for explaining this devotion in aesthetic *Rasa* Theory.

Originating at least textually in an early treatise on dramaturgy, Bharata Muni's *Natya-shastra* (an aphoristic text that is open to interpretation), *Rasa* Theory has been adopted and adapted through a lively discussion among aestheticians over the next few centuries.[25] Among these later thinkers, the two that stand out as profoundly influencing Jiva's tradition are Bhoja Raja, an eleventh century king and patron of poets, and Vishvanatha Kaviraja, a fourteenth-century Oriyan.[26]

The following first offers a brief overview of Bharata's, Bhoja's, and Vishvanatha's secular *rasa* theories that inform Jiva and Rupa's expression of mature devotion. Next, the devotional *rasa* Jiva and Rupa develop from these theories is described. Finally, it is shown how this devotional *rasa* is anticipated in Jiva's expression of the meditation rituals, affecting his statement regarding a non-imaginative object of imagination.

Secular *Rasa* Theories

In *Natya-shastra,* Bharata formally describes the arising of dramatic or aesthetic relish, or *rasa*, as a transformation of ordinary emotion by way of an

[24] In *Bhagavata-purana* all *rasas* are said to be possessed by Krishna (10.87.34), who also bestows *rasa* (10.42.1). His devotees know *rasa* (1.1.19, 1.5.19, 1.18.14, 3.15.48, 3.20.6, 4.31.21), long for it (4.4.15), and are immersed in it (5.1.5, 6.3.28). Vyāsa and Shastri, *Bhāgavata-Purāṇa of Kṛṣṇa Dvaipayana Vyāsa, with Sanskrit Commentary Bhāvārtha-Bodhinī of Śrīdhara Svāmī.*

[25] Sushil Kumar De, *Sanskrit Poetics as a Study of Aesthetic* (Berkeley: University of California Press, 1963), 2. See: Pollock, *A Rasa Reader: Classical Indian Aesthetics*, 5-6. Estimates dating *Natya-shastra* range from the fifth century CE back to the fifth century BCE. The text may have been revised around the ninth century CE, possibly in Kashmir.

[26] Bhoja's theory is addressed in Rūpa Gosvāmī's *Ujjvala-nīlamaṇi* 15.3, 15.102 and in Jīva's *Prīti-sandarbha* 110 as well as his commentary on *Ujjvala-nīlamaṇi* 15.185-187. Bhoja is not just a source of citations for these authors. He deeply influenced them. Rūpa Gosvāmī and Haridāsa Dāsa, *Ujjvala-Nīlamaṇi, with the Commentary of Vṣṇudāsa* (Navadvīpa: Haribol Kuṭira, 1955). Also see: Sivaprasad Bhattacharyya, "Bhoja's Rasa-Ideology and Its Influence on Bengal Rasa-Śāstra," *Journal of the Oriental Institute* 13, no. 2 (1963): 106-19. Rembert Lutjeharms essay has been of great help in understanding Rūpa and Jīva's theory of *rasa* and its antecedents: Rembert Lutjeharms, "An Ocean of Emotion: Rasa and Religious Experience in Early Caitanya Vaiṣṇava Thought," in *Caitanya Vaisnava Philosophy: Tradition, Reason and Devotion*, ed. Ravi M. Gupta (Routledge,, 2016).

assisting set of dramatic factors: "*Rasa* is produced from the combination of the *excitant*, the *ensuant*, and the *transitory-emotion*."[27]

This is a loose description of factors that combine to produce *rasa*. They assist in the transformation from a lasting *dominant-emotion*[28] that is implicitly referred to in this aphorism. A *dominant-emotion* defines the mood of a play, and Bharata lists eight kinds: love, humour, sorrow, anger, courage, fear, disgust, and astonishment,[29] to which later thinkers add a ninth, tranquillity. When *rasa* eventually arises, it essentially amounts to a heightened aesthetic appreciation of one of these *dominant-emotions*.

Bharata considers the *excitants* to be excited or enhanced emotions that occur in response to a scene in a drama. They arise out of or help to develop the *dominant-emotion*. For example, the *excitant* for the *dominant-emotion* of love could be the appearance of the beloved; for fear, it could be a dangerous situation or the possibility of death; and so on. Later thinkers categorise these *excitants* into two types: *direct-excitants*,[30] which could be certain characters that appear in the drama; and *indirect-excitants*,[31] as in, for instance, the setting in which a scene or the play itself takes place.[32] Actors also respond to emotions. The depiction of their responses are the *ensuants*, these occurring voluntarily towards certain characters or events. They can comprise words, gestures, or responses such as laughing, frowning, showing disdain, etc. A further set of elements that also assists in the development of *rasa*, which Bharata does not mention in this aphorism but discusses elsewhere, are involuntary *psycho-physical reactions*,[33] such as bliss, anxiety, fainting, and crying.[34] Finally, there are *transitory* or *secondary-emotions*[35] that support or engage with the *dominant-emotion*. These can be, for example, arrogance, jealousy, or idleness.[36]

---

[27] *Naṭya-shastra*: part of the explanation of sentiments immediately prior to 6.32. Muni Bharata et al., *Nátyasāstra, with the Commentary of Abhinavagupta*, Gaekwad's Oriental Series, (Baroda: Central library, 1926). The English terms in italics throughout the rest of this chapter indicate translations of technical Sanskrit terms employed by Bharata, Bhoja, Viṣvanātha, Rūpa, and Jīva. On the first mention of each term, the Sanskrit equivalent is then given in a footnote. In this case, the "excitant" is *vibhāva*, the "ensuant" is "*anubhāva*," and the "transitory-emotion" is *vyabhicāri-bhāva*.

[28] The "dominant-emotion" is *sthāyi-bhāva.*

[29] *Nāṭya-śāstra* 6.17. Pollock posits that this seemingly limited list of eight can be justified by virtue of its being a categorization only of emotions that are communicable during the performance of a drama. Pollock, *A Rasa Reader: Classical Indian Aesthetics*, 8.

[30] The "direct-excitant" is *ālambana.*

[31] The "indirect-excitant" is *uddīpana*

[32] Lutjeharms, "An Ocean of Emotion: Rasa and Religious Experience in Early Caitanya Vaiṣṇava Thought," 179.

[33] The "psycho-physical reaction" is *sāttvikā-bhāva*.

[34] *Nāṭya-śāstra* 7.94

[35] The "transitory- [or] secondary-emotion" is *vyabhicāri-bhāva*.

[36] *Nāṭya-śāstra* 6.18-21

All five of the above factors are normal emotions or emotional responses. When all together they are properly nurtured and experienced in the setting of a drama, they become aesthetically enriched and palatable, at this stage having been transformed into *rasa*. The difference between ordinary emotion and *rasa* is that the latter enables a person to be enjoyably immersed in a play even when experiencing its disturbing emotions, such as anger and sorrow.[37]

Bhoja Raja and Vishvanatha Kaviraja apply Bharata's *Rasa* theory to poetics. Bhoja sees *rasa* as a peculiar state of mind, a *sense-of-self*,[38] which he equates both with passion and love, its causing an experience of being conscious of pleasure inasmuch as it is agreeable to the mind.[39] Moreover, this passionate *sense-of-self* is expressed in a variety of emotional moods, such as affinities or inclinations for love, strife, vexation, and joking.[40] It also brings about a comportment that can intensify and manifest Bharata's listed emotions.[41] Bhoja thinks that this is all not yet beyond the reader's thinking faculties. The emotions are only experienced via *bhavana*, which he considers to be a kind of contemplation, and so exist merely as *secondary* rather than *dominant-emotions*.[42] He uses "*bhavana*" in reference to these emotions inasmuch as they are 'brought into being' or 'produced' and, yet, are still contemplated or objectively observed rather than fully and subjectively enjoyed.[43]

---

[37] In this way, a *dominant-emotion* is able to transform in a very specific way, i.e.: the *dominant-emotion* of love turns into the amorous *rasa*, humour into the comic *rasa*, sorrow into the compassionate *rasa*, anger into the furious *rasa*, courage into the heroic *rasa*, fear into the fearful *rasa*, disgust into the horrific *rasa*, and wonder into the marvelous *rasa*. *Nāṭya-śāstra* 6.15.

[38] The "sense-of-self" is *abhimāna*

[39] *Śṛṅgāra-prakāśa* 1.8. Bhojarāja and V. Raghavan, *Śṛṅgāra-Prakāśā*, Harvard Oriental Series (Cambridge, Mass.: Dept. of Sanskrit and Indian Studies, Harvard University; London, 1998).
Bhoja's *Śṛṅgāra-prakāśa* comprises both verses and prose. I cite verse numbers where appropriate and page numbers in Raghavan's printed version when it is the prose that I am citing.

[40] Ibid., 662.

[41] *Śṛṅgāra-prakāśa* 1.4

[42] Technically the term with its diacritics is "*bhāvanā*." On the difference between *bhāvanā* and *rasa*, Pollock, commenting on Bhoja's concept of *rasa* in *Śṛṅgāra-prakāśa* writes: "..."tasting" may refer to the character's capacity for experiencing, by way of the epiphenomena that manifest it (erotic desire and all the other factors), the primal Passion that otherwise "transcends the plane of the coming-into-being of feeling (*bhāvanā*)" (vs. 10)." Sheldon I. Pollock, "Bhoja's Śṛṅgāraprakāśa and the Problem of Rasa: A Historical Introduction and Annotated Translation," *Asiatische Studien* 52, no. 1 (1998): 130-31.

[43] "*Bhāvanā*" is typically translated as "imagining; contemplating; reflecting; effecting; producing; [or] causing to be." However, it literally connotes an emerging into being, this being derived from its verbal root "*bhū*," meaning "to be; exist." Hence, rather than referring to a passive reception of memories or an imaginative generation of images, "*bhāvanā*" connotes

At the *bhavana* stage, any actual experiencing of *rasa* is only in potentiality.[44] When an emotion is no longer affected by mental processes, it can then be fully relished in the heart that is endowed with ego and, as such, is considered *rasa* proper.[45] *Rasa* is the *sense-of-self* that actually experiences pleasure, even in pain.[46] *Bhavana* is missing this fully experiencing *sense-of-self*, for it is still conceptual or contemplative. It lacks the immersive experience.

Bhoja qualifies *rasa* as singular in terms of love, though it has different flavours.[47] Any one of the *dominant-emotions* can become absorbed into this singular *rasa* of love, which is enhanced with that *dominant-emotion's* unique flavour along with Bharata's other emotional components.[48] This *rasa* of love is considered *rasa* proper because it is tasted; in other words, it cannot be fully grasped other than through its experience.[49]

Vishvanatha Kaviraja challenges the idea that *rasa* is merely an intensification of emotion, claiming that it is instead a transformation of emotion into something else, like milk into yoghurt.[50] Despite *rasa* resembling a character's ordinary emotions, it is distinct from them because it comprises "self-luminous consciousness and bliss" with an "otherworldly or extraordinary essence."[51] After all, actors and audiences react to dramatic scenes differently to the way people respond to quotidian experiences.

While explaining the *excitants*, *ensuants*, and so on, Vishvanatha proposes the idea of "*commonization*," a kind of impersonal generalization.[52] This is the

---

a becoming or arriving into existence. Monier Monier-Williams, Ernst Leumann, and Carl Cappeller, *A Sanskrit-English Dictionary: Etymologically and Philologically Arranged with Special Reference to Cognate Indo-European Languages*, New ed. (Oxford: Oxford University Press, 1960).

[44] *Śṛṅgāra-prakāśa* 1.3

[45] Ibid.,1.10

[46] Bhojarāja and Raghavan, *Śṛṅgāra-Prakāśā*, 664.

[47] Ibid., 5. This is one of Bhoja's most explicit statement regarding the singularity of *rasa*. Still, his entire analysis is hedged towards this view.

[48] Ibid., 662.
Pollock translates this: "Now, rasa in this treatise is defined as love. For all forms of emotion, desire and everything else, once they reach their full development, ultimately turn out to be nothing but this. Thus people are said to "love sex," to "love quarreling" or anger or joking." Pollock, *A Rasa Reader: Classical Indian Aesthetics*, 124.

[49] Bhojarāja and Raghavan, *Śṛṅgāra-Prakāśā*, 5.

[50] *Sāhitya-darpaṇa* 3.1. Viśvanātha Kavirāja and Durgaprasad Dvivedi, *Sāhitya-Darpaṇa* (New Delhi: Daryaganj, 1982).

[51] *Sāhitya-darpaṇa* 3.19.

[52] *Sāhitya-darpaṇa* 3.9-11. The Anglicized term "*commonization*," referring to the Sanskrit "*sādhāraṇī-kṛtī*" or "*sādhāraṇī-karaṇa*," is Sheldon Pollock's. See: Pollock, *A Rasa Reader: Classical Indian Aesthetics*, xv, 261-63. The implicit example Viṣvanātha uses is of Hanumān in *Rāmāyaṇa* who jumps over the ocean between India and Lanka. The use of

means through which an audience can find common emotional ground in a drama. It enables the audience to imaginatively share in the characters' experiences despite being incapable of genuinely owning them. Through *commonization*, all personal possessiveness is bracketed.[53] Many experiences in a play, as in for instance those between a husband and a wife or those concerning fear for a monster, are either inappropriate or non-genuine for an audience to own.[54] However, the audience also cannot fail to identify with the characters' emotions as they occur as a result of such experiences, for otherwise, there would be no aesthetic participation, or *rasa*.[55] The *commonization* of these experiences, which is expressed as a total experience, thus enables the audience to have its own genuine emotional response. Members of the audience can thus, in their own way, mimic the character's total emotional experience, and it is this that transforms into *rasa*. Hence, according to Vishvanatha, *rasa*, an extraordinary combination that only a literary experience can provide, can belong to the audience solely by means of this necessary factor of *commonization*.

Devotional *Rasa*

Secular *Rasa* Theory including some of its later developments, i.e., the transformation of emotional factors into *rasa*, the *sense-of-self*, *rasa* singularly qualified as love which manifests in a variety of flavours, and the *commonization* of emotional experience, all find currency in Rupa and Jiva's devotional *rasa*. In *Bhakti-rasamrita-sindhu*, Rupa analogically utilizes *Rasa* Theory to map out the landscape of devotion with its divine characters and settings so that practitioners can psychologically navigate it and understand the culture in which a mature participatory relationship with Krishna takes place. Although Rupa's general analysis of (what becomes known as) *bhakti-rasa* (*devotional-rasa*) is informed by Bharata's, Bhoja's, and Vishvanatha's models, it is distinct from ordinary *Rasa* Theory insofar as his is of religious life framed in aesthetics; in other words, the experience of devotion is described though defined dramaturgical categories.[56]

Like Bhoja, Rupa sees *rasa* proper to be the *rasa* of love. The emotion of love arises as a result of the right kind of *memory-imprints*,[57] accumulated

---

commonization makes Hanumān not a distant divine being but a person with whom the audience can intimately relate. Hanumān's "monkey jumping" is also the example that Jīva uses in excerpt V.

[53] *Sāhitya-darpaṇa* 3.12.

[54] Ibid.,3.11

[55] Ibid.,3.11

[56] Wulff, *Drama as a Mode of Religious Realization: The Vidagdhamādhava of Rūpa Gosvāmi*, 27.

[57] The "memory-imprint" is *vāsanā* or *saṁskāra*.

during a person's life or previous lives.[58] Again, love is the only *dominant-emotion*.[59] When it is developed through religious praxis (from service and rituals through to deep meditations on Krishna) up to a point where it is heightened by the meditation on or experience of other associated affections, which are of the same nature as Bharata's *excitants*, *ensuants*, etc., then it becomes devotional *rasa*.

When mature practitioners contemplate or visualize Krishna or anyone closely associated with him, their love naturally becomes coloured by one of five possible general emotions or flavours. Rupa lists these as tranquillity, affection, friendship, parental affection, and amorous love.[60] Tranquillity is the least developed or expressive, arising mainly in sages and ascetics not participating in devotion.[61] The other four, which are listed in order of being successively sweeter,[62] are developed from a sentiment of goodwill towards Krishna and are characterised by a sense of possessiveness, or *myness*.[63] This *myness* is a *sense-of-self* (similar to Bhoja's) that is determined by one of the above four emotional flavours.[64]

Rupa also transposes all the aesthetic emotional factors leading to *rasa* into a devotional setting. Together, the possessor and the object of devotional affections, i.e. the devotee and Krishna, are the *direct-excitants*.[65] The form, qualities, beauty, activities, possessions, residences, and everything else related to Krishna, either physical, vocal, or mental, that further stimulate the devotee's love are the *indirect-excitants*.[66] Both kinds of *excitant* give rise to depicted devotional responses, such as singing, dancing, etc., these being the *ensuants*.[67] Sometimes the responses involuntarily burst out from the devotees. These are categorised into eight kinds: paralysis, perspiring, hair standing on end, choking voice, trembling, changing complexion, crying, and fainting.[68] The responses can be further agitated to manifest a continued responsive relishing, encompassing related words, movements of the eye brows, and other

---

[58] *Bhakti-rasāmṛta-sindhu* 1.2.264. The residual impressions inspire a preferred type of service or practice.

[59] *Bhakti-rasāmṛta-sindhu* 2.5.2. Also see *Bhakti-rasāmṛta-sindhu* 1.2.2, 1.3.10, 1.3.13

[60] Ibid., 2.5.6

[61] Ibid., 2.5.17-18. Interestingly, here Jīva equates sages and ascetics with monist Advaitins and impersonal yogīs, placing them on a lower rung even to non-ascetic devotees.

[62] Ibid., 2.5.38. This similarly occurs with *rasa* as mentioned in *Bhakti-rasāmṛta-sindhu* 2.5.115

[63] Ibid., 2.5.22. "Myness" is *mamatā*

[64] *Prīti-sandarbha* 84. Jīva Gosvāmī and Haridāsaśāstrī, *Śrī-Prīti-Sandarbhaḥ* (Vṛndāvana, Jillā Mathurā, Uttara Pradeśa: Śrīgadādharagauraharipresa, 1986).

[65] Ibid., 112

[66] Ibid., 116

[67] Ibid., 158, citing *Bhakti-rasāmṛta-sindhu* 2.2.2.

[68] Ibid., 158, citing *Bhakti-rasāmṛta-sindhu* 2.3.16.

bodily indications.[69] These responses can also be jarring to the *dominant-emotion*, assisting it in unusual ways.[70] The coexistence of all these factors fills the heart of the devotee with *rasa*, similar to Vishvanatha's extraordinary relish.[71] This marks the culmination of Rupa and Jiva's expression of devotion. After amassing all the elements, the original *dominant-emotion* condenses, softens the heart, is characterised by possessiveness, and so is known as the *rasa* of "love."[72] Once attaining a state of *rasa*, this love maintains one of its previously mentioned five primary flavours, but enhanced. In a similar way to Bhoja, Rupa additionally holds that despite its flavours, the *rasa* of love is a singular *dominant-em*otion.[73]

The practitioner therefore really or imaginatively participates in Krishna's divine play via a *dominant-emotion* with a particular flavour, interacts with Krishna and his companions as the *excitants*, reciprocates with him via the *ensuants* such as singing and dancing, enables the specific flavour of love for him to be enhanced by the *transient-emotions* such as words and facial expressions, and subsequently realizes *rasa* in the heart. Moreover, rather than the *excitants*, *ensuants*, and so on being the causes of emotional love for Krishna, Rupa sees it as the opposite. For him, an extraordinary love for Krishna, the origins of which are Krishna's own intrinsic divine potency, initiates its own causes, turning Krishna, etc. into the *excitants*, *ensuants*, and so on. To illustrate this, Rupa employs the analogy of clouds that fill an ocean using the same water that they collected from it.[74] Hence, love for Krishna is the origin of *rasa* and not its result.[75] *Rasa* reveals Krishna as charming, which increases that love.[76]

Jiva notes the two kinds of devotee who experience *rasa*: those participating in Krishna's play in reality and those that imagine participating in it.[77] For the latter, there are two ways of acquiring *rasa*: hearing of Krishna's and his companions' activities or hearing of his attributes.[78] It is in regard to the former, and specifically in terms of the activities of Krishna's companions, that Vishvanatha's *commonization* in *rasa* becomes relevant, for the companions being described could be exhibiting a different *dominant-emotion* to the hearer, the practitioner. This could cause confusion regarding whose *dominant-emotion* determines the nature of the *rasa* experience – that of the characters in the poem

---

[69] Ibid., 158, citing *Bhakti-rasāmṛta-sindhu* 2.4.2.

[70] *Bhakti-rasāmṛta-sindhu* 2.4.1

[71] *Bhakti-rasāmṛta-sindhu* 2.1.10; *Prīti-sandarbha* 110

[72] Ibid., 1.4.1

[73] Ibid., 2.5.132. The other seven of Bharata's emotions become secondary: *Bhakti-rasāmṛta-sindhu* 2.5.39-41.

[74] Ibid., 2.5.94-5

[75] *Prīti-sandarbha* 110

[76] *Bhakti-rasāmṛta-sindhu* 2.5.98

[77] *Prīti-sandarbha* 111

[78] Ibid.

or cosmic drama or that of the hearer or audience. Jiva clarifies that it is the audience's, or the imaginatively participating devotee's, *dominant-emotion* that defines the nature of the *rasa* experience. This is because both characters and audience possess a similar general, or common, proclivity, this being love of Krishna. So the audience is able through this to generalize the *excitants* etc., and hence imagine itself in a way that can bring about an enhanced emotional relishing of the situations in which the characters find themselves.[79] Rupa, in a similar way to Vishvanatha while ascribing the idea to Bharata, who also touches on it,[80] describes this *commonization* in terms of removing the restraints between self and other so that the self can identify with the *excitants*.[81] However, Jiva notes that since *rasa* is considered a permanent and ubiquitous fixture of the devotee's existence, *rasa* experienced via *commonization* can only be obtained if the characters and the hearing devotee are of a similar nature, that is, defined by the same *dominant-emotion*.[82] Otherwise, the emotion will be enhanced, but it will not manifest *rasa*. This view of Rupa and Jiva's regarding *commonization* incorporates both of the secular views – that *rasa* exists in the characters as well as in the audience.

Rasa Anticipated in the Meditation Rituals

Striking consistencies are found when mapping the Gaudiya explanation of *rasa* and its elements as part of mature devotional praxis onto Jiva's description of the meditation rituals. This is not to say that Jiva considers *rasa* to be part of the rituals *per se,* for they are not solely for the mature practitioner. What can be inferred is that Jiva's descriptions of the practitioner's exchanges with ritual objects of the imagination, such as Krishna and his companions, anticipates his later explanation or mapping out of mature devotion via *Rasa* theory.

Jiva's treatise describes a developing love for Krishna through service and praxis. This evolving love is essentially the *dominant-emotion* of which *rasa* is eventually informed or arises. The *dominant-emotion* of love can exist in the practitioner or through the practitioner's exchanges with Krishna, the latter being prevalent throughout Jiva's explication of the meditation rituals.

Jiva proposes conceptual abstractions as part of the ritual visualizations. Both the demons and the monkey jumping that are part of Rama's story are conceptually transposed onto characters and scenes in Krishna's dramas with his friends that are performed as part of their perennial empirically non-manifest cosmic play (excerpt V). This is similar to Viśvanatha's *commonization*, which enables members of an audience to become emotionally engaged in a dramatic act based on a different *dominant-emotion* to their own. Throughout

[79] Ibid.

[80] This is not found in the extant editions of *Nāṭya-śāstra*.

[81] *Bhakti-rasāmṛta-sindhu* 2.5.103

[82] See *Prīti-sandarbha* 111

his treatise, Jiva is focused on Krishna's perennial non-manifest acts, for these comprise the direct visual goal of his devotional process. Krishna and his expansions, like Rama, perform earthly acts that often involve maleficent beings, towards which the practitioner cannot project loving emotion. So Jiva asks the ritual practitioner to see them figuratively as enacted characters depicted in dramas that are part of Krishna's perennial activities. This reconceptualization is of the nature of *commonization*, allowing the *dominant-emotion* of love of Krishna to flourish in and be owned by practitioners despite their being informed by descriptions of Krishna's terrestrial acts depicting maleficent beings that would ordinarily disrupt *rasa*. Still, such *commonization* cannot bring about *rasa* because it does not enhance but instead diffuses the diverse emotive responses between devotees and demons. It does not describe the mature stage wherein Krishna's perennial acts are naturally experienced. This effectively explains Jiva's use of "*bhavana*" to describe imagination in the rituals and throughout his treatise. Rupa, like Bhoja, considers that *rasa* surpasses *bhavana* because it produces wonder and is relished in the heart of those who are qualified by purity.[83] *Bhavana*, on the other hand, remains conceptual or contemplative – a looking in from the outside. The progression from *bhavana* to *rasa* is of an intensity in emotion leading to an immersion in emotion. Pollock, commenting on Bhoja's use of "*bhavana*," notes, with respect to its being preliminary to *rasa*, that it connotes "the coming-into-being of feeling."[84] Similarly, Rupa connects *bhavana* with the emerging of feeling or emotion, which is prior to any experiencing of a mature emotional relish. Jiva's use of "*bhavana*" in his descriptions of the rituals can thus be interpreted as a precursor to *rasa*.

Krishna as the object of love is reinforced in the rituals through Jiva's arguing that the representative image is non-different from this deity, for, he notes, thinking otherwise disrupts devotion (excerpt II). Throughout Jiva's treatise, the *dominant-emotion* is always the love of Krishna. This love resides in the devotee's exchanges with Krishna and in Krishna himself, the object of love, both of which qualify as *excitants* that evoke an intensification of love. The *direct-excitants* in the rituals are drawn out by the meditations on Krishna and his companions. The *indirect-excitants* are the qualities, activities, ornaments, scenes, and all else that is connected with Krishna, all these being explicitly described in Jiva's explanation of ritual meditation. Jiva also refers to Krishna's realms (implicitly in excerpt V and explicitly elsewhere in the same section of his treatise)[85] as objects of meditation, also *indirect-excitants*.

---

[83] *Bhakti-rasāmṛta-sindhu* 2.5.132

[84] Pollock, "Bhoja's Śṛṅgāraprakāśa and the Problem of Rasa: A Historical Introduction and Annotated Translation," 130-31.

[85] In *Bhakti-sandarbha* 286, Jīva refers to Krishna's lands, Vṛndāvana and Mathurā, as part of the ritual visualization.

Interestingly, in Jiva's explanation of the rituals there is no mention of *ensuants*, i.e., responses to the emotions or *excitants*, such as singing, dancing, perspiring, crying, or fainting.[86] This is testimony to the deficiency of factors that lead to *rasa* at the stage of ritual visualization.

Although *bhavana* does not evoke *rasa*, it does imply an emerging of feeling that leads to an intensification of emotion. Its effect is similar to *rasa* in that it brings the practitioner closer to the object that excites love. Jiva's use of the term "*bhavana*" for ritual imagination along with his focus on religious experience implies that the imaginal of Krishna engaged with as part of the ritual visualization should be understood in terms of a devotional and emotional exchange, one that is contemplated as part of the ritual meditation. Since the image is imaginative, the means for this exchange is the aesthetic excitant. In other words, it involves an imaginative participation that is real in the same way as an audience's actual participation in a drama. Yet, and importantly, this participation is not fully mature and so is not fully immersive.

The Role of Imagination in the Meditation Rituals

The original problem addressed by this article is that on face value, Jiva's statement regarding an imagination praxis that yields non-imaginative or real objects seems paradoxical. Two viable explanations for the author's statements were offered but turned out to be philosophically unsatisfactory. Instead, through noting Jiva's anticipating of *Rasa* Theory in his description of the meditation rituals, it can be understood that his statements on imagination are coloured by his use of "*bhavana*," which is about an emerging real emotional and aesthetic engagement with an object or image. His descriptions express an embryonic form of *rasa* that carries a similar but less intense and truncated set of mechanisms.

Although *rasa* does not arise during ritual visualization, the *dominant-emotion*, *direct-* and *indirect-excitants*, and *ensuants* are prevalent throughout Jiva's descriptions of it. These factors are meant to enhance the intensity of the practitioner's experience with Krishna. Since devotion requires a real and not a fictitious participatory relationship, the object of any visualization needs to be established in reality. It is therefore not surprising that Jiva claims just this, although it initially seems paradoxical due to the imaginative element. However, it is only a paradox when reality is applied to the images or objects of imagination in and of themselves. If the reality that Jiva speaks of is a reference to the practitioner's real aesthetic comportment towards these objects, whether attained through images that capture the real Krishna or directly via the mind-*murti*, the inconsistencies dissolve.

---

[86] Singing is, however, treated in Jīva's treatise as another practice that is both preliminary and independent to *mūrti* worship: *Bhakti-sandarbha* 262-5.

The *dominant-emotion* in Jiva's expression of *rasa* theory belongs to the practitioner's exchanges with Krishna as well as to Krishna himself, the actor in both the imaginative and the real perennial 'non-manifest' play. It is through this *dominant-emotion* that the object of visualization can be engaged with in a real way. By means of the different *excitants* and *ensuants*, this emotion is enhanced. Through a kind of *commonization*, it is owned. The reality of the exchange is thus in the practitioner's engagement. In other words, the same *real* engagement would occur if the practitioner were to see Krishna externally and directly. Hence, the object or image of visualization is non-imaginative inasmuch as it evokes real emotion towards an object consistent with reality. Therefore, the positive role of imagination in the rituals comprises a means for generating as many factors leading to *rasa* as possible by way of an imaginal so as to bring about a real *rasa*-lite emotional exchange with the object of meditation, this acting as a segue to devotional maturity.

Nordic Studies in Theology / Nordische Studien zur Theologie

Edited by / hrsg. von Prof. Dr. Kirsten Busch Nielsen (University of Copenhagen), Prof. Dr. Dr. Jan-Olav Henriksen (MF Norwegian School of Theology, Religion and Society, Oslo), Dr. Hans Bringeland (NLA University College, Bergen)

Sasja Mathiasen Stopa
Soli Deo Honor et Gloria
Honour and Glory in the Theology of Martin Luther
Sasja E.M. Stopa explores the influence of honour and glory on Martin Luther's theology. Luther's works overflow with terminology of honour and glory. Analysing a broad selection hereof, Stopa argues that his doctrine of justification centers on a soteriological concern for the recreation of human glory lost in the Fall and a doxological concern for God's glory stolen by sinners. Stopa shows how this relation to God patterns Luther's understanding of social relations and discusses justification as a process of mutual recognition translating Luther's theology of glory into contemporary theology.
vol. 7, 2021, ca. 248 pp., ca. 39,90 €, br., ISBN-CH 978-3-643-91272-5

Fredrik Saxegaard
Realizing Church
Parish Clergy as Contributors to Leadership in Congregations
Realizing Church is an empirial investigation into how three Norwegian parish priests take part in congregational leadership. Based on Cultural-Historical Activity Theory, leadership is viewed as intimately connected to mundane routines and material objects. The book finds that the priests contribute to leadership through their work to give differing communities a coherent shape, negotiation of their own leader subject nodes, and through discussions, processings and realizations of the object of activity – of Church.
Realizing Church contributes to pastoral theology, and to the fields of leadership-as-practice and religious leadership.
vol. 6, 2021, ca. 280 pp., ca. 39,90 €, br., ISBN-CH 978-3-643-91177-3

Jan-Olav Henriksen
Representation and Ultimacy
Christian Religion as Unfinished Business
Bd. 5, 2019, 278 S., 69,90 €, br., ISBN 978-3-643-91168-1

Asle Eikrem; Atle O. Søvik (Eds.)
Talking Seriously About God
Philosophy of Religion in the Dispute between Theism and Atheism
Bd. 4, 2016, 184 S., 29,90 €, br., ISBN 978-3-643-90741-7

Hans Bringeland
Die Theologie Ole Hallebys
Norwegischer Pietismus in erfahrungstheologischer und kantianischer Prägung
Bd. 3, 2021, 256 S., 39,90 €, gb., ISBN-CH 978-3-643-90385-3

Gunnar Innerdal
Hans Urs von Balthasar on Spirit and Truth
A Systematic Reconstruction in Connection to the Theoretical Framework of Lorenz B. Puntel
Bd. 2, 2016, 328 S., 49,90 €, br., ISBN 978-3-643-90628-1

Jonna Bornemark; Mattias Martinson; Jayne Svenungsson (Eds.)
Monument and Memory
Bd. 1, 2015, 272 S., 49,90 €, gb., ISBN 978-3-643-90467-6

LIT Verlag Berlin – Münster – Wien – Zürich – London
Auslieferung Deutschland / Österreich / Schweiz: siehe Impressumsseite

Nordic Studies in Religion and Culture / Nordische Studien zur Religion und Kultur

edited by /hrsg. von Dr. Hans Bringeland (NLA University College, Bergen), Prof. Dr. Ingvild S. Gilhus (University of Bergen)

Kai Merten
Ïch habe im Himmel keine Spur von dir gesehen."
Religionsbegegnung in Grönland im 18. Jahrhundert
Dänisch-norwegische und deutsche Missionare kamen im 18. Jahrhundert erstmals nach Grönland. Sie trafen dort auf Menschen, deren kulturelle und religiöse Vorstellungen ihnen völlig fremd waren. So wurden sie z. B. mit dem Vorwurf konfrontiert: „Ich habe im Himmel keine Spur von dir gesehen." Andere Einheimische trieb die Sorge um, wie sie trotz ihres Übertritts zum Christentum weiter Kontakt zu ihren ungetauft verstorbenen Angehörigen halten konnten, und sie fanden ihre spezielle Antwort auf diese Frage.
Das vorliegende Buch analysiert die Gespräche zwischen europäischen Missionaren und indigenen Grönländern in dieser ersten Zeit der Religionsbegegnung anhand zeitgenössischer Quellen und bietet auf dieser Grundlage eine Deutung an, wie der Prozess der Christianisierung Grönlands verstanden werden kann.
Bd. 7, 2020, 578 S., 49,90 €, br., ISBN 978-3-643-14638-0

Hans Bringeland; Arve Brunvoll (Eds.)
What on Earth is 'Religion'?
Religion, the Name and the Concepts. NLA Hogskolen, Bergen, 12. – 13. November 2019
What has been the role and understanding of religion in the last hundred years, and what can be the meaning of religion today? There is a well-known ongoing process of secularization in the Western world. Is there also a return of religion? And what does the fate of religion mean for an understanding of the Christian faith? These are topics of this book. The articles originate from the actual fields of research of an interdisciplinary group of scholars, who took part in a symposium held in Bergen Nov. 2019. The contributions relate to specific contexts in the modern history of religion from the perspective of religious studies, theology, philosophy and sociology.
vol. 6, 2021, ca. 360 pp., ca. 39,90 €, br., ISBN-CH 978-3-643-91139-1

Kaarlo Arffman
Revolution des Helfens
Der Versuch des Luthertums, die Probleme der Armut zu lösen
Bd. 5, 2019, 344 S., 29,90 €, br., ISBN 978-3-643-91122-3

Kai Merten
Färöische Religionsgeschichte
Von den Anfängen bis zur Gegenwart
Bd. 4, 2017, 320 S., 29,90 €, br., ISBN 978-3-643-13580-3

Peter Nynäs; Ruth Illman; Tuomas Martikainen (Eds.)
On the outskirts of "the church"
Diversity, fluidities and new spaces of religion in Finland
Bd. 3, 2015, 288 S., 34,90 €, br., ISBN 978-3-643-90571-0

Nils G. Holm
The Human Symbolic Construction of Reality
A Psycho-Phenomenological Study
Bd. 2, 2014, 152 S., 34,90 €, br., ISBN 978-3-643-90526-0

Hans Bringeland; Arve Brunvoll (Hg.)
Die Religion und das Wertefundament der Gesellschaft
Studien zum 200. Jahrestag des norwegischen Grundgesetzes 2014
Bd. 1, 2015, 278 S., 34,90 €, br., ISBN 978-3-643-90466-9

LIT Verlag Berlin – Münster – Wien – Zürich – London
Auslieferung Deutschland / Österreich / Schweiz: siehe Impressumsseite

Forum Religionsphilosophie

Adolf Hochmuth
Evolutives Christentum
Versuch einer Kritik der christlichen Vernunft
Die religiöse, die christliche und kirchliche Großwetterlage erscheint am Beginn des 3. Jahrtausends unübersehbar eingetrübt. Als die größte Konfession tritt der Agnostizismus zumindest in der westlichen Welt auf. Christliche Vernunft muss sich als mit den Natur- und den Humanwissenschaften vereinbar erweisen und muss eine immer schon in ihr angelegte evolutive DNA zu Wort kommen lassen. Die aufklärerischen Impulse des Christentums dürfen in großem Selbstbewusstsein allen anderen Religionen und einer billigen Wellness-Esoterik gegenüber intellektuell offen bekannt werden.
Bd. 41, 2021, ca. 296 S., ca. 39,90 €, br., ISBN 978-3-643-14915-2

Matthias Vonarburg
Der Mensch und seine Vollendung
Die Frage nach der Himmelsehe im Kontext christlicher Eschatologie
Das hier vorliegende Werk ist ein Beitrag zur christlichen Eschatologie und geht der Frage nach, ob es bei den Beziehungen unter den Heiligen von Gott intendierte Unterschiede qualitativer Art gibt. Über das Vorstellungsmodell der Himmelsehe wird dabei eine mögliche Beantwortung hergeleitet und der spekulativ gewonnene Topos von der praegerichtlichen Offenlegung als Novum in die Diskussion eingeführt.
Bd. 40, 2021, 152 S., 24,90 €, br., ISBN 978-3-643-80319-1

Udo Kern
Das Leben, das Sein und das Nichts
Ein philosophisch-theologischer Diskurs
Bd. 39, 2020, 336 S., 39,90 €, br., ISBN 978-3-643-14618-2

Robert Ernst
Theologische Fragen im Lichte mystischer Offenbarungen
Herausgegeben von Matthias Bücker-de Silva
Bd. 38, 2020, 186 S., 24,90 €, br., ISBN 978-3-643-14366-2

Christos Retoulas
God's Gift, World's Deception
Dr Eben Alexander's Proof of Heaven in the Light of the Real
vol. 37, 2021, ca. 160 pp., ca. 34,90 €, br., ISBN-CH 978-3-643-91111-7

Hinderk M. Emrich
Re-Formation der Reformation
Das Wort und die ursprüngliche Geste. Posthum herausgegeben von Lydia-Maria Emrich und Cornelia Gerbothe
Bd. 36, 2020, 184 S., 39,90 €, br., ISBN 978-3-643-14072-2

Richard Glöckner
Meister Eckhart – Philosoph und Mystiker des Christentums
Aus den deutschsprachigen Predigten und Traktaten. Texte und Interpretationen
Bd. 35, 2. Aufl. 2019, 244 S., 29,90 €, br., ISBN 978-3-643-14532-1

Eva Kaminski; Gerhard Schreiber; Heiko Schulz
Søren Kierkegaard in deutscher Sprache
Eine Gesamtbibliographie der Quellen und Sekundärliteratur von 1855 – 2015
Bd. 34, 2016, 304 S., 34,90 €, br., ISBN 978-3-643-13284-0

LIT Verlag Berlin – Münster – Wien – Zürich – London
Auslieferung Deutschland / Österreich / Schweiz: siehe Impressumsseite